COOK'S
ILLUSTRATED

~1993-1997~

Published by
Boston Common Press Limited Partnership
17 Station Street
Brookline, Massachusetts 02146

ISBN: 0-9640179-9-7
ISSN: Pending

To get home delivery of future issues of *Cook's Illustrated*
magazine, call 1-800-526-8442 or write to the above address.

$12.95

Cook's Illustrated 1993–1997 Index

Achiote

Achiote Paste (Notes). . . . . Sep/Oct 94   3

Discount Spices (S&R). . . . . Sep/Oct 94   32

Almonds

ALMOND COOKIES . . . . Nov/Dec 96   9

ALMOND FILLING WITH
CURRANTS . . . . Sep/Oct 95   15

ALMOND MACAROONS . . . . Sep/Oct 96   6

ALMOND MADELEINES . . . . Mar/Apr 96   21

ALMOND MERINGUE CAKE WITH STRAWBERRY
AND VANILLA ICE CREAM . . . May/Jun 95   13

BLOND PANFORTE . . . . Nov/Dec 94   13

DRIED PEACH AND APPLE SALAD WITH
ALMONDS AND CUMIN. . . . . . . Jul/Aug 94   20

FRIED ALMONDS. . . . . Mar/Apr 95   13

FUDGE-ALMOND MACAROONS . Sep/Oct 96   6

LEMON-ALMOND MACAROONS . Sep/Oct 96   7

ORANGE-ALMOND BISCOTTI . . . Jan/Feb 94   12

PANFORTE DI SIENNA . . . . Nov/Dec 94   12

PINE NUT–CRUSTED ALMOND
MACAROONS . . . . Sep/Oct 96   7

RASPBERRY-ALMOND COFFEE
CAKE . . . . Mar/Apr 95   21

RASPBERRY-ALMOND FILLING May/Jun 95   19

RICE PUDDING WITH ORANGE AND TOASTED
ALMONDS. . . . . Sep/Oct 96   25

RUM-BAKED APPLES WITH MASCARPONE
AND ALMONDS . . . . Sep/Oct 95   13

STEAMED COUSCOUS WITH MOROCCAN
LAMB BROTH, GLAZED ONIONS, AND
FRIED ALMONDS . . . . Mar/Apr 95   12

SWEET BREAD WITH ALMONDS AND DRIED
CHERRIES. . . . . May/Jun 94   29

Amaretti

AMARETTI COOKIES (S&R). . . . . Jul/Aug 97   32

VANILLA SEMIFREDDO WITH ALMONDS
AND AMARETTI . . . . Jul/Aug 97   23

Anchovies

BROCCOLI-ANCHOVY SAUCE
WITH ZITI . . . . Sep/Oct 94   22

Angel Food Cake

Cutting Another Cake (Notes) . . . . Nov/Dec 96   2

Anise

LEMON-ANISE BISCOTTI . . . . . . Jan/Feb 94   12

RED LENTIL PUREE WITH CUMIN AND
ANISE . . . . Mar/Apr 95   25

Appetizers

ARTICHOKE CROSTINI. . . . . . . May/Jun 96   17

Assembling Spring Rolls
Quickly (QT) . . . . May/Jun 96   5

CRISPY CHEESE WAFERS . . . . . May/Jun 96   17

GRILLED MOZZARELLA AND SUN-DRIED
TOMATO SKEWERS . . . . May/Jun 96   17

MARINATED ZUCCHINI WITH
PARMESAN . . . . May/Jun 96   16

PARMESAN-PAPRIKA PALMIERS Mar/Apr 94   16

PARMESAN-PAPRIKA PASTRY
STRAWS . . . . Mar/Apr 94   16

PARMESAN WITH DATES . . . . . May/Jun 96   16

PROSCIUTTO AND GOAT CHEESE
ROULADES . . . . May/Jun 96   16

Quick and Easy Antipasti . . . . . . May/Jun 96   16

SMOKED SALMON AND CHIVE MILLE
FEUILLE . . . . Mar/Apr 94   17

Apples (*See also* Cider; Fruit, Fresh)

APPLE-BEET SALAD WITH CREAMY DILL
DRESSING . . . . Nov/Dec 96   21

APPLE-CINNAMON COFFEE
CAKE . . . . Mar/Apr 95   21

APPLE-CRANBERRY SALAD WITH CREAMY
LEMON VINAIGRETTE. . . . . . . Nov/Dec 96   21

Apple Parer (Notes). . . . . Sep/Oct 93   2

APPLE PIE WITH CRYSTALLIZED
GINGER . . . . Nov/Dec 97   22

APPLE PIE WITH DRIED FRUIT Nov/Dec 97   22

APPLE PIE WITH FRESH
CRANBERRIES . . . . Nov/Dec 97   22

APPLE TARTLETS . . . . Mar/Apr 94   17

APPLE UPSIDE-DOWN
GINGERBREAD . . . . Nov/Dec 95   23

APPLE-WALNUT WHEAT
BREAD . . . . May/Jun 94   29

BACON AND APPLE STUFFING, MASTER
RECIPE FOR. . . . . Nov/Dec 97   9

BAKED APPLES WITH
CRANBERRIES . . . . Sep/Oct 94   BC

THE BEST APPLE PIE. . . . . Sep/Oct 94   8

The Best Baked Apple. . . . . Sep/Oct 95   12

The Best Way to Peel, Core,
and Slice Apples . . . . Nov/Dec 97   22

BISTRO APPLE TART. . . . . Mar/Apr 94   17

Boutique Apples (S&R) . . . . Sep/Oct 95   32
BRANDIED FALL FRUITS. . . . . . Sep/Oct 95   BC
BREAKFAST BAKED APPLES WITH YOGURT
     AND GRANOLA. . . . . Sep/Oct 95   13
CHICKEN SAUSAGE WITH APPLES
     AND SAGE . . . . Mar/Apr 96   12
CIDER-BAKED APPLES WITH CINNAMON
     SUGAR. . . . . Sep/Oct 95   13
CLASSIC APPLE PIE, MASTER
     RECIPE FOR. . . . . Nov/Dec 97   21
Coring Apple Quarters (QT). . . . . . Jan/Feb 96   4
CORNBREAD-APPLE STUFFING Nov/Dec 95   26
CREAM PAN SAUCE WITH APPLES
     AND SAGE . . . . Jul/Aug 97   19
Crisps and Betties. . . . . Sep/Oct 93   26
CURRIED APPLE-CRANBERRY
     CHUTNEY. . . . . Nov/Dec 94   14
CURRIED COLESLAW WITH
     APPLES AND RAISINS. . . . . . . Jul/Aug 95   13
Do-Ahead Fresh Baked Apple Pie . Nov/Dec 97   19
DRIED PEACH AND APPLE SALAD WITH
     ALMONDS AND CUMIN. . . . . . Jul/Aug 94   20
Fruit Sorbets at a Glance . . . . Jul/Aug 95   25
GREEN APPLE CHUTNEY WITH APRICOTS
     AND GINGER. . . . . Nov/Dec 97   11
HONEY-BAKED APPLES WITH CRÈME
     FRAÎCHE. . . . . Sep/Oct 95   13
How to Poach Fruit . . . . May/Jun 93   24
MASHED POTATOES AND APPLES WITH BACON
     AND BROWNED ONIONS . . . . Nov/Dec 93   11
REUBEN'S LEGENDARY APPLE
     PANCAKE . . . . Charter Issue   19
ROAST GOOSE WITH PRUNE AND APPLE
     STUFFING AND RED WINE
     GIBLET GRAVY . . . . Nov/Dec 94   7
RUM-BAKED APPLES WITH MASCARPONE
     AND ALMONDS . . . . Sep/Oct 95   13
SPICED APPLE-RAISIN FILLING Nov/Dec 95   15
TARTE TATIN . . . . Jan/Feb 96   15
Tasting the Perfect Apple . . . . Nov/Dec 97   20
Varieties . . . . Nov/Dec 97   21
WALNUT-RAISIN BAKED APPLES WITH
     MAPLE SYRUP . . . . Sep/Oct 95   13
YOGURT-CREAMED OATS WITH BERRIES
     AND APPLES. . . . . May/Jun 94   BC

Apricots (*See* also Fruit)
APRICOT-JICAMA SALSA . . . . Jul/Aug 94   20
BRAISED BUTTERNUT SQUASH WITH

DRIED APRICOTS, RAISINS, AND MADRAS
     SPICES . . . . Jan/Feb 96   26
CREAM-FILLED APRICOTS . . . . . Jan/Feb 97   BC
DRIED APRICOT COMPOTE WITH
     BALSAMIC VINEGAR AND JUNIPER
     BERRIES . . . . Jan/Feb 95   23
Poaching. May/Jun 93   26
Preparing Fruit for Crisps and
     Betties . . . . Sep/Oct 93   26

Arctic Char
Steaming Times for Fish Fillets and
     Steaks . . . . Mar/Apr 95   20

Artichokes
ARTICHOKE CROSTINI. . . . . . . May/Jun 96   17
ARTICHOKE CUPS WITH SEAFOOD SALAD
     AND HERB VINAIGRETTE. . . . May/Jun 93   BC
BRAISED ARTICHOKE SAUCE WITH WHITE
     WINE, GARLIC, AND LEMON. . Mar/Apr 95   11
BRAISED ARTICHOKES WITH TOMATOES
     AND GARLIC. . . . . May/Jun 94   12
California Artichokes (S&R) . . . . . May/Jun 94   32
PRESSURE-STEAMED
     ARTICHOKES. . . . . Jul/Aug 96   11
SKEWERED GRILLED SHRIMP WITH
     ARTICHOKE HEARTS. . . . . . . Mar/Apr 94   BC
SPAGHETTI WITH ARTICHOKE-LOBSTER
     SAUCE . . . . May/Jun 94   12
Steam, Don't Boil, Artichokes . . . . May/Jun 94   10
STEAMED ARTICHOKE HEARTS, MASTER
     RECIPE FOR . . . . May/Jun 94   11
STEAMED WHOLE ARTICHOKES, MASTER
     RECIPE FOR . . . . May/Jun 94   11
Trimming and Coring
     Artichokes (QT). . . . . May/Jun 93   5

Arugula
ARUGULA SALAD WITH GARLIC
     CROUTONS, GRUYÈRE, AND HARD-BOILED
     EGGS . . . . May/Jun 95   23
ARUGULA SALAD WITH GRILLED FIGS
     AND ROASTED PEPPER
     VINAIGRETTE . . . . Sep/Oct 96   BC
FRESH TOMATO PIZZA WITH ARUGULA AND
     PROSCIUTTO . . . . May/Jun 95   11
FUSILLI WITH ARUGULA AND TOMATO
     SAUCE. . . . . Jan/Feb 94   21
PEAR SALAD WITH ARUGULA, WALNUTS, AND

Cook's Illustrated 1993–1997 Index

GORGONZOLA . . . . Nov/Dec 96   21
TOMATO SAUCE WITH ARUGULA AND BLACK
   OLIVES . . . . Mar/Apr 95   11

Asiago
Asian Ingredients (S&R) . . . . Sep/Oct 94   32
ROASTED TOMATO PIZZA TOPPING WITH
   FENNEL AND ASIAGO . . . . May/Jun 93   9

Asparagus
ALFRED PORTALE'S JUMBO ASPARAGUS
   SALAD WITH PARMA HAM, PARMESAN, AND
   LEMON VINAIGRETTE . . . . . . May/Jun 93   7
ASPARAGUS AND MUSHROOM SAUCE WITH
   CARAMELIZED SHALLOTS . . . Mar/Apr 95   11
ASPARAGUS FRITTATA WITH MINT AND
   PARMESAN . . . . Mar/Apr 96   11
ASPARAGUS OMELET . . . . Sep/Oct 93   22
ASPARAGUS VINAIGRETTE WITH SIEVED EGG
   AND PICKLED PINK ONIONS . May/Jun 95   23
GRILLED ASPARAGUS . . . . May/Jun 93   7
HEARTY CHICKEN SOUP WITH ORZO AND
   SPRING VEGETABLES . . . . Mar/Apr 96   15
How to Cook Asparagus . . . . May/Jun 93   7
RISOTTO WITH ASPARAGUS AND WILD
   MUSHROOMS . . . . Mar/Apr 94   19
STEAMED ASPARAGUS, MASTER
   RECIPE FOR . . . . May/Jun 93   7
THAI-STYLE ASPARAGUS WITH CHILES,
   GARLIC, AND BASIL . . . . May/Jun 93   7
VEGETABLE RISOTTO IN CARROT AND
   CELERY BROTH . . . . Jan/Feb 94   27

Avocado
AVOCADO BASIL DRESSING . . Charter Issue   30
AVOCADO-CORN SALSA . . . . Jul/Aug 96   21
Extracting the Meat From
   Avocados (QT) . . . . Sep/Oct 94   4
Pitting Avocados (Notes) . . . . Jan/Feb 94   3
Pitting Avocados (QT) . . . . Sep/Oct 93   5
Preparing Guacamole
   Quickly (QT) . . . . May/Jun 96   5

Bacon
BACON AND APPLE STUFFING, MASTER
   RECIPE FOR . . . . Nov/Dec 97   9
BACON-WRAPPED MEAT LOAF WITH BROWN-
   SUGAR KETCHUP GLAZE . . . . . Sep/Oct 96   22
BAKED LEEKS WITH BACON AND

GRUYÈRE . . . . Mar/Apr 95   15
BEEF STEW WITH BACON, MUSHROOMS, AND
   PEARL ONIONS . . . . Jan/Feb 96   20
CORNBREAD-APPLE STUFFING Nov/Dec 95   26
Disposing of Bacon Fat (QT) . . . . . . Jul/Aug 97   4
Easy Bacon Bits (QT) . . . . Sep/Oct 97   4
GERMAN-STYLE POTATO SALAD WITH BACON
   AND BALSAMIC VINEGAR . . . . Jul/Aug 94   8
GOLDEN CORNBREAD WITH
   BACON . . . . Sep/Oct 95   21
GREEN BEANS WITH BACON AND
   ONIONS . . . . Nov/Dec 96   7
LOAF PAN VARIATION FOR MEAT
   LOAF . . . . Sep/Oct 96   22
MASHED POTATOES AND APPLES WITH BACON
   AND BROWNED ONIONS . . . . . Nov/Dec 93   11
ORECCHIETTE WITH CAULIFLOWER
   AND BACON . . . . Jan/Feb 94   21
QUICK-COOKED GREENS WITH BACON
   AND BLACK-EYED PEAS . . . . . Jan/Feb 95   14
QUICK-COOKED GREENS WITH BACON
   AND ONION . . . . Jan/Feb 95   13
ROASTED POTATOES WITH ONION, BACON,
   AND THYME . . . . Jan/Feb 94   11
WARM BALSAMIC VINEGAR SAUCE
   WITH BACON . . . . Jul/Aug 93   25

Bagels
The Best Way to Slice a Bagel . . . . Sep/Oct 97   14
CINNAMON RAISIN BAGELS . . . Sep/Oct 97   15
Forming and Cooking . . . . Sep/Oct 97   15
MASTER RECIPE FOR PLAIN
   BAGELS . . . . Sep/Oct 97   14
Safe Bagel Slicing (QT) . . . . Sep/Oct 97   4
TOPPED BAGELS . . . . Sep/Oct 97   15

Baking
Always Ready to Dip and
   Sweep (Flour) . . . . Sep/Oct 97   5
Are Oven Tiles Safe? (Notes) . . . . . . Jul/Aug 95   3
Avoiding a Floury Mess (Notes) . . . Mar/Apr 94   3
Avoiding Soggy Muffin
   Bottoms (QT) . . . . Jan/Feb 97   5
Avoiding Splatters When
   Mixing (QT) . . . . May/Jun 94   4
Bakewell Cream (Notes) . . . . Jul/Aug 96   3
Basic Sandwich Style Loaf . . . . Jan/Feb 97   13
Batter Skimmers (S&R) . . . . Nov/Dec 95   32
Bread Blowout (on Tearing During

Cook's Illustrated 1993–1997 Index

Baking) (Notes) . . . . Mar/Apr 97   2
Choosing Your Mixing Method . . . . Jan/Feb 97   19
Citrus Oils (S&R) . . . . Nov/Dec 93   32
CLASSIC MERINGUE . . . . May/Jun 95   12
Commercial Parchment
    Paper (S&R). . . . . Nov/Dec 93   32
Cotton Pastry Cloth (S&R) . . . . Jan/Feb 95   32
Cutting Butter into Flour (QT) . . . . Jan/Feb 95   5
Dinner Rolls . . . . Jan/Feb 97   13
Doing Upside-Down Cake Right . . . Jul/Aug 97   25
Do Muffin Papers Help? . . . . Jan/Feb 97   19
Easy Dusting Technique (QT) . . . . . Jul/Aug 97   4
Egg (Pastry) Doughs Lift Off . . . . . Sep/Oct 97   11
Fearless Phyllo . . . . Nov/Dec 95   15
Filling a Pastry Bag (QT). . . . . May/Jun 97   5
Fitting Pastry into Pie Dishes . . . . Sep/Oct 97   10
Foil-lining Springform Pans . . . . . . Sep/Oct 95   7
Folding Egg Whites Gently (QT). . . Nov/Dec 95   4
Forming and Cooking
    (Bagel Dough). . . . . Sep/Oct 97   15
FREE-FORM MERINGUE SHELLS FILLED WITH
    STRAWBERRIES AND PAPAYA May/Jun 95   13
Freezing Pie Pastry (QT) . . . . Nov/Dec 97   4
Gingerbread Coiffure (QT) . . . . Nov/Dec 97   4
Grease Pans, Mess-Free (QT). . . . . Mar/Apr 95   5
Greasing Cookie Sheets (Notes) . . . Mar/Apr 94   3
Hand Mixers (S&R) . . . . May/Jun 95   32
Homemade Condensed Milk
    (Notes) . . . . Nov/Dec 94   2
How to Measure (Notes). . . . . Mar/Apr 95   2
Indenting Cookies for Filling (QT) . Nov/Dec 97   4
Instant Cooling Rack (QT). . . . . . . Sep/Oct 97   5
Keeping Dough from Sticking (QT). Jan/Feb 97   5
Leaving Visual Cues When Baking
    (QT) . . . . Nov/Dec 97   4
LIGHTENED PASTRY CREAM . . . Sep/Oct 95   15
Lightening Batters Without Waste
    (QT) . . . . Jul/Aug 97   5
Loading a Pastry Bag (QT) . . . . . . Jan/Feb 95   4
Loosening a Sticky Mixing Bowl
    (QT) . . . . Nov/Dec 97   5
Making Cookie Crumbs (QT). . . . . Sep/Oct 94   5
Making Your Own Baking Powder. May/Jun 93   12
Measuring Cake Batter (QT). . . . . . Jul/Aug 94   5
Measuring Dough Height (QT) . . . . Sep/Oct 94   5
Measuring Extracts (QT). . . . . Jul/Aug 95   5
Measuring Flour (Notes) . . . . Jul/Aug 95   3
Measuring Shortening (Notes). . . . May/Jun 95   2
Measuring Shortening (Notes) . . . . Sep/Oct 94   2

New Uses for Your Cake Tester
    (QT) . . . . Jan/Feb 97   5
Oatmeal Cookie Woes (Notes) . . . . . Jul/Aug 97   2
On Cocoa in Cake (Notes) . . . . Mar/Apr 96   3
Pastry Board (S&R). . . . . Jul/Aug 95   32
Pouring Boiling Water into a Pan in the
    Oven (QT). . . . . Sep/Oct 95   5
Proper Handling for a Proper Irish
    Bread. . . . . Mar/Apr 97   13
Protein Content of Flour (Notes). . . Jan/Feb 96   3
Questioning Cocoa (Notes) . . . . Mar/Apr 96   3
Quick Cake Decorations (QT) . . . . . Jul/Aug 97   4
Quick (Muffin) Topping (QT) . . . . . Mar/Apr 97   4
Ramekins (S&R). . . . . Mar/Apr 95   32
Rating Handheld Mixers (ER) . . . . May/Jun 95   28
Rating Vanilla Extracts (BT) . . . . . May/Jun 95   26
Recipes That Mix Oil and Other
    Liquids (Notes) . . . . May/Jun 95   2
The Right Speed to Knead (Notes) . Jan/Feb 97   2
Rolling Out Sticky Dough (QT) . . . Mar/Apr 97   5
Shapely Biscotti (Notes). . . . . Mar/Apr 97   3
Shaping Focaccia Dough . . . . May/Jun 97   7
Shaping Foolproof Meringues,
    Master Class. . . . . May/Jun 95   12
Shaping Lace Cookies . . . . May/Jun 97   21
Sizing a Parchment Paper
    Liner (QT) . . . . May/Jun 93   4
Packed Brown Sugar (QT) . . . . Mar/Apr 97   5
Softening Brown Sugar (Notes). . . . Sep/Oct 94   3
Softening Butter for Mixing (QT) . . Jul/Aug 94   4
Specialty Flours and Baking
    Equipment (S&R). . . . . Jan/Feb 95   32
Springform Pan (S&R). . . . . Sep/Oct 95   32
Steadying Your Work Surface
    (Notes) . . . . Sep/Oct 96   3
Substituting Baking Pans (Notes). . Jan/Feb 95   3
Three Great Baking Shortcuts
    (Notes). Nov/Dec 96   2
Twisted Loaf Baked in a Pan . . . . . Jan/Feb 97   13
Unsalted Butter for Greasing Pans
    (Notes) . . . . Sep/Oct 95   3
The Water in Bread . . . . Sep/Oct 97   2
(The Water in) Pastry Dough
    (Notes) . . . . Sep/Oct 97   3
West Coast Specialty Flours
    (S&R) . . . . Jan/Feb 95   32
Wet and Dry Measures (Notes) . . . . Sep/Oct 94   3
Working with Phyllo (QT) . . . . Mar/Apr 97   4

Cook's Illustrated 1993–1997 Index

Balsamic Vinegar

Balsamic Vinegar Fraud (Notes) . . . Sep/Oct 95   3
BRAISED FENNEL AND BITTER GREENS
   SAUCE WITH BALSAMIC
   VINEGAR . . . . Mar/Apr 95   11
DRIED APRICOT COMPOTE WITH BALSAMIC
   VINEGAR AND JUNIPER
   BERRIES . . . . Jan/Feb 95   23
RED PEPPER–BASIL SAUCE WITH BALSAMIC
   VINEGAR . . . . May/Jun 95   22
TOMATO SAUCE WITH BELL PEPPERS AND
   BALSAMIC VINEGAR . . . . Mar/Apr 95   20
Traditional Balsamic
   Vinegars (S&R) . . . . Mar/Apr 95   32
WARM BALSAMIC VINEGAR WITH
   HERBS . . . . Sep/Oct 95   24
With Balsamic Vinegar, Price Equals
   Quality (BT) . . . . Mar/Apr 95   26

Bananas

BANANA BERRY POPOVER . . . Charter Issue   18
BANANA CREAM PIE . . . . Mar/Apr 96   24
BANANA-NUT CHIFFON
   CAKE . . . . May/Jun 96   8
BANANA-PAPAYA FOOL . . . . Jan/Feb 95   BC

Barbecue (See also Smoke Cooking; Spice Rubs and Pastes)

ALL-PURPOSE BARBECUE RUB . Jul/Aug 95   21
BARBECUE SAUCE, MASTER
   RECIPE FOR . . . . Jul/Aug 94   13
BARBECUE SAUCE
   WITH ASIAN FLAVORS . . . . Jul/Aug 97   15
BARBECUE SAUCE WITH MEXICAN
   FLAVORS . . . . Jul/Aug 97   15
Barbecue Sauces (S&R) . . . . Jul/Aug 94   32
Barbecue-Style Dry Rub . . . . Jul/Aug 94   13
BASIC BARBECUE SAUCE . . . . . Jul/Aug 97   15
Chimney Starter (S&R) . . . . Jul/Aug 97   32
Chimney Starter (S&R) . . . . Jul/Aug 93   32
Chinese Tip for Ribs (Notes) . . . . . . Jan/Feb 95   2
Cuts of Pork for Barbecue . . . . Jul/Aug 97   19
EASTERN NORTH CAROLINA–STYLE
   BARBECUE SAUCE . . . . Jul/Aug 97   20
Essential Steps to Homemade Pork
   Barbecue . . . . Jul/Aug 97   20
Grill Products (S&R) . . . . Jul/Aug 94   32
How to Make Authentic Barbecued
   Ribs at Home . . . . Jul/Aug 94   10

KENTUCKY SMOKED BARBECUE
   SAUCE . . . . Jul/Aug 94   13
LOUISIANA SWEET BARBECUE
   SAUCE . . . . Jul/Aug 94   13
MID–SOUTH CAROLINA MUSTARD
   SAUCE . . . . Jul/Aug 97   20
Parboiling Ribs (Notes) . . . . Jan/Feb 95   2
PULLED PORK, MASTER RECIPE
   FOR . . . . Jul/Aug 97   19
SPICY CHILI RUB . . . . Jul/Aug 97   20
SPICY RIO GRANDE BARBECUE
   SAUCE . . . . Jul/Aug 94   13
Tasting Barbecue Sauces (BT) . . . . . Jul/Aug 95   26
WESTERN SOUTH CAROLINA–STYLE
   BARBECUE SAUCE . . . . Jul/Aug 97   20

Basil

AVOCADO BASIL DRESSING . . Charter Issue   30
BASIL CURRY DRESSING . . . . . . Jan/Feb 94   23
BASIL SAUCE WITH SAUTÉED
   SHRIMP . . . . Mar/Apr 96   9
BRUSCHETTA WITH TOMATOES AND
   BASIL . . . . Sep/Oct 96   8
CURRIED CHICKEN FILLING WITH
   CARROTS AND BASIL . . . . Sep/Oct 94   15
GARLIC AND BASIL ROAST CHICKEN
   WITH LEMON PAN SAUCE . . . . Sep/Oct 93   20
Keeping the Green (Notes) . . . . May/Jun 97   3
MEAT AND RICOTTA FILLING WITH
   BASIL FOR PASTA . . . . Sep/Oct 93   18
MUSSELS STEAMED IN WHITE WINE
   WITH CURRY AND BASIL . . . . Nov/Dec 96   15
PESTO . . . . Jul/Aug 96   29
Pesto at Its Best . . . . Jul/Aug 96   29
POTATO GNOCCHI WITH
   PESTO . . . . Mar/Apr 95   10
PROVENÇAL TOMATO SAUCE WITH
   BASIL AND ORANGE . . . . Sep/Oct 95   24
PUREED BROCCOLI SOUP WITH
   BASIL . . . . Nov/Dec 96   23
GRILLED ZUCCHINI SALAD WITH
   TOMATOES AND BASIL . . . . . . Jul/Aug 95   9
RED PEPPER–BASIL SAUCE WITH
   BALSAMIC VINEGAR . . . . May/Jun 95   22
RISOTTO WITH TOMATOES AND
   BASIL . . . . Mar/Apr 94   19
SAUSAGE AND BELL PEPPER PIZZA WITH
   BASIL AND MOZZARELLA . . . . May/Jun 95   11
SAUTÉED CHICKEN CUTLETS WITH

BROCCOLI-BASIL SAUCE . . . . . Jan/Feb 94   27
SAUTÉED EGGPLANT IN TOMATO
   SAUCE WITH BASIL . . . . Jul/Aug 93   7
STEWED TOMATO SAUCE WITH BASIL
   AND OLIVE OIL . . . . Mar/Apr 94   26
SUMMER HARVEST SOUP WITH
   BASIL . . . . Charter Issue   29
THAI-STYLE ASPARAGUS WITH CHILES,
   GARLIC, AND BASIL . . . . May/Jun 93   7
TOMATO BASIL SAUCE WITH
   CAPERS . . . . Sep/Oct 93   11

Beans (*See* also Green Beans; Lentils)
Bean Nutrition (Notes) . . . . Mar/Apr 97   2
BLACK BEAN–MANGO SALSA . . . Jul/Aug 96   21
BLACK BEAN SAUCE . . . . May/Jun 93   19
Boston Baked Beans . . . . Sep/Oct 96   14
BOSTON BAKED BEANS . . . . Sep/Oct 96   15
BRAISED LAMB SHANKS WITH WHITE
   BEANS, SWISS CHARD, AND
   MARJORAM . . . . Jan/Feb 95   19
BROWN RICE AND CHICKPEA
   SALAD . . . . Jan/Feb 94   23
CANNELLINI BEANS . . . . Jan/Feb 95   19
CAVATELLI WITH WHITE BEANS AND
   CLAMS . . . . Jan/Feb 94   19
COOKED DRIED BEANS . . . . Jan/Feb 95   14
Cooking Beans in Tuscany (Notes)
   . . . . Charter Issue   2
ESCAROLE AND WHITE BEAN SAUCE WITH
   GARLIC AND OREGANO . . . . . Sep/Oct 94   22
Flavoring Bean Soups (Notes) . . . . Mar/Apr 97   3
Foam on Beans and Stock (Notes) . May/Jun 94   2
MOROCCAN LAMB BROTH WITH CHICKPEAS
   AND VEGETABLES . . . . Mar/Apr 95   13
QUICK-COOKED GREENS WITH BACON
   AND BLACK-EYED PEAS . . . . . Jan/Feb 95   14
QUICK-COOKED GREENS WITH WHITE
   BEANS AND ROSEMARY . . . . . Jan/Feb 95   14
Preparing Fava Beans (QT) . . . . . . Jul/Aug 95   5
Rating Canned Beans (BT) . . . . . . Sep/Oct 97   27
The Real McCoy: An American
   Bean Pot (S&R) . . . . Sep/Oct 96   32
TUSCAN BEANS WITH SAGE
   (Notes) . . . . Charter Issue   2
What Makes Good Beans? . . . . Sep/Oct 97   26
WHITE BEAN AND TOMATO
   CASSEROLE . . . . Charter Issue   9

Bean Sprouts
MUNG BEAN SAUCE WITH GINGER,
   CILANTRO, AND SOY . . . . Sep/Oct 95   24

Beef
BEEF CURRY WITH CRUSHED SPICES
   AND CHANNA DAL . . . . Jan/Feb 97   9
A Better Burger . . . . Jul/Aug 95   14
A BETTER BURGER . . . . Jul/Aug 95   15
Carving a Rib Roast (QT) . . . . Nov/Dec 93   5
GRILL-ROASTED BEEF
   TENDERLOIN . . . . Jul/Aug 93   20
GRILL-ROASTED SPARERIBS WITH
   BARBECUE SAUCE . . . . Jul/Aug 93   20
How to Roast a Cheap Cut of Beef . Sep/Oct 96   10
Ice in Your Ground Beef (Notes) . . . Mar/Apr 96   2
Perfect Prime Rib . . . . Nov/Dec 95   12
PERFECT PRIME RIB . . . . Nov/Dec 95   14
SAUERBRATEN . . . . Jan/Feb 94   9
SESAME BEEF AND CABBAGE
   FILLING . . . . Sep/Oct 94   15
SLOW-ROASTED BEEF WITH RED
   WINE PAN JUICES . . . . Sep/Oct 96   13
Smoke-Cooking Times . . . . Jul/Aug 95   20
When to Carve Prime Rib (Notes) . Mar/Apr 96   3
brisket
BRAISED BEEF BRISKET . . . . . . Mar/Apr 95   23
BRAISED BRISKET, OAXACAN
   STYLE . . . . Mar/Apr 95   24
BRAISED BRISKET, SOUTHERN
   ITALIAN STYLE . . . . Mar/Apr 95   24
Brisket Under Pressure (Notes) . . . Nov/Dec 95   3
Cooking Brisket in a Foil Pouch
   (Notes) . . . . Nov/Dec 95   2
HOME-CORNED BEEF BRISKET
   . . . . Mar/Apr 97   11
HOME-CORNED BEEF BRISKET AND CABBAGE,
   NEW ENGLAND STYLE . . . . . . Mar/Apr 97   11
Juicy, Flavorful Brisket . . . . Mar/Apr 95   22
meatloaf
BACON-WRAPPED MEAT LOAF WITH BROWN-
   SUGAR KETCHUP GLAZE . . . . . Sep/Oct 96   22
LOAF PAN VARIATION FOR MEAT
   LOAF . . . . Sep/Oct 96   22
Meat Loaf Pan (S&R) . . . . Sep/Oct 96   32
Meat Loaf Pan Update (S&R) . . . . Mar/Apr 97   32
Memorable Meat Loaf . . . . Sep/Oct 96   22
pot roast
MASTER RECIPE FOR POT

Cook's Illustrated 1993–1997 Index

ROAST . . . . Jan/Feb 94   9
POT ROAST IN RED WINE . . . . . . Jan/Feb 94   9
Pot Roast Perfected . . . . Jan/Feb 94   6
POT ROAST WITH PORCINI
   MUSHROOMS . . . . Jan/Feb 94   9
PRESSURE-COOKED POT
   ROAST . . . . Jul/Aug 96   11
SOUTHWESTERN POT ROAST . . Jan/Feb 94   9
safety
Bacteria in Beef (Notes) . . . . Jan/Feb 96   3
Raw Beef Safety (Notes) . . . . Jan/Feb 97   3
steak
GRILLED PORTERHOUSE OR T-BONE
   STEAK . . . . May/Jun 96   25
GRILLED STRIP SIRLOIN STEAK, MASTER
   RECIPE FOR . . . . May/Jun 96   25
Grilling Steaks (on Cast-Iron Grate)
   (Notes) . . . . Jul/Aug 97   3
and HORSERADISH CREAM . . . May/Jun 97   9
How to Grill a Steak . . . . May/Jun 96   23
and MUSTARD SAUCE . . . . May/Jun 97   9
and ROQUEFORT BUTTER . . . . May/Jun 97   9
SPICY SOUTHWESTERN FLANK
   STEAK . . . . Jul/Aug 93   12
Tasting Mail-Order Steaks (BT) . . May/Jun 96   26
stew
BEEF STEW WITH BACON, MUSHROOMS,
   AND PEARL ONIONS . . . . Jan/Feb 96   20
BEEF STEW WITH TOMATOES, CINNAMON,
   AND CLOVES . . . . Jan/Feb 96   20
BEEF STEW WITH TOMATOES, ORANGE ZEST,
   AND OLIVES, ... Jan/Feb 96   20
HEARTY BEEF STEW . . . . Jan/Feb 96   19
Simple, Satisfying Beef Stew . . . . . Jan/Feb 96   18

Beer
Rating the Beers (BT) . . . . Jul/Aug 97   26

Beets
APPLE-BEET SALAD WITH CREAMY DILL
   DRESSING . . . . Nov/Dec 96   21
BEET AND POTATO ROESTI WITH CHIVES
   . . . . Jan/Feb 95   22
BEETS ROESTI . . . . Mar/Apr 94   11
How to Cook Beets . . . . Mar/Apr 94   11
PICKLED BEETS WITH ORANGE AND
   ROSEMARY . . . . Mar/Apr 94   11
Removing the Peels from Cooked
   Beets (QT) . . . . Mar/Apr 94   5

ROASTED BEETS,
   MASTER RECIPE FOR . . . . Mar/Apr 94   11
STEAMED BEETS,
   MASTER RECIPE FOR . . . . Mar/Apr 94   11

Belgian Endive
SMOKED SALMON–FILLED BELGIAN
   ENDIVE . . . . Nov/Dec 95   BC

Berries
Crisps and Betties . . . . Sep/Oct 93   26
YOGURT-CREAMED OATS WITH BERRIES
   AND APPLES . . . . May/Jun 94   BC

Beverages (See also Coffee; Tea)
Making a Low-Tech
   Milkshake (QT) . . . . May/Jun 97   4
Making Decorative Citrus
   Spirals (QT) . . . . Jul/Aug 95   5
Rating Orange Juices (BT) . . . . . . May/Jun 97   29
Taste-Testing Sparkling
   Waters (BT) . . . . Jul/Aug 93   21

Biscotti
CAPPUCCINO SEMIFREDDO
   WITH ALMOND BISCOTTI, MASTER
   RECIPE FOR . . . . Jul/Aug 97   23
HONEY-LAVENDER BISCOTTI . . Jan/Feb 94   12
LEMON-ANISE BISCOTTI . . . . . . Jan/Feb 94   12
Making Crisp, Long-lasting Biscotti . . . .
   . . . . Jan/Feb 94   12
ORANGE-ALMOND BISCOTTI . . . Jan/Feb 94   12
Shapely Biscotti (Notes) . . . . Mar/Apr 97   3
SPICED BISCOTTI . . . . Jan/Feb 94   12

Biscuits
The Art of Biscuit Making . . . . May/Jun 93   10
Bakewell Cream (Notes) . . . . Jul/Aug 96   3
CHEDDAR BISCUITS . . . . May/Jun 93   12
CREAM BISCUITS WITH
   HERBS . . . . Nov/Dec 93   13
FLAKY BISCUITS . . . . May/Jun 93   12
FLUFFY BISCUITS . . . . May/Jun 93   12
FLUFFY BUTTERMILK
   BISCUITS . . . . May/Jun 96   13
HERB BISCUITS . . . . May/Jun 93   12
RICH SHORTCAKE TOPPING . . . Jul/Aug 96   20
STRAWBERRY SHORTCAKE . . . . May/Jun 93   12

Cook's Illustrated 1993–1997 Index

Black Beans

BLACK BEAN–MANGO SALSA. . . Jul/Aug 96   21

BLACK BEAN SAUCE . . . . May/Jun 93   19

Blackberries

Fruit Sorbets at a Glance . . . . Jul/Aug 95   25

Black-Eyed Peas

COOKED DRIED BEANS. . . . . . . Jan/Feb 95   14

QUICK-COOKED GREENS WITH BACON

   AND BLACK-EYED PEAS . . . . . Jan/Feb 95   14

Blueberries

BLUEBERRY PANCAKES . . . . Jan/Feb 96   8

CLASSIC BLUEBERRY PIE. . . . . . Jul/Aug 95   6

Fruit Sorbets at a Glance . . . . Jul/Aug 95   25

Bok Choy

QUICK-BRAISED BOK CHOY, TURNIPS, AND

   WATERCRESS WITH GINGER AND

   SOY . . . . Jan/Feb 96   26

Books (*See* also CD-ROMs)

Baking with Julia (BR) . . . . May/Jun 97   31

Bitter Almonds (BR) . . . . Jan/Feb 95   31

The Bold Vegetarian (BR) . . . . May/Jun 95   31

Book of Tarts (BR). . . . . Sep/Oct 95   31

Chez Panise Vegetables (BR) . . . . . May/Jun 96   31

Chocolate and the Art of Low-Fat Desserts

   (BR). . . . . Mar/Apr 95   31

The Complete Idiot's Guide to Cooking

   Basics (BR). . . . . Sep/Oct 97   31

Cooking for Dummies (BR) . . . . . . Sep/Oct 97   31

The Cooking of the Eastern Mediterranean

   (BR). . . . . Jul/Aug 94   31

Cooking Under Wraps (BR) . . . . . May/Jun 93   30

Cooking with Daniel Boulud (BR). . Jan/Feb 94   31

Culinary Notecards (S&R) . . . . . . May/Jun 93   32

The Dean & DeLuca Cookbook

   (BR). . . . . Jan/Feb 97   31

Delia Smith's Summer Collection

   (BR). . . . . Jul/Aug 95   31

Dumplings and Breads (BR) . . . . . May/Jun 93   21

Emeril's New New Orleans Cooking

   (BR). . . . . May/Jun 93   30

The Essential Thai Cookbook (BR) . Jan/Feb 95   31

The Everyday Cookbooks (BR) . . . . Nov/Dec 95   31

Everybody Eats Well in Belgium

   Cookbook (BR) . . . . Jan/Feb 96   31

Fast & Fresh (BR). . . . . Nov/Dec 96   31

Fear of Wine: An Introductory Guide

   to the Grape (BR) . . . . Jan/Feb 96   31

Fifty Ways to Cook Most Everything

   (BR) . . . . Charter Issue   31

Fish and Shellfish (BR). . . . . Jul/Aug 96   31

Flatbreads and Flavors (BR) . . . . . Mar/Apr 95   31

Florence Lin's Complete Book of

   Chinese Noodles . . . . May/Jun 93   21

The Foods of Greece (BR) . . . . Nov/Dec 93   31

Four Star Desserts (BR) . . . . Nov/Dec 96   31

From the Earth to the Table (BR). . Jan/Feb 96   31

Gather 'Round the Grill (BR). . . . . Jul/Aug 95   31

Great Food Almanac (BR). . . . . . . Nov/Dec 94   31

Great Good Food (BR) . . . . Jul/Aug 93   31

Grow Your Own Chinese Vegetables

   (BR) . . . . Charter Issue   7

Guide to Cooking Schools (BR) . . . May/Jun 93   32

The Heart of Sicily (BR). . . . . Mar/Apr 94   31

Home Food (BR) . . . . May/Jun 96   31

How to Bake (BR) . . . . Nov/Dec 95   31

In a Shaker Kitchen: 100 Recipes from

   the Shaker Tradition (BR) . . . . . Sep/Oct 95   31

In Nonna's Kitchen (BR). . . . . Nov/Dec 97   31

James Beard's Simple Foods (BR). . Sep/Oct 93   31

Jaques Pépin's Table (BR) . . . . May/Jun 97   32

The Joy of Coffee (BR) . . . . Nov/Dec 95   31

Keeping a Cookbook Flat (QT). . . . Mar/Apr 97   4

Ken Hom's Quick and Easy Chinese

   Cooking (BR). . . . . May/Jun 93   21

The Key to Chinese Cooking (BR) . May/Jun 93   21

La Vera Cucina (BR) . . . . Sep/Oct 96   31

Larousse Gastronomique (S&R) . . . Sep/Oct 97   32

Marcella Cuchina . . . . Nov/Dec 97   31

The Mediterranean Diet

   Cookbook (BR) . . . . Sep/Oct 94   31

Mediterranean Hot (BR) . . . . Sep/Oct 96   31

Mesa Mexicana (BR) . . . . Jan/Feb 95   31

Miami Spice: The New Florida

   Cuisine (BR). . . . . Jan/Feb 94   31

Michel Richard's Home Cooking With a

   French Accent (BR) . . . . Sep/Oct 93   31

The Modern Art of Chinese

   Cooking . . . . May/Jun 93   21

Moosewood Restaurant Low-Fat

   Favorites (BR) . . . . Jul/Aug 97   31

The New German Cookbook (BR) . . Sep/Oct 93   31

The New Southern Cook (BR) . . . . . Sep/Oct 95   31

New York Cookbook (BR) . . . . . . Charter Issue   31

New York Cookbook (Review)... Charter Issue   31
Nicole Routhier's Fruit
    Cookbook (BR) .... Jul/Aug 96   31
The Occasional Vegetarian (BR) .. May/Jun 95   31
Out of Print Cookbooks (S&R)..... Jul/Aug 94   32
Panini, Bruschetta, Crostini (BR) .. Jul/Aug 94   31
Provence the Beautiful
    Cookbook (BR).............. Nov/Dec 93   31
Red Hot Peppers (BR) .... Mar/Apr 94   31
Red, White, and Greens (BR)..... Sep/Oct 96   31
Roasting (BR)................ Mar/Apr 96   31
Roasting, a Simple Art (BR)..... Mar/Apr 96   31
Roger Verge's Vegetables in the
    French Style (BR) .... Mar/Apr 95   31
Salse di Pomodoro (BR).......... Sep/Oct 96   31
Savoring Herbs and Spices (BR) ... Jul/Aug 96   31
The Savory Way (BR) .... Jul/Aug 97   31
Soup Suppers (BR)............ Mar/Apr 94   31
Sunset Series: Casual Cuisines of the
    World (BR)................ Jan/Feb 97   31
A Taste of Old Cuba (BR) .... Nov/Dec 94   31
Treasures of the Italian Table
    (BR) .... Jan/Feb 94   31
A Treasury of Southern Baking
    (BR)..................... May/Jun 93   30
Unplugged Kitchen (BR) .... Jul/Aug 97   31
The Vegetarian Feast (BR)....... May/Jun 95   31
The Vegetarian Hearth (BR) ..... Jul/Aug 97   31
Vegetarian Planet (BR) .... Jul/Aug 97   31
Vegetarian Table: Italy (BR)...... Nov/Dec 94   31
A Well-Seasoned Appetite (BR).... Jul/Aug 95   31
With the Grain (BR) .... May/Jun 96   31
The World of Curries (BR)....... May/Jun 94   31

Bourbon

BOURBON BUTTER SAUCE..... Jan/Feb 95   25
VANILLA-BOURBON PUDDING
    CAKE .... Jan/Feb 95   25

Braising

BASIC BRAISED BRUSSELS
    SPROUTS .... Nov/Dec 95   21
BRAISED ARTICHOKE SAUCE WITH
    WHITE WINE, GARLIC, AND
    LEMON.................. Mar/Apr 95   11
BRAISED BEEF BRISKET ...... Mar/Apr 95   23
BRAISED BRISKET, OAXACAN
    STYLE.................. Mar/Apr 95   24
BRAISED BRISKET, SOUTHERN

    ITALIAN STYLE........... Mar/Apr 95   24
BRAISED BRUSSELS SPROUTS WITH NUTMEG-
    SCENTED WHITE SAUCE..... Nov/Dec 95   21
BRAISED BRUSSELS SPROUTS WITH TARRAGON-
    MUSTARD BUTTER......... Nov/Dec 95   21
BRAISED CELERY WITH VERMOUTH-BUTTER
    GLAZE .... Mar/Apr 97   24
BRAISED FENNEL AND BITTER GREENS
    SAUCE WITH BALSAMIC VINEGAR
    .... Mar/Apr 95   11
BRAISED LAMB SHANKS WITH WHITE BEANS,
    SWISS CHARD, AND MARJORAM ....
    .... Jan/Feb 95   19
BRAISED LAMB SHOULDER CHOPS WITH
    CAPERS, BALSAMIC VINEGAR, AND RED
    PEPPERS .... Mar/Apr 97   19
BRAISED LAMB SHOULDER CHOPS WITH
    TOMATOES AND RED WINE... Mar/Apr 97   18
BRAISED SHOULDER LAMB CHOPS
    WITH FIGS AND NORTH AFRICAN
    SPICES .... Mar/Apr 97   19
BRAISED SHOULDER (LAMB) CHOPS
    WITH TOMATOES, ROSEMARY, AND
    OLIVES .... Mar/Apr 97   19
Braised Winter Vegetables .... Jan/Feb 96   26
Braising Lamb Shanks .... Jan/Feb 95   18
BRUSSELS SPROUTS BRAISED
    IN CREAM .... Nov/Dec 95   21
GLAZED BRUSSELS SPROUTS WITH
    CHESTNUTS .... Nov/Dec 95   21
How to Cook Brussels Sprouts.... Nov/Dec 95   20
Juicy, Flavorful Brisket .... Mar/Apr 95   22
SAUTÉED BRUSSELS SPROUTS WITH
    GARLIC AND PINE NUTS..... Nov/Dec 95   21

Bran

BIG BRAN MUFFINS WITH RAISINS
    AND DATES............... Sep/Oct 93   7

Bread (*See* also Bread Crumbs; Brioche; Flour; Stuffings; Yeast)

AMERICAN LOAF BREAD, FOOD PROCESSOR
    METHOD .... May/Jun 96   10
AMERICAN LOAF BREAD, MASTER
    RECIPE FOR .... May/Jun 96   10
ANADAMA LOAF BREAD ...... May/Jun 96   11
Better Way with Bread Toppings
    (Notes).................. Jul/Aug 94   2
BRAIDED CHALLAH (Notes) .... Mar/Apr 94   3

Cook's Illustrated 1993–1997 Index

Braiding Bread (QT). . . . . Mar/Apr 94   4

Bread Blowout (on Tearing During Baking)
(Notes). . . . . Mar/Apr 97   2

BUTTERMILK LOAF BREAD . . . May/Jun 96   11

Challah (Notes) . . . . Mar/Apr 94   3

Chinese Fried Bread (Notes) . . . . . . Jul/Aug 93   2

Cleaning Up After Breadmaking
(QT) . . . . Nov/Dec 96   4

Draft-Free Rising Location (QT) . . . Jan/Feb 96   4

Dusting Bread with Cornmeal
(Notes). . . . . Nov/Dec 95   2

Easter Bread Ingredients (S&R) . . Mar/Apr 94   32

Gubana: Italian Easter Bread Filled
with Nuts and Fruit . . . . Mar/Apr 94   12

Gubana: Italian Easter Bread Filled with Nuts
and Fruit, Master Class . . . . . . Mar/Apr 94   12

How to Make Bread . . . . Charter Issue   22

MASTER RECIPE FOR BASIC
BREAD . . . . Charter Issue   24

No-Knead Sandwich Bread . . . . . May/Jun 96   9

OATMEAL LOAF BREAD. . . . . . May/Jun 96   11

Proofing Bread (QT) . . . . Nov/Dec 96   4

Regional Cornbread Preferences
(Notes) . . . . Mar/Apr 96   2

Responses to Country Bread Story
(Notes). . . . . Jul/Aug 95   2

Rising Bread in the Microwave
(Notes) . . . . Nov/Dec 94   3

Rustic Country Bread . . . . Jan/Feb 95   6

RUSTIC COUNTRY BREAD . . . . . Jan/Feb 95   9

Scalding Milk for Bread (Notes) . . . Jul/Aug 94   3

Seeds for Rolls and Bread (S&R). . . Jan/Feb 94   32

Slashing Bread Dough (QT) . . . . . . Nov/Dec 94   5

Slow-Rise Breads (Notes) . . . . Nov/Dec 93   2

SLOW-RISE LOAF BREAD. . . . . . May/Jun 96   11

cornbread

The Best Northern Cornbread. . . . Sep/Oct 95   20

CORNMEAL LOAF BREAD . . . . . May/Jun 96   11

GOLDEN CORNBREAD WITH
BACON. Sep/Oct 95   21

GOLDEN CORNBREAD WITH
CHEDDAR . . . . Sep/Oct 95   21

GOLDEN CORNBREAD WITH
JALAPEÑOS . . . . Sep/Oct 95   21

GOLDEN NORTHERN
CORNBREAD. . . . . Sep/Oct 95   21

DEEP-FRIED DEVILS (Notes) . . . . Jul/Aug 93   2

dinner rolls

MASTER RECIPE FOR DINNER

ROLLS. Nov/Dec 93   15

Shaping and Baking Dinner Rolls . Nov/Dec 93   15

Shaping Individual Dinner Rolls . . Nov/Dec 93   16

equipment

Bread Pans (S&R) . . . . May/Jun 96   32

Forming Bread Shapes . . . . Jan/Feb 95   16

Guaranteed Proofing (Notes). . . . . Sep/Oct 95   2

Instant Yeast (Notes) . . . . Mar/Apr 95   3

Instant Yeast (S&R). . . . . May/Jun 96   32

Is Scalding Milk for Bread Essential?
(Notes). . . . . Jan/Feb 94   2

Keeping the Rising Temperature of Dough
Correct (Notes). . . . . May/Jun 94   3

La Cloche Maker Complaints
(Notes). . . . . Jul/Aug 95   2

La Cloche Tricks (Notes) . . . . Jul/Aug 95   2

More Cloche Comments (Notes) . . . Jul/Aug 95   2

Top of the Stove Bun Warmer
(Notes) . . . . May/Jun 96   3

Using a Food Processor to Knead
Dough (Notes). . . . . Sep/Oct 96   3

focaccia

Focaccia Pans (S&R) . . . . May/Jun 97   32

FOCACCIA WITH BLACK
OLIVES . . . . May/Jun 97   7

HAND-KNEADED FOCACCIA . . May/Jun 97   7

PARMESAN FOCACCIA . . . . May/Jun 97   7

ROSEMARY FOCACCIA, MASTER
RECIPE FOR . . . . May/Jun 97   7

SAGE FOCACCIA . . . . May/Jun 97   7

Shaping Focaccia Dough . . . . May/Jun 97   7

Irish soda bread

AMERICAN-STYLE SODA BREAD WITH
RAISINS AND CARAWAY . . . . Mar/Apr 97   13

CLASSIC IRISH SODA BREAD . . Mar/Apr 97   13

Cream of Tartar (in) (Notes) . . . . . Jul/Aug 97   2

Flour Flavor (Notes) . . . . Jul/Aug 97   2

IRISH BROWN SODA BREAD . . . Mar/Apr 97   13

OATMEAL-WALNUT SODA
BREAD . . . . Mar/Apr 97   13

Proper Handling for a Proper
Irish Bread . . . . Mar/Apr 97   13

salads

Bread Salads . . . . Sep/Oct 95   14

BREAD SALAD WITH ROASTED PEPPERS
AND SICILIAN OLIVES . . . . . . Sep/Oct 95   14

BREAD SALAD WITH TOMATOES, HERBS,
AND RED ONIONS . . . . Sep/Oct 95   14

PITA BREAD SALAD WITH CUCUMBERS,

Cook's Illustrated 1993–1997 Index

CHERRY TOMATOES, AND FRESH
HERBS . . . . Sep/Oct 95   14

whole wheat bread
Basic Sandwich Style Loaf . . . . Jan/Feb 97   13
Dinner Rolls . . . . Jan/Feb 97   13
HAND-KNEADED WHOLE
WHEAT BREAD . . . . Jan/Feb 97   14
Sandwich Style . . . . Jan/Feb 97   13
Twisted Loaf Baked in a Loaf Pan . Jan/Feb 97   13
The Water in Bread (Notes) . . . . . . Sep/Oct 97   2
When Things Go Wrong . . . . Jan/Feb 97   14
WHOLE WHEAT BREAD WITH
WHEAT GERM AND RYE . . . . . Jan/Feb 97   14
WHOLE WHEAT LOAF BREAD . . May/Jun 96   11

Bread Crumbs
SPAGHETTI WITH FENNEL AND BREAD
CRUMBS . . . . May/Jun 95   25
TOASTED BREAD CRUMBS, MASTER RECIPE
FOR . . . . May/Jun 95   25
TOASTED BREAD CRUMBS WITH CRACKED
BLACK PEPPER . . . . May/Jun 95   25
TOASTED BREAD CRUMBS WITH MARJORAM,
THYME, AND LEMON ZEST . . May/Jun 95   25
TOASTED BREAD CRUMBS WITH RED PEPPER
FLAKES AND GARLIC . . . . May/Jun 95   25
TOASTED BREAD CRUMBS WITH WHITE
WINE AND BUTTER . . . . May/Jun 95   25
The Virtues of Bread Crumbs . . . . May/Jun 95   24

Bread Machines
APPLE-WALNUT WHEAT
BREAD . . . . May/Jun 94   29
Are Bread Machines Worth the Dough?
(ER) . . . . May/Jun 94   26
Bread Machines (S&R) . . . . May/Jun 94   32
Foolproof Bread Machine Recipes . May/Jun 94   28
SWEET BREAD WITH ALMONDS AND
DRIED CHERRIES . . . . May/Jun 94   29
WHEAT BREAD, MASTER RECIPE
FOR BASIC . . . . May/Jun 94   29

Brining
BRINED SHRIMP, MASTER RECIPE
FOR . . . . Jul/Aug 94   19
Brining Thawed Shrimp (Notes) . . May/Jun 95   2
Gravlax Made Easy, Master Class . . Jan/Feb 96   12
A New Way to Prepare Shrimp . . . . Jul/Aug 94   18
Roasted Turkey Revisited . . . . Nov/Dec 95   9

The Science of Brining Turkey . . . . Nov/Dec 93   19

Brioche
Brioche Desserts . . . . Sep/Oct 95   16
BRIOCHE LOAF . . . . Sep/Oct 95   17
BRIOCHE PLUM TART . . . . Sep/Oct 95   16
BRIOCHE RING . . . . Sep/Oct 95   16
Quick and Easy Brioche . . . . Sep/Oct 95   15
QUICK BRIOCHE . . . . Sep/Oct 95   15
RASPBERRY BRIOCHE
SHORTCAKE . . . . Sept/Oct 95   17

Broccoflower
BROCCOFLOWER AND CELERY
SALAD . . . . May/Jun 95   23

Broccoli
BROCCOLI-ANCHOVY SAUCE
WITH ZITI . . . . Sep/Oct 94   22
BROCCOLI-BASIL SAUCE . . . . . . Jan/Feb 94   27
BROCCOLI WITH LIME-CUMIN
DRESSING . . . . Sep/Oct 97   8
BROCCOLI WITH ORANGE-GINGER
DRESSING AND WALNUTS . . . Sep/Oct 97   8
BROCCOLI WITH SPANISH GREEN
HERB SAUCE . . . . Sep/Oct 97   8
BROCCOLI WITH SPICY BALSAMIC DRESSING
AND BLACK OLIVES . . . . Sep/Oct 97   8
BROWN RICE PILAF WITH
BROCCOLI . . . . Jan/Feb 94   23
Keeping Broccoli Fresh (QT) . . . . . Jan/Feb 97   4
Keeping Broccoli Green (Notes) . . . Nov/Dec 93   2
MASTER RECIPE FOR STEAMED
BROCCOLI . . . . Sep/Oct 97   8
PUREED BROCCOLI SOUP
WITH BASIL . . . . Nov/Dec 96   23
PUREE OF BROCCOLI SOUP WITH GARLIC
AND HOT RED PEPPER . . . . Charter Issue   29
Quick Broccoli Prep . . . . Sep/Oct 97   8
SAUTÉED CHICKEN CUTLETS WITH
STEAMED/BOILED BROCCOLI . Sep/Oct 95   9
6-Minute Broccoli . . . . Sep/Oct 95   9
STIR-FRIED BROCCOLI WITH
ORANGE SAUCE . . . . Sep/Oct 95   9

Broccoli Rabe
ORECCHIETTE WITH BROCCOLI
RABE . . . . Jan/Feb 94   21

Cook's Illustrated 1993–1997 Index

Broth (*See* also Soup; Stock)

BROTH OF BLACK BASS AND MINCED
VEGETABLES . . . . Charter Issue   9

Chicken Broth Questions (Notes) . . Jul/Aug 94   3

Clarifying Broth (Notes) . . . . Nov/Dec 96   3

QUICK BROTH . . . . Charter Issue   28

Quick Homemade Chicken Soup . . Mar/Apr 96   14

Quick Salmon Broth . . . . Jul/Aug 93   25

SLOW-COOKED BROTH . . . . . Charter Issue   29

Taking Stock of Chicken
Broth (BT) . . . . Jan/Feb 94   24

VEGETABLE BROTH . . . . Charter Issue   29

VEGETABLE RISOTTO IN CARROT AND
CELERY BROTH . . . . Jan/Feb 94   27

What's the Difference Between
Broth and Stock? . . . . Charter Issue   28

Brownies

Basic Brownies Are Best . . . . Mar/Apr 94   22

THE BEST BROWNIES . . . . Mar/Apr 94   23

LOWER-FAT COCOA
BROWNIES . . . . Mar/Apr 94   23

Brown Rice

Aromatic Brown Rice (S&R) . . . . . Jan/Feb 94   32

BASIC BROWN RICE . . . . Jan/Feb 94   23

BROWN RICE AND CHICKPEA
SALAD . . . . Jan/Feb 94   23

BROWN RICE PILAF WITH
BROCCOLI . . . . Jan/Feb 94   23

Foolproof Brown Rice . . . . Jan/Feb 94   22

Brown Sugar

BROWN SUGAR AND HONEY
MUSTARD GLAZE . . . . Nov/Dec 93   12

QUICK-COOKED CARROTS WITH MUSTARD-
BROWN SUGAR GLAZE . . . . . . Mar/Apr 96   25

Packed Brown Sugar (QT) . . . . Mar/Apr 97   5

Softening Brown Sugar (Notes) . . . . Sep/Oct 94   3

Bruschetta (*See* also Crostini)

BAKED PEACH BRUSCHETTA . . . Sep/Oct 97   BC

Bruschetta: Italian Garlic Bread . . . Sep/Oct 96   8

BRUSCHETTA WITH FRESH
HERBS . . . . Sep/Oct 96   8

BRUSCHETTA WITH GRILLED PORTOBELLO
MUSHROOMS . . . . Sep/Oct 96   8

BRUSCHETTA WITH RED ONIONS,
HERBS, AND PARMESAN . . . . . Sep/Oct 96   8

BRUSCHETTA WITH TOMATOES
AND BASIL . . . . Sep/Oct 96   8

Brussels Sprouts

BASIC BRAISED BRUSSELS
SPROUTS . . . . Nov/Dec 95   21

BRAISED BRUSSELS SPROUTS WITH NUTMEG-
SCENTED WHITE SAUCE . . . . . Nov/Dec 95   21

BRAISED BRUSSELS SPROUTS WITH TARRAGON-
MUSTARD BUTTER . . . . Nov/Dec 95   21

BRUSSELS SPROUTS BRAISED
IN CREAM . . . . Nov/Dec 95   21

GLAZED BRUSSELS SPROUTS WITH
CHESTNUTS . . . . Nov/Dec 95   21

How to Cook Brussels Sprouts . . . . Nov/Dec 95   20

Preparing Brussels Sprouts (QT) . . Jan/Feb 94   5

SAUTÉED BRUSSELS SPROUTS WITH GARLIC
AND PINE NUTS . . . . Nov/Dec 95   2

Bulgar

Bulgar for Tabbooleh (S&R) . . . . . . Jul/Aug 94   32

Real Tabbooleh . . . . Jul/Aug 94   9

TABBOOLEH . . . . Jul/Aug 94   9

Butter

BOURBON BUTTER SAUCE . . . . Jan/Feb 95   25

BROWN BUTTER AND PINE
NUT SAUCE . . . . Sep/Oct 93   18

BUTTER COOKIE DOUGH
TOPPING . . . . Jul/Aug 96   19

BUTTER FROSTING . . . . May/Jun 95   19

Clarifying Butter (Notes) . . . . Jan/Feb 97   3

Cutting Butter for Pastry (QT) . . . May/Jun 94   5

GINGER BEURRE BLANC . . . . . . May/Jun 93   28

GRILLED LEEKS WITH ORANGE-
CHIVE BUTTER . . . . Mar/Apr 95   15

MARGARINE . . . . May/Jun 93   28

Melting Butter . . . . Nov/Dec 95   7

MULTIPURPOSE BUTTER COOKIE
DOUGH . . . . Nov/Dec 96   19

New Uses for Cheese Slicer (QT) . . Jan/Feb 97   4

Roquefort Butter . . . . May/Jun   9

The Science of Butter (Notes) . . . Charter Issue   2

Softening Butter for Mixing (QT) . . Jul/Aug 94   4

SPICY RED PEPPER BUTTER . . . Mar/Apr 95   20

Unsalted Butter for Greasing Pans
(Notes) . . . . Sep/Oct 95   3

Unsalted vs. Salted Butter
(Notes) . . . . Sep/Oct 94   2

Cook's Illustrated 1993–1997 Index

WHITE WINE–BUTTER SAUCE WITH
CAPERS . . . . Mar/Apr 95   19

Buttercream
Coffee Buttercream Frosting . . . . . . Jul/Aug 94   24

Buttermilk
BUTTERMILK-FRIED
CHICKEN . . . . May/Jun 94   9
BUTTERMILK LOAF BREAD . . . May/Jun 96   11
BUTTERMILK PECAN PIE WITH
RAISINS . . . . Nov/Dec 95   8
Clabbered Milk (Notes) . . . . Jul/Aug 96   2
FLUFFY BUTTERMILK
BISCUITS . . . . May/Jun 96   13
The Science of Buttermilk . . . . Jul/Aug 93   1
SPICY BUTTERMILK FRIED
CHICKEN . . . . Charter Issue   21

Butternut Squash (See Squash)

Butterscotch
BUTTERSCOTCH COOKIES . . . . Nov/Dec 96   20
BUTTERSCOTCH CREAM PIE . . Mar/Apr 96   24

Cabbage
BRAISED CABBAGE WITH PARSLEY
AND THYME . . . . Sep/Oct 96   9
CREAM-BRAISED CABBAGE WITH
LEMON AND SHALLOTS . . . . . Sep/Oct 96   9
CREAMY COLESLAW . . . . Jul/Aug 95   13
CURRIED COLESLAW WITH APPLES
AND RAISINS . . . . Jul/Aug 95   13
Five Chinese Cabbages . . . . Charter Issue   6
Grow Your Own Chinese Cabbages
(S&R) . . . . Charter Issue   7
HOME-CORNED BEEF BRISKET AND CABBAGE,
NEW ENGLAND STYLE . . . . . . Mar/Apr 97   11
HOT AND SOUR BOK CHOY . . Charter Issue   7
How to Cook Cabbage . . . . Sep/Oct 96   9
No More Watery Coleslaw . . . . Jul/Aug 95   12
PAN-BRAISED ROOT VEGETABLES WITH RED
CABBAGE AND ROSEMARY . . . Jan/Feb 96   26
Removing Leaves from Cabbage
(QT) . . . . Sep/Oct 95   4
RISOTTO WITH CABBAGE AND
COUNTRY HAM . . . . Mar/Apr 94   19
SEAFOOD CABBAGE
CASSEROLE . . . . Charter Issue   6

SESAME BEEF AND CABBAGE
FILLING . . . . Sep/Oct 94   15
STIR-FRIED CABBAGE . . . . . . Charter Issue   7
STIR-FRIED SHANGHAI BOK CHOY WITH
CRABMEAT . . . . Charter Issue   7
SWEET-AND-SOUR COLESLAW . . Jul/Aug 95   12
Wilting Cabbage Leaves for Stuffing
(Notes) . . . . May/Jun 97   3

Cakes (See also Decorating)
All-Purpose Birthday Cake . . . . . . May/Jun 95   18
ALMOND MERINGUE CAKE WITH
STRAWBERRY AND VANILLA ICE
CREAM . . . . May/Jun 95   13
Batter Skimmers (S&R) . . . . Nov/Dec 95   32
BRIOCHE RING . . . . Sep/Oct 95   16
CLASSIC GENOISE . . . . Nov/Dec 95   11
CLASSIC WHITE LAYER CAKE WITH BUTTER
FROSTING AND RASPBERRY-ALMOND
FILLING . . . . May/Jun 95   18
Cutting Another Cake (Notes) . . . . Nov/Dec 96   2
English Cake Mixer (Notes) . . . . . . Nov/Dec 93   3
English Cake Whisk (S&R) . . . . . . Nov/Dec 93   32
Foolproof Genoise, Master Class . . Nov/Dec 95   10
GRAND MARNIER CAKE WITH GRANNY'S
SPECKLED COCONUT CAKE . Mar/Apr 94   21
Keep Cake Filling from Bleeding into
Frosting (QT) . . . . Mar/Apr 95   4
Leveling a Cake Layer (QT) . . . . . . Mar/Apr 96   4
Magi-Cake Strips . . . . Jul/Aug 96   17
Make Even Layer Cake (QT) . . . . . May/Jun 95   4
Making a Jelly Roll . . . . Jan/Feb 94   15
Measuring Cake Batter (QT) . . . . . Jul/Aug 94   5
MISSISSIPPI MUD CAKE . . . . . . Jul/Aug 93   3
Moving Cake Layers (QT) . . . . Sep/Oct 94   5
NEAPOLITAN ORANGE
CAKE . . . . Charter Issue   15
NEOCLASSIC ORANGE BUTTER
CREAM . . . . Nov/Dec 95   11
On Cocoa in Cake (Notes) . . . . Mar/Apr 96   3
A Piece of Cake (Notes) . . . . Nov/Dec 96   2
RASPBERRY BRIOCHE
SHORTCAKE . . . . Sep/Oct 95   17
RASPBERRY CHARLOTTE
ROYALE . . . . Jan/Feb 94   14
Removing Cake from a Bundt
Pan (QT) . . . . Nov/Dec 96   5
Replicate Magi-Cake Strips (QT) . . Mar/Apr 95   5
Sizing a Parchment Paper Liner . . May/Jun 93   4

SPONGE SHEET CAKE . . . . Nov/Dec 96   9
STRAWBERRY SHORTCAKE. . . . May/Jun 93   12
Torting a Cake (QT) . . . . Jan/Feb 94   5
Tube Pans (S&R) . . . . May/Jun 96   32

angel food
THE BEST ANGEL FOOD
   CAKE. . . . . Charter Issue   12
The Perfect Angel Food Cake . . . Charter Issue   10

cheesecake
Cheesecake: One Recipe, Three
   Textures. . . . . Sep/Oct 95   6
Cheesecake Slicing (Notes) . . . . Sep/Oct 97   2
DENSE AND FIRM
   CHEESECAKE. . . . . Sep/Oct 95   8
LIGHT AND AIRY
   CHEESECAKE. . . . . Sep/Oct 95   8
RICH AND CREAMY
   CHEESECAKE. . . . . Sep/Oct 95   8

chiffon
BANANA-NUT CHIFFON CAKE . May/Jun 96   8
CHIFFON CAKE, MASTER
   RECIPE FOR . . . . May/Jun 96   7
CHOCOLATE MARBLE CHIFFON
   CAKE . . . . May/Jun 96   8
CRANBERRY-ORANGE CHIFFON
   CAKE . . . . May/Jun 96   8
DATE-SPICE CHIFFON CAKE . . May/Jun 96   8
LEMON-COCONUT CHIFFON
   CAKE. May/Jun 96   8
MOCHA-NUT CHIFFON CAKE . . May/Jun 96   8
ORANGE CHIFFON CAKE. . . . . . May/Jun 96   8
RED VELVET CHIFFON CAKE . . May/Jun 96   8
Secrets of Chiffon Cake . . . . May/Jun 96   6

chocolate
CHOCOLATE PUDDING CAKE . . Jan/Feb 95   25
CLASSIC DEVIL'S FOOD LAYER CAKE
   WITH WHIPPED CREAM . . . . . Jul/Aug 94   24
GERMAN CHOCOLATE–STYLE LAYER
   CAKE WITH COCONUT-PECAN
   FILLING . . . . Jul/Aug 94   25
MISSISSIPPI MUD CAKE (Notes) . Jul/Aug 93   3
OLD-FASHIONED CHOCOLATE
   LAYER CAKE WITH CHOCOLATE
   CREAM FROSTING . . . . Jul/Aug 94   24
On Cocoa in Cake (Notes) . . . . Mar/Apr 96   3
REDUCED-GUILT CHOCOLATE LAYER CAKE
   WITH MERINGUE FROSTING . Jul/Aug 94   25
Six Chocolate Cakes . . . . Jul/Aug 94   22
SOUR CREAM-FUDGE LAYER CAKE WITH

CHOCOLATE BUTTER ICING . . Jul/Aug 94   25
VELVET DEVIL'S FOOD LAYER CAKE
   WITH COFFEE BUTTERCREAM
   FROSTING . . . . Jul/Aug 94   24

coffee cakes
APPLE-CINNAMON COFFEE
   CAKE. . . . . Mar/Apr 95   21
COCONUT CHOCOLATE CHIP COFFEE
   CAKE. . . . . Mar/Apr 95   21
Quick Crumb Coffee Cake . . . . Mar/Apr 95   21
QUICK CRUMB COFFEE CAKE . Mar/Apr 95   21
RASPBERRY-ALMOND COFFEE
   CAKE. . . . . Mar/Apr 95   21

gingerbread
APPLE UPSIDE-DOWN
   GINGERBREAD . . . . Nov/Dec 95   23
GINGERBREAD WITH DRIED
   FRUIT . . . . Nov/Dec 95   23
Old-Fashioned Gingerbread . . . . . . Nov/Dec 95   22
OLD-FASHIONED
   GINGERBREAD . . . . Nov/Dec 95   23

panforte
Authentic Panforte Di Siena,
   Master Class . . . . Nov/Dec 94   12
BLOND PANFORTE . . . . Nov/Dec 94   13
CHOCOLATE PANFORTE. . . . . . Nov/Dec 94   13
DRIED FRUIT PANFORTE. . . . . . Nov/Dec 94   13
PANFORTE DI SIENA. . . . . Nov/Dec 94   12
Panforte Essentials (S&R) . . . . Nov/Dec 94   32

poundcake
The Best Poundcake. . . . . May/Jun 94   18
THE BEST POUNDCAKE. . . . . . May/Jun 94   20
CITRUS POUNDCAKE. . . . . May/Jun 94   20
GINGER POUNDCAKE . . . . May/Jun 94   20
ROSE WATER POUNDCAKE. . . . May/Jun 94   20
SEED CAKE . . . . May/Jun 94   20

pudding cakes
CHOCOLATE PUDDING CAKE . . Jan/Feb 95   25
COFFEE PUDDING CAKE . . . . . . Jan/Feb 95   25
LEMON PUDDING CAKE . . . . . . Jan/Feb 95   24
The Magic of Pudding Cakes. . . . . . Jan/Feb 95   24
ORANGE PUDDING CAKE . . . . . Jan/Feb 95   25
Pudding Cake Ramekins (S&R) . . . Jan/Feb 95   32
VANILLA-BOURBON PUDDING
   CAKE. . . . . Jan/Feb 95   25

Cannellini (*See* **White Beans**)

Capers

Cook's Illustrated 1993–1997 Index

CHICKEN IN THE POT WITH TOMATOES,
BLACK OLIVES, AND CAPERS . Sep/Oct 95 19
LEMON-CAPER SAUCE......... Sep/Oct 93 10
ONION, BLACK OLIVE, AND CAPER
COMPOTE .... May/Jun 94 13
PANFRIED SOFT-SHELL CRABS WITH LEMONS,
CAPERS, AND HERBS........ May/Jun 95 7
Removing Capers from the Jar ... May/Jun 97 5
ROAST LEG OF LAMB WITH PIQUANT
CAPER SAUCE............. Mar/Apr 94 10
SAUTÉED PORK CHOPS WITH MUSTARD AND
CAPERS.................... Sep/Oct 94 13
TOMATO-BASIL SAUCE WITH
CAPERS.................... Sep/Oct 93 11
WHITE WINE–BUTTER SAUCE WITH
CAPERS .... Mar/Apr 95 19

Carambola
Preparing Tropical Fruit......... Jan/Feb 94 16

Caraway
FRENCH LENTIL SALAD WITH CARAWAY
AND RADISH .... Mar/Apr 95 25

Cardamom
PUREE OF CAULIFLOWER SOUP WITH
CARDAMOM AND MACE.... Charter Issue 29

Carrots
BRAISED CARROTS WITH SOUR
CREAM–CILANTRO SAUCE ... Jan/Feb 96 BC
CHICKEN IN THE POT WITH CARROTS,
MUSHROOMS, AND THYME ... Sep/Oct 95 19
CURRIED CHICKEN FILLING WITH CARROTS
AND BASIL .... Sep/Oct 94 15
How to Quick-Cook Carrots ...... Mar/Apr 96 25
PAN-BRAISED ROOT VEGETABLES WITH RED
CABBAGE AND ROSEMARY ... Jan/Feb 96 26
PUREED CARROT SOUP WITH
NUTMEG .... Nov/Dec 96 23
QUICK-COOKED CARROTS WITH
BUTTER AND PARSLEY...... Mar/Apr 96 25
QUICK-COOKED CARROTS WITH MUSTARD-
BROWN SUGAR GLAZE ...... Mar/Apr 96 25
QUICK-COOKED CARROTS WITH ORANGE
AND PISTACHIO .... Mar/Apr 96 25
QUICK-COOKED CARROTS WITH VINEGAR
AND THYME .... Mar/Apr 96 25
ROASTED CARROTS AND PARSLEY

ROOTS .... Jul/Aug 93 25
ROASTED CARROTS AND RED ONION WITH
BALSAMIC VINEGAR......... Jan/Feb 94 11
ROASTED FENNEL WITH RED ONIONS
AND CARROTS .... May/Jun 96 19
SHREDDED ZUCCHINI AND CARROT SAUTÉ
WITH GARLIC AND HERBS ... Jul/Aug 95 9
VEGETABLE RISOTTO IN CARROT AND
CELERY BROTH............. Jan/Feb 94 27

Carving
Carve a Half-Ham (QT) .... Charter Issue 5
Carve a Whole Ham (QT) ...... Charter Issue 5
Carve It Simply .... Nov/Dec 95 13
Carving a Rib Roast (QT)....... Nov/Dec 93 5
Cleaning, Boning, and Carving a
Leg of Lamb .... Mar/Apr 94 9
How a Chef Carves a Chicken .. Charter Issue 26
How to Carve Turkey and Goose .. Nov/Dec 94 16
Two-Part Steaks.............. May/Jun 96 24
When to Carve Prime Rib (Notes) . Mar/Apr 96 3

Cauliflower
Breaking Cauliflower into
Florets (QT)................ Sep/Oct 93 5
ORECCHIETTE WITH CAULIFLOWER
AND BACON .... Jan/Feb 94 21
Pickled Curried Cauliflower ...... Sep/Oct 94 19
PUREED CAULIFLOWER SOUP
WITH CORIANDER .... Nov/Dec 96 23
PUREE OF CAULIFLOWER SOUP WITH
CARDAMOM AND MACE.... Charter Issue 29

Caviar
Caviar by Mail (S&R).......... Nov/Dec 93 32
Caviar Tasting Finds Quality
Disappointing (BT) .... Nov/Dec 93 26

CD-ROMs
Better Homes and Gardens Healthy
Cooking Deluxe............. Mar/Apr 97 31
Elle Cooking................. Mar/Apr 97 31
4 Paws of Crab .... Mar/Apr 97 31
John Ash's Wine Country
Cuisine .... Mar/Apr 97 31
Julia Child: Home Cooking with
the Master Chefs .... Mar/Apr 97 31
Vegetarian Delights .... Mar/Apr 97 31
Williams-Sonoma Guide to

Cook's Illustrated 1993–1997 Index

Good Cooking . . . . Mar/Apr 97   31
World Cuisine Chinese . . . . Mar/Apr 97   31

Celery
BRAISED CELERY . . . . Jul/Aug 93   25
BRAISED CELERY WITH VERMOUTH-
    BUTTER GLAZE . . . . Mar/Apr 97   24
BROCCOFLOWER AND CELERY
    SALAD . . . . May/Jun 95   23
CELERY-ROQUEFORT GRATIN . Mar/Apr 97   24
Chopping Celery Quickly (QT) . . . . Nov/Dec 94   5
GLAZED CELERY WITH
    PARMESAN CHEESE . . . . Mar/Apr 97   24
VEGETABLE RISOTTO IN CARROT
    AND CELERY BROTH . . . . Jan/Feb 94   27

Celery Root
CELERY ROOT AND POTATO ROESTI WITH
    LEMON AND PARSLEY . . . . . . Jan/Feb 95   22
PAN-BRAISED ROOT VEGETABLES WITH RED
    CABBAGE AND ROSEMARY . . . Jan/Feb 96   26

Ceviche
BASIC CEVICHE . . . . Jul/Aug 96   15
SCALLOP CEVICHE WITH SWEET
    PEPPER CONFETTI . . . . Jul/Aug 96   15
Simple Scallop Ceviche . . . . Jul/Aug 96   15
SOY-GINGER SCALLOP
    CEVICHE . . . . Jul/Aug 96   15

Champagne
Tasting True Champagnes (BT) . . . Nov/Dec 96   30

Cheddar Cheese
GOLDEN CORNBREAD WITH
    CHEDDAR . . . . Sep/Oct 95   21
HERBED ROESTI WITH SMOKED
    CHEDDAR . . . . Jan/Feb 95   22
SPOON BREAD WITH CHEDDAR
    CHEESE . . . . Nov/Dec 96   25

Cheese (See also specific kinds)
BROILED EGGPLANT SLICES
    WITH TWO CHEESES . . . . Jul/Aug 93   7
Cheese Grater (S&R) . . . . Sep/Oct 94   32
CHEESE OMELET . . . . Sep/Oct 93   22
CRISPY CHEESE WAFERS . . . . . May/Jun 96   17
FRITTATA WITH CHEESE AND
    FRESH HERBS . . . . Mar/Apr 96   11

Grating Hard Cheeses (QT) . . . . . . Sep/Oct 95   4
GRILLED SHRIMP PIZZA TOPPING WITH
    ROASTED TOMATOES AND FARMER'S
    CHEESE . . . . May/Jun 93   9
Homemade Yogurt Cheese
    (Notes) . . . . May/Jun 95   2
Making Yogurt Cheese (QT) . . . . . Mar/Apr 96   4
Making Yogurt Cheese (QT) . . . . . Sep/Oct 94   4
MEAT AND RICOTTA FILLING WITH
    BASIL FOR PASTA . . . . Sep/Oct 93   18
POACHED PEARS ON SALAD GREENS WITH
    WALNUTS AND STILTON . . . . . Jan/Feb 94   BC
ROASTED TOMATO PIZZA TOPPING WITH
    FENNEL AND ASIAGO . . . . . . May/Jun 93   9
SPINACH AND RICOTTA FILLING
    FOR PASTA . . . . Sep/Oct 93   18

Cheesecake
Cheesecake: One Recipe, Three
    Textures . . . . Sep/Oct 95   6
Cheesecake Slicing (Notes) . . . . Sep/Oct 97   2
DENSE AND FIRM
    CHEESECAKE . . . . Sep/Oct 95   8
LIGHT AND AIRY
    CHEESECAKE . . . . Sep/Oct 95   8
RICH AND CREAMY
    CHEESECAKE . . . . Sep/Oct 95   8

Cherimoya
Preparing Tropical Fruit . . . . Jan/Feb 94   17

Cherries (See also Fruit, Fresh)
CHERRY PIE . . . . Jul/Aug 95   7
Cherry Pitter (S&R) . . . . Jul/Aug 93   32
Cherry Pitting (Notes) . . . . Jul/Aug 94   3
Dried Sweet Cherries (S&R) . . . . . Sep/Oct 97   32
How to Poach Fruit . . . . May/Jun 93   24
PEACHES AND CHERRIES POACHED
    IN SPICED RED WINE . . . . . . May/Jun 93   26
SWEET BREAD WITH ALMONDS AND
    DRIED CHERRIES . . . . May/Jun 94   29

Chestnuts
Dried Chestnuts (S&R) . . . . Nov/Dec 95   32
GLAZED BRUSSELS SPROUTS WITH
    CHESTNUTS . . . . Nov/Dec 95   21
Peeling (QT) . . . . Jan/Feb 94   4
SAUSAGE AND PEAR STUFFING WITH
    CHESTNUTS AND PRUNES . . . Nov/Dec 95   26

Cook's Illustrated 1993–1997 Index

Chicken

BASIC RECIPE FOR ROAST
CHICKEN . . . . Charter Issue 27

Better Fried Chicken (QT) . . . . Nov/Dec 95 5

Boning a Chicken Thigh (QT). . . . . Nov/Dec 94 4

BROILED BUTTERFLIED CHICKEN WITH
PARMESAN, LEMON, AND RED PEPPER
FLAKES . . . . Sep/Oct 94 25

Butterflying a Chicken Breast
(QT). . . . . May/Jun 94 5

BUTTERMILK-FRIED
CHICKEN. . . . . May/Jun 94 9

CHICKEN AND DUMPLINGS WITH
AROMATIC VEGETABLES . . . . Mar/Apr 97 8

CHICKEN AND HERBED DUMPLINGS WITH
AROMATIC VEGETABLES . . . . Mar/Apr 97 8

CHICKEN CURRY WITH SPINACH
AND FENUGREEK . . . . Jan/Feb 97 9

CHICKEN CURRY WITH YOGURT,
CILANTRO, AND ZUCCHINI . . . Jan/Feb 97 9

Chicken in the Pot . . . . Sep/Oct 95 18

CHICKEN IN THE POT WITH CARROTS,
MUSHROOMS, AND THYME . . . Sep/Oct 95 19

CHICKEN IN THE POT WITH POTATOES
AND INDIAN SPICES . . . . Sep/Oct 95 19

CHICKEN IN THE POT WITH TOMATOES,
BLACK OLIVES, AND CAPERS . . Sep/Oct 95 19

CHICKEN IN THE POT WITH TURNIPS AND
NORTH AFRICAN SPICES . . . . . Sep/Oct 95 19

CHICKEN ROASTED IN RED
PEPPERS. . . . . Sep/Oct 93 BC

CHICKEN SAUSAGE WITH APPLES
AND SAGE. . . . . Mar/Apr 96 12

CHICKEN SAUSAGE WITH MEDITERRANEAN
FLAVORS . . . . Mar/Apr 96 12

CURRIED CHICKEN FILLING WITH CARROTS
AND BASIL . . . . Sep/Oct 94 15

EASY ROAST CHICKEN . . . . Jan/Feb 96 11

Fried Chicken Comments (Notes) . . Jan/Feb 95 3

GARLIC AND BASIL ROAST CHICKEN WITH
LEMON PAN SAUCE . . . . Sep/Oct 93 20

GRILLED BONE-IN CHICKEN BREASTS
WITH BARBECUE SAUCE . . . . . . Jul/Aug 97 15

GRILLED BUTTERFLIED CHICKEN WITH ROSE-
MARY, LEMON, AND GARLIC . . Sep/Oct 94 24

GRILLED CHICKEN WITH OLIVES, ROSEMARY,
AND GARLIC. . . . . Jul/Aug 93 12

Grilling Chicken Legs and Thighs. . Jul/Aug 96 22

GRILL-ROASTED HICKORY

CHICKEN . . . . Jul/Aug 93 20

How to Cut Up a Chicken . . . . Mar/Apr 97 7

How to Sauté Chicken. . . . . Sep/Oct 93 9

MAHOGANY GRILLED CHICKEN
THIGHS OR LEGS . . . . Jul/Aug 96 23

GRILLED BONE-IN CHICKEN BREASTS,
MASTER RECIPE FOR . . . . Jul/Aug 97 15

STIR-FRY, MASTER RECIPE
FOR. . . . . Mar/Apr 96 20

One-Pot Chicken Pot Pie . . . . May/Jun 96 12

PAELLA, CRIOLLA'S STYLE. . . . . Jan/Feb 95 11

POACHED CHICKEN WITH CREAMED
GRAVY AND AROMATIC
VEGETABLES . . . . Mar/Apr 97 8

Preflavoring Frozen Chicken
Breasts (QT). . . . . Sep/Oct 97 5

Produce Uniform Pieces of Chicken
Breast . . . . May/Jun 93 20

Rediscovering Fried Chicken . . . . . May/Jun 94 6

Removing Drumstick Tendons
(QT). . . . . Nov/Dec 96 5

Roast Chicken Reply (Notes) . . . . . May/Jun 93 3

ROAST CHICKEN WITH DIJON
MUSTARD–THYME SAUCE . . . May/Jun 93 28

ROASTED BUTTERFLIED CHICKEN
WITH TARRAGON-MUSTARD
PAN SAUCE. . . . . Sep/Oct 94 25

Roasting Chicken 14 Ways . . . . Jan/Feb 96 9

SAUTÉED BUTTERFLIED CHICKEN
WITH MUSHROOM-SAGE PAN
SAUCE. . . . . Sep/Oct 94 25

SAUTÉED CHICKEN BREAST CUTLETS,
MASTER RECIPE FOR . . . . Sep/Oct 93 10

SAUTÉED CHICKEN CUTLETS WITH
BROCCOLI-BASIL SAUCE . . . . . Jan/Feb 94 27

Secrets of Butterflied Chicken. . . . . Sep/Oct 94 23

SIMPLE CHICKEN POT PIE . . . . May/Jun 96 13

Simple Chicken Trussing (Notes) . May/Jun 93 3

SIMPLE ROAST CHICKEN
BREASTS . . . . Jul/Aug 97 8

SLOW-ROASTED CHICKEN . . . . . Jan/Feb 96 11

Specialty Chickens Win
Tasting (BT). . . . . Sep/Oct 94 26

SPICE-RUBBED GRILLED BONE-IN
CHICKEN BREASTS . . . . Jul/Aug 97 15

SPICE RUB FOR CHICKEN . . . . . Jul/Aug 95 21

SPICY BUTTERMILK FRIED
CHICKEN . . . . Charter Issue 21

Stabilizing Stuffed Chicken

Cook's Illustrated 1993–1997 Index

Breasts (QT) . . . . Nov/Dec 96   4
STOVE-TOP TEA-SMOKED
    CHICKEN. . . . . May/Jun 95   15
Taking Poultry Temperature (QT) . May/Jun 94   5
Tea-Smoked Chicken . . . . May/Jun 95   14
Tools for Butterflying Chicken
    (S&R). . . . . Sep/Oct 94   32
Trussing Needles (S&R) . . . . Sep/Oct 94   32
The Way to Roast Chicken . . . . . Charter Issue   27
salad
CHICKEN SALAD WITH HOISIN
    DRESSING . . . . Jul/Aug 97   8
CLASSIC CREAMY CHICKEN
    SALAD . . . . Jul/Aug 97   8
CURRIED CHICKEN SALAD
    WITH RAISINS AND HONEY . . . . Jul/Aug 97   8
Preparing the Chicken . . . . Jul/Aug 97   8
WALDORF CHICKEN SALAD . . . Jul/Aug 97   8
soup
HEARTY CHICKEN NOODLE SOUP,
    MASTER RECIPE FOR . . . . . . Mar/Apr 96   15
HEARTY CHICKEN SOUP WITH LEEKS, WILD
    RICE, AND MUSHROOMS . . . . Mar/Apr 96   15
HEARTY CHICKEN SOUP WITH ORZO AND
    SPRING VEGETABLES . . . . . . Mar/Apr 96   15
HEARTY CHICKEN SOUP WITH SHELLS,
    TOMATOES, AND ZUCCHINI . Mar/Apr 96   15
Quick Homemade Chicken Soup . . Mar/Apr 96   14

Chickpeas
BROWN RICE AND CHICKPEA
    SALAD . . . . Jan/Feb 94   23
MOROCCAN LAMB BROTH WITH CHICKPEAS
    AND VEGETABLES . . . . Mar/Apr 95   13

Chile Peppers
Avoiding the Burn of Chile
    Peppers (QT). . . . . Nov/Dec 95   4
BLACK BEAN–MANGO SALSA. . . Jul/Aug 96   21
BRAISED LAMB SHANKS WITH NORTH
    AFRICAN SPICES. . . . . Jan/Feb 95   19
BROILED OYSTERS TOPPED WITH ROASTED
    CHILE-CILANTRO SAUCE . . . . Nov/Dec 94   BC
CHILE DIPPING SAUCE . . . . Sep/Oct 94   15
CLASSIC RED TABLE SALSA. . . . Jul/Aug 96   21
CORN AND ZUCCHINI SAUTÉ
    WITH CHILES. . . . . Jul/Aug 93   9
Cutting and Seeding Dried
    Chiles (QT). . . . . Sep/Oct 93   4

Dried Chiles (S&R) . . . . May/Jun 93   32
GOLDEN CORNBREAD WITH
    JALAPEÑOS . . . . Sep/Oct 95   21
GRILLED JALAPEÑO SALSA . . . . Jul/Aug 96   21
Hot Peppers (S&R) . . . . Jul/Aug 96   32
Paprika Peppers (Notes). . . . . . . Charter Issue   3
PUREE OF BROCCOLI SOUP WITH GARLIC
    AND HOT RED PEPPER . . . . Charter Issue   29
Quick-Cooked Tomatillo-Chile
    Sauce . . . . Jul/Aug 94   14
Rehydrating Dried Ingredients
    (QT). Nov/Dec 95   5
ROAST LEG OF LAMB WITH RED CHILE
    CRUST AND JALAPEÑO
    PRESERVES . . . . May/Jun 93   22
Seeding Fresh Chile Peppers
    (QT) . . . . Mar/Apr 94   4
SIMPLE PEACH SALSA. . . . . Jul/Aug 96   21
Sorting Out Chiles. . . . . May/Jun 93   23
SZECHWAN CHILI SAUCE . . . . . May/Jun 93   19
THAI-STYLE ASPARAGUS WITH CHILES,
    GARLIC, AND BASIL. . . . . May/Jun 93   7
TOMATO BASE WITH POBLANOS AND
    CILANTRO. . . . . Jan/Feb 95   11

Chili
SPICY CHILI RUB . . . . Jul/Aug 97   20

Chives
CREAMY POTATO SOUP WITH
    CHIVES . . . . Nov/Dec 96   23
GRILLED LEEKS WITH ORANGE-CHIVE
    BUTTER . . . . Mar/Apr 95   15
LEMON-CHIVE VINAIGRETTE. . May/Jun 94   12
ROASTED SWEET POTATOES
    WITH CHIVES. . . . . Jan/Feb 94   11
SMOKED SALMON AND CHIVE MILLE
    FEUILLE . . . . Mar/Apr 94   17
TWO-MUSTARD DRESSING WITH
    CHIVES. . . . . Charter Issue   30

Chocolate
ALL-PURPOSE CHOCOLATE GLAZE
    AND FROSTING. . . . . Nov/Dec 96   20
Are Expensive Chocolates Worth
    the Money? (BT) . . . . Nov/Dec 94   25
Chasing the Chew (Notes) . . . . . . Jul/Aug 96   2
CHOCOLATE COCONUT
    TRUFFLES . . . . Nov/Dec 97   25

CHOCOLATE CREAM PIE . . . . . . Mar/Apr 96   24
CHOCOLATE FROZEN
   YOGURT. . . . . May/Jun 96   15
CHOCOLATE MADELEINES . . . . Mar/Apr 96   21
CHOCOLATE MOUSSE . . . . Jul/Aug 96   7
CHOCOLATE NUT TRUFFLES . . Nov/Dec 97   25
CHOCOLATE SOUFFLÉ . . . . Sep/Oct 96   19
CHOCOLATE TRINITY
   PARFAITS. . . . . Nov/Dec 93   BC
Chopping a Block of Chocolate
   (QT) . . . . Mar/Apr 94   4
Decorating with Chocolate. . . . . . May/Jun 97   21
Elegant Dipped Strawberries
   (QT) . . . . Jul/Aug 97   5
FROZEN HOT CHOCOLATE . . . . May/Jun 95   BC
FUDGE-ALMOND MACAROONS . Sep/Oct 96   6
MAKE-AHEAD CHOCOLATE
   SOUFFLÉ. . . . . Sep/Oct 96   19
Making Perfect Dipped Berries
   (QT). Mar/Apr 96   5
Mastering the Chocolate Soufflé . . Sep/Oct 96   18
Melting and Holding Chocolate
   (QT) . . . . Jan/Feb 94   4
The Perfect Chocolate Truffle . . . . Nov/Dec 97   25
PERFECT CHOCOLATE TRUFFLES,
   MASTER RECIPE FOR . . . . Nov/Dec 97   25
Rating Unsweetened (Baking)
   Chocolate (BT) . . . . Jan/Feb 97   27
Rating White Chocolate (BT) . . . . Nov/Dec 97   27
Simple Chocolate Decorations . . . . Mar/Apr 96   16
TRIPLE CHOCOLATE CHUNK
   PECAN PIE. . . . . Nov/Dec 95   8
The Ultimate Chocolate Mousse. . . Jul/Aug 96   6

brownies
Basic Brownies Are Best . . . . Mar/Apr 94   22
THE BEST BROWNIES . . . . Mar/Apr 94   23
LOWER-FAT COCOA
   BROWNIES . . . . Mar/Apr 94   23

cakes
CHOCOLATE MARBLE CHIFFON
   CAKE . . . . May/Jun 96   8
CHOCOLATE PUDDING CAKE . . Jan/Feb 95   25
CHOCOLATE PANFORTE. . . . . . Nov/Dec 94   13
CLASSIC DEVIL'S FOOD LAYER CAKE
   WITH WHIPPED CREAM . . . . . Jul/Aug 94   24
COCONUT CHOCOLATE CHIP
   COFFEE CAKE. . . . . Mar/Apr 95   21
GERMAN CHOCOLATE–STYLE LAYER
   CAKE WITH COCONUT-PECAN

FILLING . . . . Jul/Aug 94   25
MISSISSIPPI MUD CAKE (Notes) . Jul/Aug 93   3
MOCHA-NUT CHIFFON CAKE . May/Jun 96   8
OLD-FASHIONED CHOCOLATE LAYER
   CAKE WITH CHOCOLATE CREAM
   FROSTING. . . . . Jul/Aug 94   24
REDUCED-GUILT CHOCOLATE LAYER
   CAKE WITH MERINGUE
   FROSTING. . . . . Jul/Aug 94   25
RED VELVET CHIFFON CAKE . . May/Jun 96   8
Six Chocolate Cakes . . . . Jul/Aug 94   23
SOUR CREAM-FUDGE LAYER CAKE WITH
   CHOCOLATE BUTTER ICING . . Jul/Aug 94   25
VELVET DEVIL'S FOOD LAYER CAKE
   WITH COFFEE BUTTERCREAM
   FROSTING. . . . . Jul/Aug 94   24

cocoa
Cocoa Powder (Notes) . . . . Jul/Aug 94   2
Dutched vs. Natural Cocoas (BT) . . Sep/Oct 95   26
HOT COCOA WITH ORANGE . . . . Jan/Feb 97   11
HOT COCOA, MASTER RECIPE
   FOR . . . . Jan/Feb 97   11
LOWER-FAT COCOA
   BROWNIES . . . . Mar/Apr 94   23
On Cocoa in Cake (Notes) . . . . . . Mar/Apr 96   3
Questioning Cocoa (Notes) . . . . . . Mar/Apr 96   3

cookies
CHOCOLATE BUTTER COOKIE
   DOUGH. . . . . Nov/Dec 93   7
Chocolate Chip Cookie Conundrum
   (Notes). . . . . May/Jun 96   2
CHOCOLATE-CINNAMON
   COOKIES . . . . Nov/Dec 96   20
Chocolate-Coating Bar Cookies
   (QT) . . . . May/Jun 96   4
Solving the Mystery of the Chewy
   Chocolate Chip Cookie . . . . Jan/Feb 96   22
THICK AND CHEWY CHOCOLATE CHIP
   COOKIES . . . . Jan/Feb 96   23

sauces
HOT FUDGE SAUCE . . . . Jul/Aug 97   21
WARM BITTERSWEET
   CHOCOLATE SAUCE . . . . Jul/Aug 97   21

Chutney
CURRIED APPLE-CRANBERRY
   CHUTNEY . . . . Nov/Dec 94   14
CURRIED FRUIT CHUTNEY WITH LIME
   AND GINGER . . . . Jul/Aug 94   20

Cook's Illustrated 1993–1997 Index

SOUTHEAST ASIAN–STYLE COCONUT
CHUTNEY . . . . Mar/Apr 94   20

Cider

CIDER-BAKED APPLES WITH
CINNAMON-SUGAR . . . . Sep/Oct 95   13
HORSERADISH AND CIDER
CREAM SAUCE . . . . Sep/Oct 95   24

Cilantro

BRAISED CARROTS WITH SOUR
CREAM–CILANTRO SAUCE . . . Jan/Feb 96   BC
BROILED OYSTERS TOPPED WITH ROASTED
CHILE–CILANTRO SAUCE . . . . Nov/Dec 94   BC
CHILI SPICE PASTE WITH CITRUS
AND CILANTRO . . . . Jul/Aug 96   23
CILANTRO CREAM . . . . Jan/Feb 96   13
CILANTRO PESTO . . . . May/Jun 93   22
CREAM-CILANTRO SAUCE . . . . . Jan/Feb 96   BC
ED BROWN'S SEARED SCALLOPS WITH
CILANTRO PESTO . . . . Mar/Apr 96   8
MUNG BEAN SAUCE WITH GINGER,
CILANTRO, AND SOY . . . . Sep/Oct 95   24
TENDER GREENS WITH CUMIN,
TOMATOES, AND CILANTRO . . Sep/Oct 94   21
TOMATO BASE WITH POBLANOS
AND CILANTRO. . . . . Jan/Feb 95   11

Cinnamon

APPLE-CINNAMON COFFEE
CAKE . . . . Mar/Apr 95   21
BEEF STEW WITH TOMATOES, CINNAMON,
AND CLOVES . . . . Jan/Feb 96   20
CHOCOLATE-CINNAMON
COOKIES . . . . Nov/Dec 96   20
CIDER-BAKED APPLES WITH
CINNAMON-SUGAR . . . . Sep/Oct 95   13
CINNAMON-WALNUT FILLING . . Sep/Oct 95   15
OAXACAN-STYLE SAUCE WITH
CLOVES AND CINNAMON . . . . . Sep/Oct 93   10
RICE PUDDING WITH CINNAMON
AND DRIED FRUIT . . . . Sep/Oct 96   25

Citrus Fruit

Bowls. . . . . Jan/Feb 97   17
CHILI SPICE PASTE WITH CITRUS
AND CILANTRO . . . . Jul/Aug 96   23
Citrus as Cleaner (QT) . . . . Jan/Feb 97   4
CITRUS POUNDCAKE . . . . May/Jun 94   20

CORNMEAL-CITRUS COOKIES. . Nov/Dec 96   20
Decorative Slices . . . . Jan/Feb 97   16
Juice . . . . Jan/Feb 97   17
Juicing Lemons (Notes) . . . . Mar/Apr 94   2
Rating Orange Juices (BT). . . . . . May/Jun 97   29
Sections. . . . . Jan/Feb 97   17
Wedges . . . . Jan/Feb 97   17
Zest . . . . Jan/Feb 97   16
Zesters. . . . . Jan/Feb 97   16

Citrus Oils

CITRUS BUTTER COOKIE
DOUGH. . . . . Nov/Dec 93   7
Citrus Oils (S&R) . . . . Nov/Dec 93   32
Clabbered Milk
Clabbered Milk (Notes) . . . . Jul/Aug 96   2
More Details on Clabbered Milk
(Notes) . . . . Nov/Dec 96   2

Clams

CAVATELLI WITH WHITE BEANS
AND CLAMS. . . . . Jan/Feb 94   19
CLAM SAUCE WITH TOMATOES
AND GARLIC . . . . Mar/Apr 96   9
CORN AND CLAM CHOWDER WITH
ROASTED PARSNIPS . . . . Jul/Aug 93   9
PASTA WITH FRESH CLAM
SAUCE . . . . Nov/Dec 97   14
Cleanup and Mess Control Avoiding
Splatters when Mixing (QT) . . . . May/Jun 94   4
Citrus as Cleaner (QT) . . . . Jan/Feb 97   4
Cleaning a Burr Coffee Grinder,
Carefully (Notes) . . . . Jan/Feb 97   2
Cleaning Burr Coffee Grinders
(Notes) . . . . Nov/Dec 95   2
Cleaning Coffee Grinders (QT) . . . Jul/Aug 95   4
Cleaning Out a Meat Grinder
(QT). . . . . Jan/Feb 97   4
Cleaning the Trifle Bowl (QT) . . . . Nov/Dec 96   4
Disposing of Bacon Fat (QT) . . . . . Jul/Aug 97   4
Espresso Spick-and-Span (Notes). . Nov/Dec 97   3
For Dirty Blade-Type Coffee
Grinders (Notes). . . . . Jan/Feb 97   2
Grease Pans, Mess-Free (QT) . . . . Mar/Apr 95   5
Grinding without mess (QT) . . . . . Mar/Apr 96   4
Keeping the Cake Plate
Clean (QT) . . . . May/Jun 97   4
Mess-Free Piping (QT) . . . . Nov/Dec 97   4
Salad Without the Bowl (Notes) . . . Jul/Aug 97   3

Splatter-Free Mixing (QT)........ Jul/Aug 97   5
Stain-Free Plastic Containers
    (QT)..................... Nov/Dec 97   4

Clotted Cream
Clotted Cream (Notes).......... Jan/Feb 95   2
HOMEMADE CLOTTED CREAM
    (Notes).................... Jan/Feb 95   3

Cloves
OAXACAN-STYLE SAUCE WITH CLOVES
    AND CINNAMON .... Sep/Oct 93   10

Cocoa
Cocoa Powder (Notes) .... Jul/Aug 94   2
Dutched vs. Natural Cocoas (BT) .. Sep/Oct 95   26
HOT COCOA WITH ORANGE .... Jan/Feb 97   11
HOT COCOA, MASTER RECIPE
    FOR .... Jan/Feb 97   11
LOWER-FAT COCOA
    BROWNIES .... Mar/Apr 94   23
On Cocoa in Cake (Notes) .... Mar/Apr 96   3
Questioning Cocoa (Notes)....... Mar/Apr 96   3

Coconut
AMBROSIA .... Mar/Apr 94   21
COCONUT CHOCOLATE CHIP
    COFFEE CAKE.............. Mar/Apr 95   21
COCONUT COOKIES .... Nov/Dec 96   20
COCONUT CREAM PIE .... Mar/Apr 96   24
COCONUT CURRY SAUCE ..... May/Jun 93   19
DELICATE COCONUT
    MACAROONS .... Sep/Oct 96   6
LEMON-COCONUT CHIFFON
    CAKE.................... May/Jun 96   8

Coffee (*See* also Espresso)
The Best Coffee-Brewing
    Method (ER) .... Jan/Feb 96   27
Cappuccino Comments (Notes) ... May/Jun 94   3
Coffee Buttercream Frosting...... Jul/Aug 94   24
COFFEE FROZEN YOGURT .... May/Jun 96   15
COFFEE PUDDING CAKE ...... Jan/Feb 95   25
Cold-Brewing Coffee (Notes) ..... May/Jun 96   2
House Blend Coffee Tasting Finds Wide
    Divergence of Styles (BT)....... Jan/Feb 95   26
MOCHA-NUT CHIFFON CAKE .. May/Jun 96   8
Retro-Brewing Coffee (Notes) .... May/Jun 96   2
Roasting Coffee Beans at Home

(Notes) .... Sep/Oct 94   2
Storing Coffee Beans (Notes)..... Sep/Oct 95   2
Undiluted Ice Drinks (Notes) ..... Jul/Aug 97   2

equipment
Cleaning Burr Coffee Grinders
    (Notes).................... Nov/Dec 95   2
Cleaning Coffee Grinders (QT) .... Jul/Aug 95   4
Coffee Equipment (S&R)........ Jan/Feb 96   32
Coffee Grinders (S&R) .... Jan/Feb 95   32
Drip-Brewing Coffee (Notes) ..... May/Jun 96   2
Rating Electric Coffee Grinders
    (ER)..................... Jan/Feb 95   28

Coleslaw
CREAMY COLESLAW .... Jul/Aug 95   13
CURRIED COLESLAW WITH APPLES
    AND RAISINS.............. Jul/Aug 95   13
No More Watery Coleslaw....... Jul/Aug 95   12
SWEET-AND-SOUR COLESLAW.. Jul/Aug 95   12

Compotes
DRIED APRICOT COMPOTE WITH
    BALSAMIC VINEGAR AND JUNIPER
    BERRIES .... Jan/Feb 95   23
DRIED PEACH COMPOTE WITH MINT
    AND WHISKEY............. Jan/Feb 95   23
DRIED PEAR AND ORANGE COMPOTE
    WITH HONEY AND SAGE ..... Jan/Feb 95   23
ONION, BLACK OLIVE, AND CAPER
    COMPOTE .... May/Jun 94   13
ORANGE COMPOTE WITH STAR
    ANISE.................... Mar/Apr 96   BC
POACHED PLUM AND RASPBERRY COMPOTE
    IN SWEET WINE SYRUP ..... Jul/Aug 96   BC
RAISIN COMPOTE WITH ROSEMARY
    AND THYME .... Jan/Feb 95   23
Savory Dried Fruit Compotes ..... Jan/Feb 95   23
STRAWBERRY AND RHUBARB COMPOTES
    WITH SUGARED PECANS.... May/Jun 93   25

Condensed Milk
Homemade Condensed Milk
    (Notes).................... Nov/Dec 94   2
Thickening Without Cooking ..... Mar/Apr 97   23
Condiments and Side Dishes
APRICOT-JICAMA SALSA....... Jul/Aug 94   20
AVOCADO-CORN SALSA........ Jul/Aug 96   21
BARBECUE SAUCE, MASTER

Cook's Illustrated 1993–1997 Index

RECIPE FOR . . . . Jul/Aug 94   13
BLACK BEAN–MANGO SALSA. . . Jul/Aug 96   21
BLACK OLIVE PASTE . . . . Mar/Apr 95   19
CHILE DIPPING SAUCE . . . . Sep/Oct 94   15
CILANTRO CREAM . . . . Jan/Feb 96   13
CLASSIC RED TABLE SALSA . . . . Jul/Aug 96   21
CRANBERRY-GREEN GRAPE
   RELISH . . . . Nov/Dec 97   11
Cranberry-Onion Confit . . . . Nov/Dec 94   14
CRANBERRY-ONION CONFIT . . . Nov/Dec 94   14
CRANBERRY-PEAR BUTTER . . . . Nov/Dec 94   14
CRANBERRY-RED PEPPER
   RELISH . . . . Nov/Dec 94   14
CHILE DIPPING SAUCE . . . . Sep/Oct 94   15
CREAMY DIPPING SAUCE . . . . . Jul/Aug 95   23
CUMIN-SPIKED ORANGE-RED-
   ONION RELISH . . . . Nov/Dec 97   11
CURRIED APPLE-CRANBERRY
   CHUTNEY. . . . . Nov/Dec 94   14
CURRIED FRUIT CHUTNEY WITH LIME
   AND GINGER . . . . Jul/Aug 94   20
CURRIED SWEET POTATO
   CHUTNEY . . . . Nov/Dec 97   11
DRIED PEACH AND APPLE SALAD WITH
   ALMONDS AND CUMIN. . . . . . Jul/Aug 94   20
Easy Summer Salsas. . . . . Jul/Aug 96   21
FENNEL-TANGERINE SLAW . . . Nov/Dec 97   11
GREEN APPLE CHUTNEY
   WITH APRICOTS AND GINGER . Nov/Dec 97   11
GRILLED JALAPEÑO SALSA . . . . Jul/Aug 96   21
HOISIN-SESAME SAUCE . . . . . . May/Jun 94   13
HORSERADISH CREAM . . . . . . May/Jun 97   9
KENTUCKY SMOKED BARBECUE
   SAUCE . . . . Jul/Aug 94   13
LIME-GINGER VINAIGRETTE . . May/Jun 94   13
LOUISIANA SWEET
   BARBECUE SAUCE . . . . Jul/Aug 94   13
MEXICAN-STYLE SALSA
   CRUDA . . . . Jul/Aug 93   14
ONION, BLACK OLIVE, AND CAPER
   COMPOTE. . . . . May/Jun 94   13
ONION RELISH . . . . Jan/Feb 96   13
PEACH SALSA . . . . Sep/Oct 93   11
PEPPERED OVEN-DRIED
   TOMATO RELISH . . . . Sep/Oct 96   21
PICKLED GRAPE RELISH . . . . . Mar/Apr 97   BC
PINEAPPLE SALSA. . . . . Sep/Oct 94   13
PIQUANT PLUM SAUCE WITH
   SESAME OIL AND GINGER. . . . Jul/Aug 94   20

PLUM TOMATO SALSA WITH
   SHERRY VINEGAR . . . . May/Jun 94   13
QUICK-COOKED TOMATILLO-
   CHILE SAUCE. . . . . Jul/Aug 94   14
Rating Dijon Mustards (BT). . . . . . Jan/Feb 96   24
ROASTED CORN SALSA . . . . Jul/Aug 93   8
Roasted Red Pepper Rouille . . . . . . Nov/Dec 94   21
SIMPLE PEACH SALSA. . . . . Jul/Aug 96   21
Simple Tomato Sauce . . . . Nov/Dec 94   11
SOUTHEAST ASIAN–STYLE
   COCONUT CHUTNEY. . . . . . . Mar/Apr 94   20
SOY-GINGER DIPPING SAUCE . . Sep/Oct 94   15
Stone Fruit Relishes . . . . Jul/Aug 94   20
Tasting Barbecue Sauces (BT). . . . . Jul/Aug 95   26
TOMATO SAUCE WITH BELL
   PEPPERS AND BALSAMIC
   VINEGAR . . . . Mar/Apr 95   20
TOMATO YOGURT SAUCE . . . . . Jul/Aug 93   14
WARM CUCUMBER/RED ONION
   RELISH WITH MINT. . . . . May/Jun 94   13

Confit
Cranberry-Onion Confit . . . . Nov/Dec 94   14

Cookies
ALL-PURPOSE CHOCOLATE GLAZE
   AND FROSTING . . . . Nov/Dec 96   20
All-Purpose Holiday Cookies . . . . . Nov/Dec 96   18
ALMOND COOKIES . . . . Nov/Dec 96   9
BUTTERSCOTCH COOKIES . . . . Nov/Dec 96   20
Chasing the Chew (Notes). . . . . Jul/Aug 96   2
Chocolate Chip Cookie
   Conundrum (Notes) . . . . May/Jun 96   2
CHOCOLATE-CINNAMON
   COOKIES . . . . Nov/Dec 96   20
Chocolate-Coating Bar Cookies
   (QT). . . . . May/Jun 96   4
CLASSIC CUT-OUTS. . . . . Nov/Dec 93   8
COCONUT COOKIES . . . . Nov/Dec 96   20
Cookie Cutters (S&R) . . . . Nov/Dec 93   32
Cookie Press (Notes,) . . . . Jul/Aug 95   3
CORNMEAL-CITRUS COOKIES. . Nov/Dec 96   20
Cutting Bar Cookies (QT). . . . . . . Mar/Apr 96   5
Decorating Cookies (QT). . . . . Nov/Dec 94   5
DECORATIVE ICING . . . . Nov/Dec 93   9
DELICATE COCONUT
   MACAROONS . . . . Sep/Oct 96   6
Form Icebox Cookies (QT) . . . . . . Mar/Apr 95   5
Freestyle Cookie Decorating. . . . . . Nov/Dec 96   16

Cook's Illustrated 1993–1997 Index

GINGER COOKIES . . . . Nov/Dec 96   20
Indenting Cookies for Filling (QT) . Nov/Dec 97   4
LADYFINGERS (Notes) . . . . Jan/Feb 94   2
LEMON-POPPY SEED COOKIES. Nov/Dec 96   20
LINZER COOKIES. . . . . Nov/Dec 93   9
Making Cookie Crumbs (QT). . . . . . Sep/Oct 94   5
Making Thin Sugar Cookies (QT). . Nov/Dec 95   4
MINCEMEAT OR JAM
    TURNOVERS . . . . Nov/Dec 93   8
MOCK THUMBPRINTS. . . . . Nov/Dec 93   8
One Dough, Many Cookies . . . . . . Nov/Dec 93   6
ORANGE-NUT COOKIES . . . . Nov/Dec 96   20
PEANUT BUTTER COOKIES . . . . Nov/Dec 96   20
PETTICOAT TAILS . . . . Nov/Dec 93   9
PINE NUT–CRUSTED ALMOND
    MACAROONS . . . . Sep/Oct 96   7
PINWHEELS . . . . Nov/Dec 93   8
Preserving the Chew (Notes). . . . . Jul/Aug 96   2
RAISIN-SPICE COOKIES . . . . Nov/Dec 96   20
Rolling Out Perfect Cookie
    (or Pie) Dough (QT) . . . . Jan/Feb 96   5
Solving the Mystery of the Chewy Chocolate Chip
    Cookie. Jan/Feb 96   22
SPICE COOKIES . . . . Nov/Dec 96   20
THICK AND CHEWY CHOCOLATE
    CHIP COOKIES. . . . . Jan/Feb 96   23
VIENNESE CRESCENTS . . . . Nov/Dec 93   9
WALNUT WAFERS . . . . Charter Issue   15

amaretti
Amaretti Cookies (S&R) . . . . Jul/Aug 97   32
BAKED PEACHES WITH AMARETTI
    COOKIES. . . . . Jul/Aug 94   BC
VANILLA SEMIFREDDO WITH
    ALMONDS AND AMARETTI . . Jul/Aug 97   23

biscotti
MASTER RECIPE FOR CAPPUCCINO
    SEMIFREDDO WITH ALMOND
    BISCOTTI . . . . Jul/Aug 97   23
Shapely Biscotti (Notes). . . . . Mar/Apr 97   3

butter cookies
CHOCOLATE BUTTER
    COOKIE DOUGH. . . . . Nov/Dec 93   7
CITRUS BUTTER COOKIE
    DOUGH. . . . . Nov/Dec 93   7
HOLIDAY BUTTER COOKIE DOUGH,
    MASTER RECIPE FOR . . . . . . Nov/Dec 93   7
LEMON BUTTER COOKIES. . . . . Nov/Dec 96   20
MULTIPURPOSE BUTTER COOKIE
    DOUGH . . . . Nov/Dec 96   19

NUT BUTTER COOKIE DOUGH . Nov/Dec 93   7
ORANGE BUTTER COOKIES. . . . Nov/Dec 96   20
SPICE BUTTER COOKIE
    DOUGH. . . . . Nov/Dec 93   7

gingerbread house
Gingerbread Coiffure (QT) . . . . Nov/Dec 97   4

lace
MASTER RECIPE FOR LACE
    COOKIES . . . . May/Jun 97   20
Shaping Lace Cookies . . . . May/Jun 97   21

macaroons
ALMOND MACAROONS . . . . Sep/Oct 96   6
FUDGE-ALMOND MACAROONS . Sep/Oct 96   6
LEMON-ALMOND MACAROONS . Sep/Oct 96   7
Macaroons Six Ways . . . . Sep/Oct 96   6
PISTACHIO MACAROON
    BUTTONS . . . . Sep/Oct 96   7

oatmeal
BIG CHEWY OATMEAL-RAISIN
    COOKIES . . . . Jan/Feb 97   23
CHOCOLATE CHIP OATMEAL
    COOKIES . . . . Jan/Feb 97   23
DATE OATMEAL COOKIES . . . . . Jan/Feb 97   23
GINGER OATMEAL COOKIES . . . Jan/Feb 97   23
NUT OATMEAL COOKIES . . . . . . Jan/Feb 97   23
Oatmeal Cookie Woes (Notes) . . . . Jul/Aug 97   2
ORANGE AND ALMOND OATMEAL
    COOKIES . . . . Jan/Feb 97   23

Coriander
PURÉED CAULIFLOWER SOUP WITH
    CORIANDER. . . . . Nov/Dec 96   23

Corn
AVOCADO-CORN SALSA. . . . . . . Jul/Aug 96   21
BOILED CORN ON THE COB . . . . Jul/Aug 95   22
Cooking Corn on the Cob. . . . . Jul/Aug 95   22
CORN AND CLAM CHOWDER WITH
    ROASTED PARSNIPS . . . . Jul/Aug 93   9
CORN AND ZUCCHINI SAUTÉ
    WITH CHILES. . . . . Jul/Aug 93   9
Corn-Kernel Cutter (S&R). . . . . . . Jul/Aug 93   32
Corn off the Cob . . . . Jul/Aug 93   8
Corn-on-the-Cob Dishes (S&R) . . . Jul/Aug 95   32
Corn Poster (S&R). . . . . Jul/Aug 93   32
DOUBLE-CORN MUFFINS . . . . . . Sep/Oct 93   7
Fresh Corn Tamales with Tomatillo-
    Chile Sauce, Master Class . . . . . . Jul/Aug 94   14
GRILLED CORN ON THE COB . . . Jul/Aug 95   22

Cook's Illustrated 1993–1997 Index

MICROWAVED CORN ON
THE COB . . . . Jul/Aug 95   22
Microwaving Corn (Notes) . . . . Jan/Feb 96   2
Other Ideas for Cooking Corn
(Notes). . . . . Jan/Feb 96   2
ROASTED CORN SALSA . . . . Jul/Aug 93   8
SHAKER-STYLE CREAMY
CORN PUDDING. . . . . Jul/Aug 93   9
STEAMED CORN ON THE COB . . Jul/Aug 95   22

Cornbread
The Best Northern Cornbread. . . . . Sep/Oct 95   20
CORNBREAD-APPLE
STUFFING . . . . Nov/Dec 95   26
CORNMEAL LOAF BREAD . . . . . May/Jun 96   11
GOLDEN CORNBREAD WITH
BACON. Sep/Oct 95   21
GOLDEN CORNBREAD WITH
CHEDDAR . . . . Sep/Oct 95   21
GOLDEN CORNBREAD WITH
JALAPEÑOS . . . . Sep/Oct 95   21
GOLDEN NORTHERN
CORNBREAD. . . . . Sep/Oct 95   21
SOUTHERN SPOON BREAD . . . . Nov/Dec 96   25
SPOON BREAD WITH CHEDDAR
CHEESE . . . . Nov/Dec 96   25

Corned Beef (*See* Beef, brisket)

Cornish Hens (*See* also Poultry)
Bird Size and Meat Yield. . . . . Sep/Oct 97   22
Hens for Two . . . . Sep/Oct 97   22
ROAST STUFFED CORNISH
HENS . . . . Sep/Oct 97   21
SIMPLE ROAST BUTTERFLIED
CORNISH HENS . . . . Sep/Oct 97   22

Cornmeal
ANADAMA LOAF BREAD . . . . . . May/Jun 96   11
Another Way to Cook Polenta
(Notes). . . . . Nov/Dec 95   2
Cornmeal by Mail (S&R) . . . . Sep/Oct 95   32
CORNMEAL-CITRUS
COOKIES . . . . Nov/Dec 96   20
Dusting Bread With Cornmeal
(Notes). . . . . Nov/Dec 95   2
Mail-Order Cornmeal (S&R). . . . . Nov/Dec 96   32
Polenta vs. Cornmeal (Notes) . . . . Mar/Apr 96   2

Cornstarch
Cornstarch Connection . . . . Nov/Dec 93   9
Cornstarch Problems (Notes). . . . . Sep/Oct 94   3

Couscous
Couscoussier (S&R) . . . . Mar/Apr 95   32
Moroccan Lamb Couscous, Master
Class . . . . Mar/Apr 95   12
SHIITAKE-STUFFED SALMON ROLLS WITH
TARRAGON-TOMATO SAUCE . . . Jul/Aug 95   11
STEAMED COUSCOUS . . . . Mar/Apr 95   13
STEAMED COUSCOUS WITH MOROCCAN
LAMB BROTH, GLAZED ONIONS, AND
FRIED ALMONDS . . . . Mar/Apr 95   12

Crab
Cleaning Shrimp, Squid, and Soft-
Shell Crab. . . . . May/Jun 94   17
Dungeness Crabs (Notes). . . . . . . Mar/Apr 95   2
Fresh Crabmeat and Seasoning
(S&R) . . . . Jul/Aug 95   32
How to Cook Soft-Shell Crabs . . . . May/Jun 95   6
How to Make Crab Cakes . . . . Jul/Aug 95   23
Making Crab Cakes (Notes). . . . . . May/Jun 97   2
PANFRIED CRAB CAKES WITH OLD
BAY SEASONING . . . . Jul/Aug 95   23
PANFRIED SOFT-SHELL CRABS ON A BED OF
SPINACH . . . . May/Jun 95   7
PANFRIED SOFT-SHELL CRABS WITH
LEMONS AND HERBS . . . . . . May/Jun 95   7
Soft-Shell Crabs (S&R) . . . . May/Jun 95   32
STIR-FRIED SHANGHAI BOK CHOY
WITH CRABMEAT . . . . Charter Issue   7

Crackers
Common Crackers (S&R) . . . . Jan/Feb 97   32

Cranberries
APPLE-CRANBERRY SALAD WITH
CREAMY BAKED APPLES WITH
CRANBERRIES . . . . Sep/Oct 94   BC
Cranberry-Onion Confit . . . . Nov/Dec 94   14
CRANBERRY-ORANGE CHIFFON
CAKE . . . . May/Jun 96   8
Cranberry-Pear Butter . . . . Nov/Dec 94   14
CRANBERRY-PEAR SALSA IN
PEAR SHELLS . . . . Nov/Dec 96   BC
Cranberry-Red Pepper Relish. . . . . Nov/Dec 94   14
Curried Apple-Cranberry Chutney . Nov/Dec 94   14

Cook's Illustrated 1993–1997 Index

Dried Cranberries (S&R) . . . . Nov/Dec 94   32
Halving Cranberries (QT) . . . . Jan/Feb 95   4
LEMON VINAIGRETTE . . . . Nov/Dec 96   21
New Uses for Cranberries . . . . Nov/Dec 94   14

Cream
BANANA-PAPAYA FOOL . . . . Jan/Feb 95   BC
Bel Cream Maker (Notes) . . . . Jul/Aug 94   3
BRANDIED WHIPPED CREAM . . Nov/Dec 93   23
BRUSSELS SPROUTS BRAISED
    IN CREAM . . . . Nov/Dec 95   21
CILANTRO CREAM . . . . Jan/Feb 96   13
Clotted Cream (Notes). . . . . Jan/Feb 95   2
CREAM-BRAISED CABBAGE WITH
    LEMON AND SHALLOTS. . . . . . Sep/Oct 96   9
GREEN BEANS AND MUSHROOMS
    BRAISED IN CREAM . . . . Nov/Dec 96   7
HOMEMADE CLOTTED
    CREAM (Notes) . . . . Jan/Feb 95   3
HONEY-BAKED APPLES WITH
    CRÈME FRAÎCHE. . . . . Sep/Oct 95   13
HORSERADISH AND CIDER
    CREAM SAUCE . . . . Sep/Oct 95   24
Keeping Whipped Cream
    (Notes) . . . . Sep/Oct 97   2
LEMON WHIPPED CREAM . . . . . Nov/Dec 96   10
LIGHTENED PASTRY CREAM . . . Sep/Oct 95   15
LINGUINE WITH GARLIC
    CREAM SAUCE. . . . . Sep/Oct 93   20
PERFECT WHIPPED CREAM . . . May/Jun 97   19
RASPBERRY ORANGE
    BAVARIAN . . . . Charter Issue   BC
SHERRY-CREAM SAUCE WITH
    MUSHROOMS . . . . Sep/Oct 93   10
TOMATO-ROSEMARY CREAM
    SAUCE . . . . May/Jun 95   22
WHIPPED CREAM . . . . May/Jun 97   19

Cream Cheese
Cheesecake: One Recipe, Three
    Textures . . . . Sep/Oct 95   6
DENSE AND FIRM
    CHEESECAKE. . . . . Sep/Oct 95   8
LIGHT AND AIRY
    CHEESECAKE. . . . . Sep/Oct 95   8
ORANGE-FLAVORED CREAM
    CHEESE FILLING . . . . Sep/Oct 95   15
RICH AND CREAMY
    CHEESECAKE. . . . . Sep/Oct 95   8

Crème Fraîche
HONEY-BAKED APPLES WITH
    CRÈME FRAÎCHE . . . . Sep/Oct 95   13

Crepes (See also Pancakes)
Crepe Pan (S&R) . . . . Mar/Apr 97   32
CREPES WITH RICOTTA, HAM,
    AND SPINACH FILLING . . . . . . Mar/Apr 97   15
CREPES WITH RICOTTA, LEMON,
    AND RAISIN FILLING . . . . Mar/Apr 97   15
Do I Need a Real Crepe Pan? . . . . Mar/Apr 97   15
Folding Crepes Step-by-Step . . . . . Mar/Apr 97   16
Freezing and Thawing Crepes . . . . Mar/Apr 97   14
Pan Technique . . . . Mar/Apr 97   15
SAVORY CREPES . . . . Mar/Apr 97   15
SESAME CREPES (Chinese Pancakes)
    (Notes). Jan/Feb 94   3
SWEET CREPES . . . . Mar/Apr 97   15

Crostini (See also Bruschetta)
ARTICHOKE CROSTINI. . . . . . . May/Jun 96   17

Croutons
GRILLED PORTOBELLO MUSHROOMS,
    RED PEPPER, AND GARLIC
    CROUTONS . . . . Jul/Aug 96   9

Cucumbers
Bread and Butter Pickles . . . . Sep/Oct 94   19
CREAMY DILL CUCUMBER
    SALAD . . . . Jul/Aug 97   11
Dégorger (Notes) . . . . Sep/Oct 97   3
How to Salt and Drain Cucumbers . Jul/Aug 97   11
Pickled Cucumber Spears . . . . Sep/Oct 94   19
PITA BREAD SALAD WITH CUCUMBERS,
    CHERRY TOMATOES, AND FRESH
    HERBS. Sep/Oct 95   14
ROASTED RED PEPPER SALAD WITH RED
    ONIONS AND CUCUMBERS . . May/Jun 96   21
Seeding Cucumbers (QT). . . . . Jul/Aug 93   4
SESAME LEMON CUCUMBER
    SALAD . . . . Jul/Aug 97   11
SWEET-AND-TART CUCUMBER
    SALAD . . . . Jul/Aug 97   11
WARM CUCUMBER/RED ONION RELISH
    WITH MINT . . . . May/Jun 94   13
YOGURT MINT CUCUMBER
    SALAD . . . . Jul/Aug 97   11

Cook's Illustrated 1993–1997 Index

Cumin

DRIED PEACH AND APPLE SALAD WITH
ALMONDS AND CUMIN...... Jul/Aug 94 20
RED LENTIL PUREE WITH CUMIN
AND ANISE .... Mar/Apr 95 25
TENDER GREENS WITH CUMIN,
TOMATOES, AND CILANTRO .. Sep/Oct 94 21

Currants

ALMOND FILLING WITH
CURRANTS .... Sep/Oct 95 15
CLASSIC BAKLAVA FILLING ... Nov/Dec 95 15
CREAM AND CURRANT
SCONES .... Mar/Apr 94 7

Curry

BASIL-CURRY DRESSING ...... Jan/Feb 94 23
BEEF CURRY WITH CRUSHED SPICES
AND CHANNA DAL .... Jan/Feb 97 9
BRAISED BUTTERNUT SQUASH WITH
DRIED APRICOTS, RAISINS, AND
MADRAS SPICES .... Jan/Feb 96 26
CHICKEN CURRY WITH SPINACH AND
FENUGREEK .... Jan/Feb 97 9
CHICKEN CURRY WITH YOGURT, CILANTRO,
AND ZUCCHINI .... Jan/Feb 97 9
COCONUT CURRY SAUCE ..... May/Jun 93 19
Cooking Spices: A Matter of
Temperature .... Jan/Feb 97 7
Curried Apple-Cranberry
Chutney................... Nov/Dec 94 14
CURRIED CHICKEN FILLING WITH
CARROTS AND BASIL .... Sep/Oct 94 15
CURRY SAUCE .... Mar/Apr 96 20
Curry Spices and Ingredients
(S&R) .... Jan/Feb 97 32
GRILLED SKEWERED LAMB WITH
YOGURT, CURRY, AND MINT .. Jul/Aug 93 12
LAMB CURRY WITH FIGS
FENUGREEK .... Jan/Feb 97 9
LAMB CURRY WITH WHOLE
SPICES .... Jan/Feb 97 9
LYNNE ARONSON'S SEARED SNAPPER
WITH PEA SHOOTS AND COCONUT
CURRY SAUCE (Notes) ...... May/Jun 93 2
MASTER RECIPE FOR CURRY... Jan/Feb 97 9
MUSSELS STEAMED IN WHITE WINE
WITH CURRY AND BASIL .... Nov/Dec 96 15
Pickled Curried Cauliflower ...... Sep/Oct 94 19

SHRIMP CURRY WITH YOGURT
AND PEAS .... Jan/Feb 97 9
SWEET-AND-SOUR CURRY
SPICE RUB .... Jul/Aug 96 23

Custards

Crème Brûlée Questions (Notes)... Sep/Oct 95 2
CRÈME CARAMEL (Notes) .... Charter Issue 3
Is Scalding Milk Necessary?
(Notes) .... Charter Issue 2
LIGHTENED PASTRY CREAM ... Sep/Oct 95 15
PEAR BRANDY CUSTARD
SAUCE .... Sep./Oct 94 11
Perfect Crème Brûlée.......... Mar/Apr 95 6
PERFECT CRÈME BRÛLÉE .... Mar/Apr 95 7
PRUNE CUSTARD PUDDING . Charter Issue 19
Ramekins (S&R)............ Mar/Apr 95 32
RASPBERRY ORANGE
BAVARIAN .... Charter Issue BC
RICH BAKED CUSTARD .... Nov/Dec 96 9
The Science of Custard......... Nov/Dec 96 9

Dates

BIG BRAN MUFFINS WITH RAISINS
AND DATES............... Sep/Oct 93 7
California-Grown (Notes) .... Jan/Feb 97 3
Medjool Dates (S&R) .... May/Jun 96 32
PARMESAN WITH DATES...... May/Jun 96 16

Decorating

ALL-PURPOSE CHOCOLATE GLAZE AND
FROSTING .... Nov/Dec 96 20
Basket Weave............... May/Jun 95 17
Borders................... May/Jun 95 17
Cake Decorating Supplies (S&R).. May/Jun 95 32
Cakes.................... Jul/Aug 94 23
Candied Violets (S&R) .... Nov/Dec 96 32
Chocolate Curls .... Mar/Apr 96 17
Chocolate Shards .... Mar/Apr 96 17
Chocolate Splinters .... Mar/Apr 96 17
Citrus Spirals (QT) .... Jul/Aug 95 5
Cookies (QT)............... Mar/Apr 97 2
Crimped Edge Decoration....... Nov/Dec 96 17
Decorating (QT) .... Nov/Dec 94 5
Decorating Cookies (QT)........ Nov/Dec 94 5
Decorating Tube, Making a
Quick (QT). .... Mar/Apr 94 5
Decorating With Chocolate ...... May/Jun 97 21
Decorative (Citrus) Slices .... Jan/Feb 97 16

Cook's Illustrated 1993–1997 Index

DECORATIVE ICING .... Nov/Dec 93   9
Decorative Melon Carving........ Jul/Aug 95   16
Diamond Cut Decoration .... Nov/Dec 96   16
Filling and Holding Pastry Bags ... May/Jun 95   16
Filling Pastry Bags (QT) .... Sep/Oct 96   5
Fine Chocolate Shavings........ Mar/Apr 96   16
Fitting Pastry Bags With Plastic
    Coupler .... May/Jun 95   16
Floral Design Decoration .... Nov/Dec 96   16
Free Decorating Bottles (QT) ..... Nov/Dec 97   4
Freestyle Cookie Decorating...... Nov/Dec 96   16
Geometric Design Decoration..... Nov/Dec 96   17
Gingerbread Coiffure (QT) .... Nov/Dec 97   4
Giving Your Cakes a Silky
    Look (QT) .... Jul/Aug 95   4
Grooved Look Decoration .... Nov/Dec 96   16
Keep Cake Filling From Blending into
    Frosting (QT). .... Mar/Apr 95   4
LEMON, ORANGE, OR PLAIN
    GLAZE. .... Nov/Dec 96   20
Making a Disposable Piping
    Cone (QT) .... Nov/Dec 93   5
Making a Quick Decorating
    Tube (QT) .... Mar/Apr 94   5
Making Decorative Citrus
    Spirals (QT) .... Jul/Aug 95   5
Mess-Free Piping (QT) .... Sep/Oct 95   5
Piping Cone, Making a Disposable
    (QT) .... Nov/Dec 93   5
Piping From Pastry Bag (QT) ..... Sep/Oct 95   5
Polka-Dot Effect .... Nov/Dec 96   16
Quick and Easy Ways to Decorate
    a Cake .... Jul/Aug 94   23
Quick Cake Decorations (QT) ..... Jul/Aug 97   4
Quilted Look.................. Nov/Dec 96   17
Ricrac Design Decoration .... Nov/Dec 96   17
Rosettes and Stars........... May/Jun 95   17
Side Swags.................... May/Jun 95   16
Simple Cake Decorating .... May/Jun 95   16
Simple Chocolate Decorations .... Mar/Apr 96   16
Spiraled Effect .... Nov/Dec 96   17
Star Pattern Decoration,........ Nov/Dec 96   17
Subtle Groove Decoration........ Nov/Dec 96   16
Tailored Crosshatch Decoration ... Nov/Dec 96   17
Thick Chocolate Shavings .... Mar/Apr 96   16
Torting (QT). .... Jan/Feb 94   5
Waffle Texture Decoration .... Nov/Dec 96   16
Wavy Pleats Decoration........ Nov/Dec 96   17
Writing....................... May/Jun 95   17

Zigzag Look Decoration......... Nov/Dec 96   17

Desserts (See also Baking; Cakes; Cookies; Doughs; Pies and Tarts)

AMBROSIA .... Mar/Apr 94   21
BAKED APPLES WITH
    CRANBERRIES .... Sep/Oct 94   BC
BAKED PEACHES WITH
    AMARETTI COOKIES......... Jul/Aug 94   BC
BANANA BERRY POPOVER... Charter Issue   18
BANANA-PAPAYA FOOL .... Jan/Feb 95   BC
BASIC BATTER .... Charter Issue   18
BASIC BETTY, MASTER
    RECIPE FOR .... Sep/Oct 93   26
BATTER FRUIT COBBLER ...... Jul/Aug 96   20
The Best Baked Apple........... Sep/Oct 95   12
BRANDIED FALL FRUITS....... Sep/Oct 95   BC
Brioche Desserts .... Sep/Oct 95   16
BRIOCHE LOAF................ Sep/Oct 95   17
BRIOCHE RING .... Sep/Oct 95   16
CHOCOLATE MOUSSE .... Jul/Aug 96   7
CHOCOLATE SOUFFLÉ .... Sep/Oct 96   19
CHOCOLATE TRINITY
    PARFAITS................... Nov/Dec 93   BC
CIDER-BAKED APPLES WITH
    CINNAMON-SUGAR.......... Sep/Oct 95   13
CLASSIC MERINGUE .... May/Jun 95   12
Classic Trifle................... Nov/Dec 96   8
Cleaning the Trifle Bowl (QT) .... Nov/Dec 96   4
CREAM-FILLED APRICOTS ..... Jan/Feb 97   BC
Crème Brûlée Questions (Notes)... Sep/Oct 95   2
CRÈME CARAMEL .... Charter Issue   3
FLAKY PASTRY TOPPING ...... Jul/Aug 96   20
FREE-FORM MERINGUE SHELLS FILLED
    WITH STRAWBERRIES AND
    PAPAYA .... May/Jun 95   13
Fresh Phyllo (S&R). .... Nov/Dec 96   32
FRESH RASPBERRY PUREE .... Nov/Dec 96   9
FROZEN HOT CHOCOLATE .... May/Jun 95   BC
FRUIT COBBLER, MASTER
    RECIPE FOR .... Jul/Aug 96   19
FRUIT CRISP, MASTER
    RECIPE FOR .... Sep/Oct 93   26
FRUIT SORBETS, MASTER
    TECHNIQUE FOR. .... Jul/Aug 95   25
HONEY-BAKED APPLES WITH
    CRÈME FRAÎCHE............ Sep/Oct 95   13
MAKE-AHEAD CHOCOLATE
    SOUFFLÉ. .... Sep/Oct 96   19

Cook's Illustrated 1993–1997 Index

Making Phyllo Pastries . . . . Nov/Dec 95   16
Mastering the Chocolate Soufflé . . . Sep/Oct 96   18
Mix-and-Match Fruit Cobblers . . . . Jul/Aug 96   18
One Batter, Many Desserts. . . . . Charter Issue   18
ORANGE COMPOTE WITH STAR
   ANISE. . . . . Mar/Apr 96   BC
POACHED PLUM AND RASPBERRY COMPOTE
   IN SWEET WINE SYRUP . . . . . . Jul/Aug 96   BC
Perfect Crème Brûlée. . . . . Mar/Apr 95   6
PERFECT CRÈME BRÛLÉE . . . . Mar/Apr 95   7
Quick and Easy Brioche . . . . Sep/Oct 95   15
QUICK BRIOCHE. . . . . Sep/Oct 95   15
RASPBERRY BRIOCHE
   SHORTCAKE . . . . Sept/Oct 95   17
Raspberry Charlotte Royale, Master
   Class. . . . . Jan/Feb 94   14
RASPBERRY CHARLOTTE
   ROYALE. . . . . Jan/Feb 94   14
RASPBERRY ORANGE
   BAVARIAN . . . . Charter Issue   BC
RASPBERRY SPRITZER . . . . Jul/Aug 97   BC
REUBEN'S LEGENDARY APPLE
   PANCAKE . . . . Charter Issue   19
RICH BAKED CUSTARD . . . . Nov/Dec 96   9
RICH SHORTCAKE TOPPING. . . . Jul/Aug 96   20
RUM-BAKED APPLES WITH MASCARPONE
   AND ALMONDS . . . . Sep/Oct 95   13
Secrets of Creamy Fruit Sorbets . . . Jul/Aug 95   24
Shaping Foolproof Meringues, Master
   Class. . . . . May/Jun 95   12
SPONGE SHEET CAKE . . . . Nov/Dec 96   9
STRAWBERRY SHORTCAKE. . . . May/Jun 93   12
The Ultimate Chocolate Mousse . . . Jul/Aug 96   6
WALNUT-RAISIN BAKED APPLES WITH
   MAPLE SYRUP . . . . Sep/Oct 95   13
YOGURT-CREAMED OATS WITH BERRIES
   AND APPLES. . . . . May/Jun 94   BC

rice pudding
Simple Stovetop Rice Pudding. . . . Sep/Oct 96   25
SIMPLE STOVETOP RICE
   PUDDING . . . . Sep/Oct 96   25
RICE PUDDING WITH CINNAMON AND
   DRIED FRUIT . . . . Sep/Oct 96   25
RICE PUDDING WITH ORANGE AND TOASTED
   ALMONDS. . . . . Sep/Oct 96   25

rugelach
Filling and Forming Rugelach . . . . Sep/Oct 97   25
Freeze-and-Bake Rugelach . . . . . . Sep/Oct 97   25
MASTER RECIPE FOR CRESCENT-SHAPED

RUGELACH WITH RAISIN-WALNUT
   FILLING . . . . Sep/Oct 97   24
ROULADE-SHAPED RUGELACH   Sep/Oct 97   25
RUGELACH WITH CHOCOLATE-WALNUT
   FILLING . . . . Sep/Oct 97   25
semifreddo
CHOCOLATE ORANGE
   SEMIFREDDO . . . . Jul/Aug 97   23
CAPPUCCINO SEMIFREDDO WITH
   ALMOND BISCOTTI, MASTER
   RECIPE FOR . . . . Jul/Aug 97   23
VANILLA SEMIFREDDO WITH ALMONDS
   AND AMARETTI . . . . Jul/Aug 97   23
WARM BITTERSWEET CHOCOLATE
   SAUCE . . . . Jul/Aug 97   23
What Is Semifreddo? . . . . Jul/Aug 97   23
strawberry shortcake
PERFECT WHIPPED CREAM . . . May/Jun 97   19
RICH AND TENDER SHORTCAKES WITH
   STRAWBERRIES AND WHIPPED
   CREAM . . . . May/Jun 97   19
STRAWBERRY SHORTCAKE. . . . May/Jun 93   12

Dill
APPLE-BEET SALAD WITH CREAMY DILL
   DRESSING . . . . Nov/Dec 96   21
CREAMY DILL CUCUMBER
   SALAD . . . . Jul/Aug 97   11

Dips
SWEET AND SPICY ROASTED RED
   PEPPER DIP . . . . May/Jun 96   21
ROASTED ONION AND BACON
   DIP . . . . Nov/Dec 97   18

Dipping Sauce (*See* also Condiments)
CHILE DIPPING SAUCE . . . . Sep/Oct 94   15
CREAMY DIPPING SAUCE . . . . . Jul/Aug 95   23
PIQUANT PLUM SAUCE WITH SESAME OIL
   AND GINGER . . . . Jul/Aug 94   20
SOY-GINGER DIPPING SAUCE . . Sep/Oct 94   15

Doughnuts
BUTTERMILK DOUGHNUTS . . . Mar/Apr 97   21
CINNAMON-SUGARED BUTTERMILK
   DOUGHNUTS. . . . . Mar/Apr 97   21
Doughnut Cutter (S&R). . . . . Mar/Apr 97   32
SUGARED BUTTERMILK
   DOUGHNUTS. . . . . Mar/Apr 97   21

Cook's Illustrated 1993–1997 Index

Doughs (*See also* Pastries)

Forming and Cooking (Bagel
  Dough) . . . . Sep/Oct 97   15
Keeping Dough from
  Sticking (QT) . . . . Jan/Feb 97   5
Rolling Out Sticky Dough (QT) . . . Mar/Apr 97   5
The Water in Bread . . . . Sep/Oct 97   2
(The Water in) Pastry Dough
  (Notes) . . . . Sep/Oct 97   3

Dried Fruit (*See* Fruits, Dried)

Duck

Mail-order Duck (S&R) . . . . Sep/Oct 95   32
PEKING DUCK. . . . . Sep/Oct 93   12
30-Minute Peking Duck. . . . . Sep/Oct 93   13
Twice-Cooked Duck, Master Class . Sep/Oct 95   10
TWICE-COOKED DUCK WITH ASIAN
  FLAVORINGS . . . . Sep/Oct 95   10

Dumplings (*See* also Gnocchi)

Asian Ingredients (S&R) . . . . Sep/Oct 94   32
BAKING POWDER DUMPLINGS Mar/Apr 97   8
BUTTERED SPATZLE (Notes) . . . May/Jun 93   2
CHICKEN AND DUMPLINGS WITH AROMATIC
  VEGETABLES . . . . Mar/Apr 97   8
CHICKEN AND HERBED DUMPLINGS WITH
  AROMATIC VEGETABLES . . . . Mar/Apr 97   8
CURRIED CHICKEN FILLING WITH CARROTS
  AND BASIL . . . . Sep/Oct 94   15
How to Make Asian Dumplings. . . . Sep/Oct 94   15
Making Spatzle (QT) . . . . Jan/Feb 96   5
SESAME BEEF AND CABBAGE
  FILLING . . . . Sep/Oct 94   15
Shaping and Filling Asian
  Dumplings . . . . Sep/Oct 94   16
SHRIMP FILLING WITH GINGER AND
  SESAME. . . . . Sep/Oct 94   14
Spatzle Machine (Notes) . . . . May/Jun 93   2
Spatzle Machine (S&R) . . . . May/Jun 93   32

Eggnog

HOLIDAY EGGNOG . . . . Nov/Dec 97   23

Eggplant

BROILED EGGPLANT SLICES, MASTER
  RECIPE FOR . . . . Jul/Aug 93   7
BROILED EGGPLANT SLICES WITH TWO
  CHEESES . . . . Jul/Aug 93   7

Gender Confusion (Notes). . . . . . . Nov/Dec 93   2
GRILLED ITALIAN VEGETABLES WITH
  THYME AND GARLIC. . . . . Jul/Aug 96   8
How to Cook Eggplant. . . . . Jul/Aug 93   7
Male vs. Female Eggplant (QT) . . . May/Jun 93   5
SAUTÉED EGGPLANT IN SPICY GARLIC
  SAUCE . . . . Jul/Aug 93   7
SAUTÉED EGGPLANT IN TOMATO SAUCE
  WITH BASIL . . . . Jul/Aug 93   7
SAUTÉED EGGPLANT, MASTER
  RECIPE FOR . . . . Jul/Aug 93   7
SAUTÉED EGGPLANT WITH CRISPED
  BREAD CRUMBS . . . . Jul/Aug 93   7
Squeezing Moisture From
  Eggplant (QT). . . . . Sep/Oct 94   4

**Eggs (*See also* Frittatas; Genoise; Meringues;
Mousse; Soufflés)**

AMERICAN-STYLE POTATO SALAD WITH EGGS
  AND SWEET PICKLES. . . . . . . Jul/Aug 94   8
ARUGULA SALAD WITH GARLIC
  CROUTONS, GRUYÈRE, AND HARD-BOILED
  EGGS . . . . May/Jun 95   23
ASPARAGUS OMELET . . . . Sep/Oct 93   22
ASPARAGUS VINAIGRETTE WITH SIEVED EGG
  AND PICKLED PINK ONIONS. May/Jun 95   23
BASIC OMELET, MASTER
  RECIPE FOR . . . . Sep/Oct 93   22
CHEESE OMELET . . . . Sep/Oct 93   22
Egg Grades and Sizes (Notes) . . . . May/Jun 94   3
Egg (Pastry) Doughs Lift Off . . . . Sep/Oct 97   11
Eggshell Cutter (Notes) . . . . Mar/Apr 96   3
ESCAROLE SALAD WITH BACON AND
  POACHED EGG . . . . May/Jun 97   24
FINES HERBES OMELET . . . . . . Sep/Oct 93   22
Folding Egg Whites Gently (QT) . . Nov/Dec 95   4
GRUYÈRE, AND HARD-BOILED
  EGGS . . . . May/Jun 95   23
Healthy Mousses? . . . . Jul/Aug 96   6
How to Fold in Egg Whites . . . . . . Sep/Oct 96   19
Making Manageable Deviled
  Eggs (QT) . . . . Sep/Oct 95   4
Omelets Revisited . . . . Sep/Oct 93   21
Pasteurized Egg Products (Notes). . Jan/Feb 97   2
Peeling Hard-Boiled Eggs (Notes) . May/Jun 95   3
POACHED EGGS, MASTER RECIPE
  FOR . . . . May/Jun 97   24
POTATO, HAM, AND PARSLEY
  OMELET . . . . Sep/Oct 93   22

Cook's Illustrated 1993–1997 Index

Quick-Chopping Hard-Boiled
Eggs (QT) . . . . Jul/Aug 96   4
RICH BAKED CUSTARD . . . . Nov/Dec 96   9
The Science of Egg Whites . . . . . Charter Issue   11
Separating Eggs (QT) . . . . Jul/Aug 93   5
SMOKED SALMON OMELET . . . . Sep/Oct 93   22
Storing Poached Eggs (QT) . . . . . . May/Jun 97   4
Whole-Egg Mayonnaise (Notes) . . . Nov/Dec 93   3
ZUCCHINI FRITTATA WITH PARMESAN
AND HERBS . . . . Jul/Aug 95   9

Equipment

Any Way You Slice It . . . . Nov/Dec 95   19
Bel Cream Maker (Notes,) . . . . Jul/Aug 94   3
But Don't Slice Yourself! (S&R) . . . Nov/Dec 95   32
Couscoussier (S&R) . . . . Mar/Apr 95   32
Heat Master (S&R) . . . . Jan/Feb 94   32
La Cloche Maker Complains (Notes) Jul/Aug 95   2
La Cloche Tricks (Notes) . . . . Jul/Aug 95   2
More Cloche Comments (Notes) . . . Jul/Aug 95   2
La Cotta (Notes) . . . . Jul/Aug 96   3
Pizza Bella Delivers Pizza Brutta . May/Jun 95   11
Vinegar Equipment (S&R) . . . . Sep/Oct 93   32
Which Tool Is Best for Pureeing? . . Nov/Dec 96   23

baking

Are Oven Tiles Safe? (Notes) . . . . . . Jul/Aug 95   3
Baguette Baking Pans (Notes) . . . . Nov/Dec 94   2
Batter Skimmers (S&R) . . . . Nov/Dec 95   32
Bread Pans (S&R) . . . . May/Jun 96   32
Cake Decorating Supplies (S&R) . . May/Jun 95   32
Commercial Muffin Tins (S&R) . . . . Sep/Oct 93   32
Commercial Parchment
Paper (S&R) . . . . Nov/Dec 93   32
Cookie Cutters (S&R) . . . . Nov/Dec 93   32
Cookie Press (Notes) . . . . Jul/Aug 95   3
Cooling Racks (S&R) . . . . Sep/Oct 96   32
Cotton Pastry Cloth (S&R) . . . . . . Jan/Feb 95   32
Do You Really Need a Tube
Pan? . . . . Charter Issue   12
English Cake Mixer (Notes) . . . . . Nov/Dec 93   3
English Cake Whisk (S&R) . . . . . . Nov/Dec 93   32
Focaccia Pans (S&R) . . . . May/Jun 97   32
Kuchen Pans (Notes) . . . . Nov/Dec 94   3
Madeleine Pans (S&R) . . . . Mar/Apr 96   32
Mini-Loaf Pans (S&R) . . . . May/Jun 94   32
Molded Baguette Pans (S&R) . . . . Nov/Dec 94   32
Pastry Board (S&R) . . . . Jul/Aug 95   32
Porcelain Quiche Dishes (S&R) . . . Sep/Oct 97   32
Pudding Cake Ramekins (S&R) . . . Jan/Feb 95   32

Ramekins (S&R) . . . . Mar/Apr 95   32
The Right Cake Pan . . . . Charter Issue   12
Rolling Pins (Notes) . . . . Sep/Oct 93   3
Specialty Flours and Baking
Equipment (S&R) . . . . Jan/Feb 95   32
Springform Pan (S&R) . . . . Sep/Oct 95   32
Stollen Mold (Notes) . . . . Nov/Dec 94   3
Substituting Baking Pans (Notes) . . Jan/Feb 95   3
Top of the Stove Bun Warmer
(Notes) . . . . May/Jun 96   3
Tube Pans (S&R) . . . . May/Jun 96   32
Upside-Down Cake Pan (S&R) . . . . Jul/Aug 97   32

blenders

Best Blenders (S&R) . . . . Jul/Aug 95   32
Blenders Prove Useful Tools (ER) . . Jul/Aug 95   28
Cleaning a Blender (Notes) . . . . . . Nov/Dec 95   3
Immersion Blenders (S&R) . . . . . . May/Jun 93   32
Using and Rating Immersion
Blenders (ER) . . . . May/June 93   28

coffee and espresso

The Best Coffee-Brewing
Method (ER) . . . . Jan/Feb 96   27
Cleaning Burr Coffee Grinders
(Notes) . . . . Nov/Dec 95   2
Cleaning Coffee Grinders (QT) . . . . Jul/Aug 95   4
Coffee Equipment (S&R) . . . . Jan/Feb 96   32
Coffee Grinders (S&R) . . . . Jan/Feb 95   32
Do Espresso Machines Under $200
Really Work? (ER) . . . . Nov/Dec   28
Espresso Aides (S&R) . . . . Sep/Oct 93   32
Espresso Machines (S&R) . . . . Nov/Dec 96   32
Espresso Machines (S&R) . . . . Sep/Oct 93   32
Rating Electric Coffee
Grinders (ER) . . . . Jan/Feb 95   28

cookware

Adjustable Roasting Rack (S&R) . . Nov/Dec 93   32
Are Oven Tiles Safe? (Notes) . . . . . Jul/Aug 95   3
Baguette Baking Pans (Notes) . . . . Nov/Dec 94   2
Basket Roasting Rack (S&R) . . . . . Jan/Feb 97   32
Bread Pans (S&R) . . . . May/Jun 96   32
Brisket Under Pressure (Notes) . . . Nov/Dec 95   3
Cast-Iron Pot (S&R) . . . . Mar/Apr 97   32
Cast-Iron Pot for Smoking (S&R) . May/Jun 95   32
Cast-Iron Skillets (S&R) . . . . May/Jun 94   32
Clay Roasters (Notes) . . . . May/Jun 94   2
Clay Roasters Revisited (Notes) . . . Nov/Dec 94   3
Commercial Muffin Tins (S&R) . . . . Sep/Oct 93   32
Conventional Saucepan (ER) . . . . . May/Jun 97   27
Cookware Pollution (Notes) . . . . . . Jul/Aug 95   2

Cookware Reactivity (Notes) . . . . . . Sep/Oct 96   2
Customizing a Roasting Pan . . . . Charter Issue   27
Dark-Finished Tart Pans (S&R) . . . Sep/Oct 97   32
Different Pans for Different
   Stoves? . . . . May/Jun 97   25
A Different Take on Vertical
   Roasters . . . . May/Jun 97   2
Do I Need a Real Crepe Pan? . . . . . Mar/Apr 97   15
Double Boilers (S&R) . . . . Jan/Feb 95   32
Do You Really Need a Tube
   Pan? . . . . Charter Issue   12
Focaccia Pans (S&R) . . . . May/Jun 97   32
Griddle Riddle (ER) . . . . May/Jun 97   23
Griddles (S&R) . . . . May/Jun 97   32
Griddles (S&R) . . . . Jan/Feb 96   32
Griddle Update (S&R) . . . . Jul/Aug 97   32
Grilling Steaks (on Cast-Iron Grate)
   (Notes) . . . . Jul/Aug 97   3
Kuchen Pans (Notes) . . . . Nov/Dec 94   3
Large Casserole Dish (S&R) . . . . . Sep/Oct 95   32
Madeleine Pans (S&R) . . . . Mar/Apr 96   32
Meat Loaf Pan (S&R) . . . . Mar/Apr 97   32
Meat Loaf Pan (S&R) . . . . Sep/Oct 96   32
Mini-Loaf Pans (S&R) . . . . May/Jun 94   32
Molded Baguette Pans (S&R) . . . . . Nov/Dec 94   32
Multipurpose Pot (S&R) . . . . Mar/Apr 95   32
Nonstick Cookware Abuse (Notes) . . Sep/Oct 97   2
Nonstick Saucepan (ER) . . . . May/Jun 97   27
Nonstick Skillets (S&R) . . . . Nov/Dec 94   32
Nonstick Skillets Come of
   Age (ER) . . . . Nov/Dec 94   27
Ovenware by Emile Henry (S&R) . May/Jun 96   32
Paella Pan (S&R) . . . . Jan/Feb 95   32
Polishing Copper (Notes) . . . . Jan/Feb 95   2
Porcelain Quiche Dishes (S&R) . . . Sep/Oct 97   32
Pressure Cookers (S&R) . . . . Jul/Aug 96   32
Pudding Cake Ramekins (S&R) . . Jan/Feb 95   32
Ramekins (S&R) . . . . Mar/Apr 95   32
Rating Nonstick Baking Sheet
   Liners (ER) . . . . May/Jun 97   20
Rating Roasting Racks for
   Poultry (ER) . . . . Jan/Feb 97   28
Rating Saucepans (ER) . . . . May/Jun 97   26
The Real McCoy: An American
   Bean Pot (S&R) . . . . Sep/Oct 96   32
The Right Cake Pan . . . . Charter Issue   12
Roasting Pan (S&R) . . . . Mar/Apr 95   32
Roasting Racks (S&R) . . . . Jan/Feb 96   32
Saucepans (S&R) . . . . May/Jun 97   32

Splatter Screen (S&R) . . . . May/Jun 97   32
Springform Pan (S&R) . . . . Sep/Oct 95   32
Spring-Valve Pressure Cookers Top
   Testing (ER) . . . . Jul/Aug 96   26
Stacking Nonstick Pans (QT) . . . . . Sep/Oct 97   5
Substituting Baking Pans (Notes) . . Jan/Feb 95   3
Throw Out Your Wok! . . . . Mar/Apr 96   18
Top of the Stove Bun Warmer
   (Notes) . . . . May/Jun 96   3
Tube Pans (S&R) . . . . May/Jun 96   32
The Truth About Pressure Cookers . Jul/Aug 96   10
Universal Pan Cover (S&R) . . . . . . Nov/Dec 97   32
Upside-Down Cake Pan (S&R) . . . . Jul/Aug 97   32
Vertical Roasters (Notes) . . . . May/Jun 95   3
We're Not High on Vertical
   Roasters . . . . Jan/Feb 97   28

electric fryers
Choosing the Right Electric Deep
   Fryer (ER) . . . . Charter Issue   20
Deep-Frying Method (Notes) . . . . . Nov/Dec 96   3
Electric Fryers Needn't Disappoint
   (Notes) . . . . May/Jun 96   3

food processors
Cuisinart Mini-Mate Plus
   Chopper/Grinder . . . . Jan/Feb 97   7
Cuisinart Mini-Mate Plus
   Chopper/Grinder (S&R) . . . . Jan/Feb 97   32
Food Processor as Grinder . . . . Jul/Aug 95   15
Food Processor Sausage,
   Master Class . . . . Mar/Apr 96   12
Food Processors (S&R) . . . . Sep/Oct 97   32
For Kneading Dough (Notes) . . . . . Sep/Oct 96   3
Lids Kept Clean (QT) . . . . Sep/Oct 96   4
Pouring from (QT) . . . . Jul/Aug 96   4
Rating Full-Size Food
   Processors (ER) . . . . Sep/Oct 97   28

gadgets, utensils, and kitchen aids
Apple Parer (Notes) . . . . Sep/Oct 93   2
Batter Skimmers (S&R) . . . . Nov/Dec 95   32
Bean Slicers . . . . Nov/Dec 96   7
The Best Way to Slice a Bagel . . . . Sep/Oct 97   14
Biscuit Cutters (S&R) . . . . May/Jun 97   32
Blistering Pepper Skins Quickly
   (Notes) . . . . Sep/Oct 96   2
Bottle Corker (Notes) . . . . Sep/Oct 95   3
Bottles for Infused Oils (S&R) . . . . . Jan/Feb 95   32
Butcher Twine (S&R) . . . . Mar/Apr 94   32
Candy/Jelly/Deep-Fry
   Thermometer (S&R) . . . . Jul/Aug 96   32

Cook's Illustrated 1993–1997 Index

Cherry Pitter (S&R) .... Jul/Aug 93   32
Chinese Skimmer (S&R) .... Jul/Aug 96   32
Cookie Decorating............. Nov/Dec 96   16
Coring Hook (Notes) .... Jan/Feb 96   3
Corkscrews (S&R)............. Nov/Dec 97   32
Corn-Kernel Cutter (S&R)....... Jul/Aug 93   32
Cutting-Board Controversy (Notes). Sep/Oct 93   2
Digital Thermometer (S&R)...... Mar/Apr 94   32
Double Boiler Stand .... Jul/Aug 96   16
Doughnut Cutter (S&R)........ Mar/Apr 97   32
Eggshell Cutter (Notes) .... Mar/Apr 96   3
Extending Spatula Life (QT) ..... Nov/Dec 97   5
Fat-Skimming Ladle (S&R) ...... Mar/Apr 96   32
Fine-Mesh Strainers (S&R) ..... May/Jun 95   32
Fish Cleaner (Notes) .... Sep/Oct 94   2
Flavor Injector (S&R).......... Nov/Dec 97   32
Food Mill .... Jul/Aug 96   17
Free Decorating Bottles (QT) ..... Nov/Dec 97   4
Garlic Peeler .... Jul/Aug 96   16
Garlic Peeling (QT) .... Sep/Oct 96   5
Garlic Slicer (Notes).......... May/Jun 95   3
Glass measuring cups (QT)...... Sep/Oct 96   5
Gnocchi Tools (S&R)........... Mar/Apr 95   32
Grain Storage Containers (S&R) .. Nov/Dec 96   32
Grapefruit Spoon (S&R)........ May/Jun 94   32
Hardtack Rolling Pin (Notes)..... Nov/Dec 97   2
Heartwatch Gourmet Fat
   Skimmer.................. Jul/Aug 96   17
Homemade Stuffing Bag (QT) .... Nov/Dec 97   4
Impromptu Steamer (QT) .... Sep/Oct 97   5
Ingenius Recipe Holder (QT) .... Nov/Dec 96   5
Instant Cooling Rack (QT)....... Sep/Oct 97   5
Guide to Marinating for Flavor.... Jul/Aug 93   11
Instant Marinating Needle (Notes). Jul/Aug 93   3
Instant-Read Thermometers (S&R). Jul/Aug 97   32
Instant-Read Thermometer (S&R). May/Jun 95   32
Italian Potato Masher (S&R) ..... Nov/Dec 93   32
Judging the Accuracy of Thermometers
   (Notes)................... Mar/Apr 96   2
Kitchen Gadgets (S&R) .... Jul/Aug 96   32
Kitchen Timers (S&R) .... Sep/Oct 96   32
Kitchen Twine (S&R).......... May/Jun 95   32
The Kitchen Whiz (Food Preparation/Conversion
   Computer) (S&R) .... Sep/Oct 96   32
Magi-Cake Strips.............. Jul/Aug 96   17
Making a Low-Tech
   Milkshake (QT).............. May/Jun 97   4
Marinating Needles (S&R) ...... Jul/Aug 93   32
Baller (S&R) .... Sep/Oct 95   32

Mesh Roasting Rack (S&R) ...... Mar/Apr 94   32
Mesh Tea Balls (S&R) .... May/Jun 95   32
Metal Dough Scrapers (S&R)..... Mar/Apr 94   32
Mexican Hand Beater (Notes) .... Mar/Apr 97   3
Mini Ice Cream Scoop (S&R) ..... Nov/Dec 97   32
More Uses for the Egg Slicer (QT) . Jan/Feb 96   4
Multicorer .... Jul/Aug 96   17
Multifeatured Electronic Timers Win
   Testing (ER) .... Sep/Oct 96   28
Multi-Purpose Ricer (S&R) ...... Sep/Oct 94   32
New Uses for Cheese Slicer (QT) .. Jan/Feb 97   4
Nutmeg and Grinders (S&R) ..... Nov/Dec 95   32
Nutmeg Grater .... Jul/Aug 96   16
Olive Picker (Notes)........... Sep/Oct 96   3
Olive Pitter .... Jul/Aug 96   16
Paper Towel Holder (QT) .... May/Jun 97   5
Pasta Partitioner (Notes)....... Sep/Oct 97   3
Pastry Bags, Filling (QT)........ Sep/Oct 96   5
Pepper Mills (S&R) .... Mar/Apr 96   32
Pie Marker (Notes)............ May/Jun 97   3
Pie Weights (S&R) .... Sep/Oct 97   32
Pizza Tools (S&R)............. May/Jun 95   32
Plättar (Notes) .... Mar/Apr 94   2
Poultry Lacers (S&R) .... Nov/Dec 97   32
Poultry Stuffing Bag (S&R) ...... Jul/Aug 95   32
Professional Ice-Cream
   Scoops (S&R) .... Sep/Oct 93   32
Rating Corkscrews (ER)........ Nov/Dec 97   28
Rating Instant-Read Thermometers
   (dial and digital) (ER)......... Jul/Aug 97   27
Ravioli Cutters (S&R) .... Sep/Oct 93   32
Recipe Card Holder (QT) .... Mar/Apr 96   5
Roast/turkey Lifters .... Nov/Dec 97   9
Salad Spinners For Drying Grated
   Potatoes (QT) .... Sep/Oct 96   5
Sharp Vegetable Peeler (S&R) .... Nov/Dec 93   32
Slice a Spud (S&R)............ Nov/Dec 95   32
Smoked Salmon Slicer (Notes) .... Nov/Dec 95   3
Spatzle Maker (Notes)......... May/Jun 93   2
Spice Grinder (Notes) .... Sep/Oct 95   2
Spiral Sauce Whisk (Notes, What
   Is It?)..................... Mar/Apr 95   3
Spring-Action Tongs (S&R) ..... May/Jun 93   32
Stainless-Steel Baster (Notes, What
   Is It?) .... Jul/Aug 93   3
Steadying Your Work Surface
   (Notes) .... Sep/Oct 96   3
Steamer, simple (QT)........... Jan/Feb 96   5
Steaming Equipment .... Mar/Apr 95   19

Cook's Illustrated 1993–1997 Index

Stuffing Bag (S&R)............ Nov/Dec 97   32

Sturdy Graters (S&R)........... Jul/Aug 95   32

Tagliapasta (Notes)............ Jan/Feb 97   3

Tea Bag Squeezer (Notes, What
  Is It?)..................... Nov/Dec 96   3

Time and Beyond
  (thermometer/timer) (S&R) ..... Sep/Oct 96   32

To Make a Cookbook
  Holder (QT)................ Mar/Apr 95   4

To Test a Meat
  Thermometer (QT) .... May/Jun 95   5

Tongs for Grilling (S&R) .... Jul/Aug 97   32

Tong Storage (QT) .... Sep/Oct 96   4

Traditional Designs Score Well in Pepper Mill
  Testing (ER) .... Mar/Apr 96   28

Truffle Slicer (Notes) .... May/Jun 94   3

Truffle Slicer (S&R)........... May/Jun 94   32

Turkey Lifters (S&R) .... Nov/Dec 97   32

Two-Legged Salamander
  (Notes)................... Charter Issue   2

Useful Kitchen Gadgets......... Jul/Aug 96   16

V-shaped Melon Cutter (Notes).... Jul/Aug 97   3

Wooden Oven Rack Adjuster ...... Jul/Aug 96   17

Zesters...................... Jan/Feb 97   16

grilling and smoking

Bamboo Skewers (S&R)......... Jul/Aug 96   32

Basic Tools .... Jul/Aug 97   16

Charcoal Baskets or Rails (S&R) .. Jul/Aug 97   32

Chimney Starter (S&R)......... Jul/Aug 97   32

Chimney Starter (S&R)........ Jul/Aug 93   32

Coal Baskets .... Jul/Aug 97   16

Grilling Rack (S&R), ... Jul/Aug 96   32

Hinged Grill Grids .... Jul/Aug 97   16

How to Check a Propane Tank
  (Notes) .... Jul/Aug 96   3

How to Smoke-Cook with a Kettle-Style
  Grill .... Jul/Aug 95   19

How to Smoke-Cook with a Water
  Smoker................... Jul/Aug 95   19

Japanese Turning Mandoline
  (Notes) .... Jan/Feb 94   3

Oven Thermometer .... Jul/Aug 97   16

Rib Racks .... Jul/Aug 97   16

Smoking Equipment (S&R)...... Jul/Aug 95   32

Tongs for Grilling (S&R) .... Jul/Aug 97   32

Wire "Fence" .... Jul/Aug 97   16

ice cream makers

Choosing an Ice Cream
  Maker (ER)................ Jul/Aug 93   28

Electric Ice Cream
  Machine (S&R).............. Jul/Aug 95   32

Electric Ice Cream
  Machine (S&R) .... May/Jun 96   32

Ice Cream Makers (S&R) .... Jul/Aug 93   32

juicers

Juice Extractors (S&R) .... Jan/Feb 94   32

Which Juice Extractor Should You
  Buy? (ER).................. Jan/Feb 94   28

knife sharpeners

Knife Sharpeners (S&R)........ Mar/Apr 97   32

Rating Electric Knife
  Sharpeners (ER) .... Mar/Apr 97   29

Will Electric Sharpeners Reduce the Life of Your
  Knives?................... Mar/Apr 97   28

knives

Anatomy of the Knife.......... Mar/Apr 97   27

Basic Knife Techniques .... Jan/Feb 96   16

Blade Guards (S&R) .... Sep/Oct 97   32

Chinese Meat and Vegetable
  Cleavers .... Sep/Oct 97   16

Meat Cleavers (S&R)........... Sep/Oct 97   32

Sharpening by Hand .... Mar/Apr 97   28

Vegetable Cleavers (S&R) .... Sep/Oct 97   32

microwaves

Microwaving Corn (Notes)....... Jan/Feb 96   2

Proofing Bread (QT) .... Nov/Dec 96   4

mixers

English Cake Mixer (Notes) ...... Nov/Dec 93   3

Hand Mixers (S&R)........... May/Jun 95   32

Rating Free-Standing Mixers (ER) May/Jun 96   28

Rating Handheld Mixers (ER).... May/Jun 95   28

Standing Mixers (S&R) .... May/Jun 96   32

parts

Appliance Replacement
  Parts (S&R)................ Mar/Apr 97   32

Replacement Parts for
  Appliances (S&R) .... Sep/Oct 93   32

pasta makers

Electric Pasta Machines (S&R).... Nov/Dec 95   32

Making Pasta Machines Work .... Nov/Dec 95   27

Pasta Machine (S&R) .... Sep/Oct 93   32

Rating Electric Pasta
  Makers (ER) .... Nov/Dec 95   28

rice makers

Rating Rice Cookers (ER)........ Mar/Apr 95   28

Rice Cookers (S&R) .... Mar/Apr 95   32

Rice Cookers (S&R)............ Jan/Feb 94   32

scales

Cook's Illustrated 1993–1997 Index

Best Kitchen Scales (S&R) . . . . Sep/Oct 95   32
Electronic Scale Batteries (Notes) . Mar/Apr 96   2
For Kitchen Scales, Go
   Electronic (ER) . . . . Sep/Oct 95   28
Kitchen Scale (S&R) . . . . May/Jun 94   32

tabletop
Bread Box (S&R) . . . . May/Jun 94   32
Home-Style Wine Cooler (QT) . . . . . Jan/Feb 97   4
Wine Tasting Wheels (S&R) . . . . . . Nov/Dec 97   32

toasters
Building a Better Toaster (ER) . . . . Sep/Oct 94   28
Dualit Toaster (Notes) . . . . Mar/Apr 95   3
More on Dualit Toasters (Notes). . . Nov/Dec 95   2
Top Toasters (S&R) . . . . Sep/Oct 94   32

waffle irons
Rating Waffle Irons (ER) . . . . Nov/Dec 93   29
Waffle Irons (S&R) . . . . Nov/Dec 93   32

Escarole (*See* also Greens)
ESCAROLE AND WHITE BEAN SAUCE WITH
  GARLIC AND OREGANO . . . . . . Sep/Oct 94   22

Espresso
COFFEE FROZEN YOGURT . . . . May/Jun 96   15
Do Espresso Machines Under $200
  Really Work? (ER) . . . . Nov/Dec 96   28
Espresso Aides (S&R) . . . . Sep/Oct 93   32
ESPRESSO GRANITA . . . . May/Jun 96   BC
Espresso Machines (S&R). . . . . . . Nov/Dec 96   32
Espresso Machines (S&R) . . . . Sep/Oct 93   32
MOCHA-NUT CHIFFON CAKE . . May/Jun 96   8
Nespresso (S&R). . . . . Nov/Dec 96   32
Secrets of Homemade Espresso. . . . Sep/Oct 93   27
ESPRESSO GRANITA . . . . May/Jun 96   BC

Fat-Free and Reduced-Fat Cooking
Heartwatch Gourmet Fat
  Skimmer. . . . . Jul/Aug 96   17
Is a Lower Fat (Key Lime) Pie Really
  Worth It?. . . . . Mar/Apr 97   22
LOWER-FAT COCOA
  BROWNIES . . . . Mar/Apr 94   23
Making Canned Broth
  Fat-Free (QT) . . . . May/Jun 97   5
Moosewood Restaurant Low-Fat
  Favorites (BR) . . . . Jul/Aug 97   31
Removing Fat From Stock (QT). . . . Sep/Oct 94   4
Separating Fat From Pan
  Drippings (QT) . . . . Sep/Oct 95   5

Fava Beans
Preparing Fava Beans (QT). . . . . . . Jul/Aug 95   5

Fennel
BRAISED FENNEL AND BITTER
  GREENS SAUCE WITH BALSAMIC
  VINEGAR . . . . Mar/Apr 95   11
BRAISED FENNEL WITH WHITE WINE
  AND PARMESAN. . . . . May/Jun 96   18
Cooking with Fennel . . . . May/Jun 96   18
FENNEL AND OLIVE SALAD WITH CREAMY
  TARRAGON VINAIGRETTE . . . May/Jun 95   23
FENNEL-ORANGE SALAD WITH BLACK
  OLIVES AND MINT. . . . . May/Jun 96   19
ORANGE PAN SAUCE WITH FENNEL AND
  GREEN OLIVES . . . . Jul/Aug 97   19
PICKLED FENNEL . . . . Sep/Oct 94   19
ROASTED FENNEL WITH RED ONIONS AND
  CARROTS. . . . . May/Jun 96   19
ROASTED TOMATO TOPPING WITH FENNEL
  AND ASIAGO . . . . May/Jun 93   9
SAUTÉED FENNEL WITH GARLIC AND
  PARSLEY . . . . May/Jun 96   19
SPAGHETTI WITH FENNEL AND BREAD
  CRUMBS . . . . May/Jun 95   25
Trimming and Slicing Fennel (QT) . Sep/Oct 93   5

Feta Cheese
FETA CHEESE FRITTATA WITH OLIVES AND
  SUN-DRIED TOMATOES. . . . . . Mar/Apr 96   11
GRAPE AND FETA SALAD WITH
  ROSEMARY . . . . Nov/Dec 96   21
SPINACH, LEEK, AND FETA
  FILLING . . . . Nov/Dec 95   15

Figs
ARUGULA SALAD WITH GRILLED FIGS
  AND ROASTED PEPPER
  VINAIGRETTE . . . . Sep/Oct 96   BC
How to Poach Fruit . . . . May/Jun 93   24

Fish (*See* also specific kinds)
BOUILLABAISSE . . . . Nov/Dec 94   20
BROTH OF BLACK BASS AND MINCED
  VEGETABLES. . . . . Charter Issue   9
CHEATER'S FISH STOCK . . . . . . Nov/Dec 94   21
Fish Cleaner (Notes) . . . . Sep/Oct 94   3
Fish Stew Basics. . . . . Nov/Dec 94   18
FISH STEW FLAVORING BASE, MASTER

Cook's Illustrated 1993–1997 Index

RECIPE FOR .... Nov/Dec 94 20
FISH STEW, MASTER
RECIPE FOR............... Nov/Dec 94 20
FISH STOCK, MASTER
RECIPE FOR............... Nov/Dec 94 20
Five Easy Sauces for Fish .... May/Jun 94 13
Freezing Fish (QT) .... Nov/Dec 94 4
Gary Kunz's Broth of Black Bass and Minced
Vegetables, Master Class..... Charter Issue 8
How to Clean Whole Fish........ Mar/Apr 95 16
How to Fillet a Roundfish
(Notes).................. Charter Issue 3
Keeping Fish Fresh (QT) .... Jan/Feb 94 4
LYNNE ARONSON'S SEARED SNAPPER WITH
PEA SHOOTS AND COCONUT CURRY
SAUCE (Notes)............. May/Jun 93 2
Preparing Monkfish (QT) .... Sep/Oct 93 4
SAUTÉED MEDIUM-THICK FISH
FILLETS .... Sep/Oct 95 24
SAUTÉED THICK FISH FILLETS. Sep/Oct 95 24
SAUTÉED THIN FISH FILLETS .. Sep/Oct 95 24
Sautéing Fish Fillets........... Sep/Oct 95 23
Scaling Fish (QT)............. May/Jun 94 5
SPICE RUB FOR OILY FISH ..... Jul/Aug 95 21
Steaming Fish Fillets and Steaks . Mar/Apr 95 18
STIR-FRY, MASTER RECIPE FOR Mar/Apr 96 20
ZARZUELA................. Nov/Dec 94 20

sauces for
HOISIN-SESAME SAUCE ...... May/Jun 94 13
LIME-GINGER VINAIGRETTE .. May/Jun 94 13
ONION, BLACK OLIVE, AND CAPER
COMPOTE .... May/Jun 94 13
PLUM TOMATO SALSA WITH SHERRY
VINEGAR................. May/Jun 94 13
Quick Pan Sauces for Sautéed Fish. Sep/Oct 95 24
Quick Seafood Pasta Sauces..... Mar/Apr 96 9
TARTAR SAUCE .... Jul/Aug 97 10
WARM CUCUMBER/RED ONION RELISH
WITH MINT............... May/Jun 94 13

Flour
Flour Flavor (Notes) .... Jul/Aug 97 2
High-Gluten Flour (S&R) .... Sep/Oct 97 32
How Much Protein Is in My Flour? May/Jun 93 10
How to Substitute Specialty
Flours .... Charter Issue 24
Measuring Flour (Notes)........ Jul/Aug 95 3
Protein Content of Flour (Notes)... Jan/Feb 96 3
Semolina Flour (S&R).......... Jan/Feb 94 32

Specialty Flours and Baking
Equipment (S&R)............ Jan/Feb 95 32
West Coast Specialty Flours (S&R). Jan/Feb 95 32
What Is Whole Wheat Flour? ..... Jan/Feb 97 12
Whole Wheat Graham Flour (S&R) Jan/Feb 97 32

Focaccia
Focaccia Pans (S&R) .... May/Jun 97 32
FOCACCIA WITH BLACK OLIVES May/Jun 97 7
HAND-KNEADED FOCACCIA .. May/Jun 97 7
MASTER RECIPE FOR ROSEMARY
FOCACCIA .... May/Jun 97 7
PARMESAN FOCACCIA .... May/Jun 97 7
SAGE FOCACCIA .... May/Jun 97 7
Shaping Focaccia Dough .... May/Jun 97 7

Fontina Cheese
POTATO GNOCCHI GRATINÉED WITH
FONTINA CHEESE .... Mar/Apr 95 10
WILD MUSHROOM PIZZA WITH SAGE,
FONTINA, AND PARMESAN .. May/Jun 95 11

Food Processors
AMERICAN LOAF BREAD, FOOD PROCESSOR
METHOD .... May/Jun 96 10
Cuisinart Mini-Mate Plus
Chopper/Grinder .... Jan/Feb 97 7
Cuisinart Mini-Mate Plus
Chopper/Grinder (S&R) .... Jan/Feb 97 32
Food Processor as Grinder........ Jul/Aug 95 15
FOOD PROCESSOR MAYONNAISE Jul/Aug 97 10
Food Processor Sausage, Master
Class .... Mar/Apr 96 12
Food Processors (S&R).......... Sep/Oct 97 32
For Kneading Dough (Notes)...... Sep/Oct 96 3
Lids Kept Clean (QT) .... Sep/Oct 96 4
Mini Food Processors (S&R) ..... Jul/Aug 94 32
Pouring from (QT)............. Jul/Aug 96 4
Rating Full-Size Food
Processors (ER) .... Sep/Oct 97 28
Rating Mini Food Processors (ER).. Jul/Aug 94 29
To Clean a Food Processor
Bowl (QT) .... Mar/Apr 95 4
Using a Food Processor to Knead
Dough (Notes)............... Sep/Oct 96 3

Food Safety
Bacteria in Beef (Notes) .... Jan/Feb 96 3
But Is It Safe? (ceviche).......... Jul/Aug 96 15

Cook's Illustrated 1993–1997 Index

Healthy Mousses? (eggs) . . . . Jul/Aug 96   6

Raw Beef Safety (Notes) . . . . Jan/Feb 97   3

Raw Fish Safety (Notes) . . . . Jan/Feb 97   3

The Real Lowdown on Turkey

   Safety . . . . Nov/Dec 97   9

Safe Bagel Slicing (QT) . . . . Sep/Oct 97   4

Slow-Roast Safety (Notes) . . . . Jan/Feb 96   3

Food Storage

Easy Rice Handling and

   Storage (QT) . . . . Sep/Oct 97   4

Freezing Stock (QT) . . . . Jul/Aug 96   3

Grain Storage Containers (S&R) . . Nov/Dec 96   32

Keeping Broccoli Fresh (QT) . . . . . Jan/Feb 97   4

Keeping Fish Fresh (QT) . . . . Jan/Feb 94   4

Keeping Herbs Fresh (QT) . . . . . . Jul/Aug 96   3

Keeping Herbs Fresh (QT) . . . . . . Mar/Apr 96   5

Keeping Strawberries Fresh (QT) . . Jul/Aug 96   3

Keeping Whipped Cream (Notes) . . Sep/Oct 97   2

Portioning Tomato Paste (QT) . . . . Jan/Feb 96   4

Preserving the Chew (Notes) . . . . . Jul/Aug 96   2

Store Vidalia Onions (QT) . . . . . . May/Jun 95   5

Storing Bacon (QT) . . . . Sep/Oct 96   4

Storing Coffee Beans (Notes) . . . . . Sep/Oct 95   2

Storing Poached Eggs (QT) . . . . . . May/Jun 97   4

Storing Roasted Peppers (Notes) . . May/Jun 95   3

French Toast

FRENCH TOAST I (FOR CHALLAH OR

   SANDWICH BREAD) . . . . May/Jun 97   23

FRENCH TOAST II (FOR FIRM EUROPEAN-

   STYLE BREAD) . . . . May/Jun 97   23

Griddle Riddle (ER) . . . . May/Jun 97   23

Oven-Baked French Toast: Just

   Say No . . . . May/Jun 97   22

Frittatas

ASPARAGUS FRITTATA WITH MINT AND

   PARMESAN . . . . Mar/Apr 96   11

FETA CHEESE FRITTATA WITH OLIVES AND

   SUN-DRIED TOMATOES . . . . . . Mar/Apr 96   11

FRITTATA WITH CHEESE AND

   FRESH HERBS . . . . Mar/Apr 96   11

FRITTATA WITH LEEKS AND

   POTATOES . . . . Mar/Apr 96   11

Frittatas Made Easy . . . . Mar/Apr 96   10

ZUCCHINI FRITTATA WITH PARMESAN

   AND HERBS . . . . Jul/Aug 95   9

Frostings, Fillings, and Glazes (See also Decorating)

ALMOND FILLING WITH

   CURRANTS . . . . Sep/Oct 95   15

ALL-PURPOSE CHOCOLATE GLAZE AND

   FROSTING . . . . Nov/Dec 96   20

BUTTER FROSTING . . . . May/Jun 95   19

Cake Frosting Tools (S&R) . . . . . . Jul/Aug 94   32

CHOCOLATE-BOURBON GLAZE . Jul/Aug 93   3

CHOCOLATE BUTTER ICING . . . Jul/Aug 94   25

CHOCOLATE CREAM FROSTING Jul/Aug 94   24

CINNAMON-WALNUT FILLING . . Sep/Oct 95   15

CLASSIC BAKLAVA FILLING . . . Nov/Dec 95   15

COCONUT-PECAN FILLING . . . . . Jul/Aug 94   25

COFFEE BUTTERCREAM

   FROSTING . . . . Jul/Aug 94   24

Confectioners' Sugar (Notes) . . . . . Mar/Apr 95   3

DECORATIVE ICING . . . . Nov/Dec 93   9

Giving Your Cakes a Silky

   Look (QT) . . . . Jul/Aug 95   4

Keep Cake Filling from Bleeding

   into Frosting (QT) . . . . Mar/Apr 95   4

LEMON, ORANGE, OR PLAIN

   GLAZE . . . . Nov/Dec 96   20

LIGHTENED PASTRY CREAM . . . Sep/Oct 95   15

NEOCLASSIC ORANGE

   BUTTERCREAM . . . . Nov/Dec 95   11

OPTIONAL GLAZE FOR CHIFFON

   CAKE . . . . May/Jun 96   8

ORANGE-FLAVORED CREAM CHEESE

   FILLING . . . . Sep/Oct 95   15

RASPBERRY-ALMOND FILLING May/Jun 95   19

RASPBERRY MOUSSE FILLING . Jan/Feb 94   14

SPECKLED COCONUT

   FROSTING . . . . Mar/Apr 94   21

SPICED APPLE-RAISIN FILLING Nov/Dec 95   15

SPINACH, LEEK, AND FETA

   FILLING . . . . Nov/Dec 95   15

Frozen Desserts

CHOCOLATE FROZEN YOGURT May/Jun 96   15

COFFEE FROZEN YOGURT . . . . May/Jun 96   15

Electric Ice Cream Machine (S&R) May/Jun 96   32

ESPRESSO GRANITA . . . . May/Jun 96   BC

Homemade Frozen Yogurt . . . . . . May/Jun 96   14

RASPBERRY FROZEN YOGURT . May/Jun 96   15

STRAWBERRY FROZEN

   YOGURT . . . . May/Jun 96   15

VANILLA FROZEN YOGURT . . . . May/Jun 96   15

Cook's Illustrated 1993–1997 Index

Frozen Foods

Cookie dough . . . . Jan/Feb 96   23
Defrosting Frozen Foods (Notes) . . . Jan/Feb 96   2
Freeze-and-Bake Rugelach . . . . . . Sep/Oct 97   25
Freezing and Peeling
   Tomatoes (Notes) . . . . Jul/Aug 94   2
Freezing and Thawing Crepes . . . . Mar/Apr 97   14
Freezing Ground Beef (QT) . . . . . . May/Jun 97   4
Freezing Lemon Zest (Notes) . . . . . Mar/Apr 95   3
Freezing Pie Pastry (QT) . . . . Nov/Dec 97   4
Freezing Stock (QT) . . . . Jul/Aug 96   3
Freezing Stock in Convenient
   Portions (QT) . . . . Nov/Dec 95   4
Frozen Bounty (fruit) . . . . Jul/Aug 96   18

Fruit, Dried (See also specific kinds)

ALMOND FILLING WITH
   CURRANTS . . . . Sep/Oct 95   15
APRICOT-JICAMA SALSA . . . . Jul/Aug 94   20
BIG BRAN MUFFINS WITH RAISINS
   & DATES . . . . Sep/Oct 93   7
BUTTERMILK PECAN PIE WITH
   RAISINS . . . . Nov/Dec 95   8
Candied Fruit Sources (S&R) . . . . . Nov/Dec 94   32
CLASSIC BAKLAVA FILLING . . . Nov/Dec 95   15
CREAM AND CURRANT SCONES Mar/Apr 94   7
CURRIED COLESLAW WITH APPLES
   AND RAISINS . . . . Jul/Aug 95   13
Cutting Up Dried Fruit (QT) . . . . . . Jan/Feb 96   5
DRIED APRICOT COMPOTE WITH
   BALSAMIC VINEGAR AND JUNIPER
   BERRIES . . . . Jan/Feb 95   23
Dried Cranberries (S&R) . . . . Nov/Dec 94   32
DRIED FRUIT PANFORTE . . . . . Nov/Dec 94   13
DRIED PEACH AND APPLE SALAD WITH
   ALMONDS AND CUMIN . . . . . . Jul/Aug 94   20
DRIED PEACH COMPOTE WITH MINT AND
   WHISKEY . . . . Jan/Feb 95   23
DRIED PEAR AND ORANGE COMPOTE WITH
   HONEY AND SAGE . . . . Jan/Feb 95   23
GINGERBREAD WITH DRIED
   FRUIT . . . . Nov/Dec 95   23
GLAZED ONIONS WITH
   RAISINS . . . . Mar/Apr 95   13
PEAR AND DRIED FRUIT
   STRUDEL . . . . Sep/Oct 94   10
Preservatives in Dried Fruits
   (Notes) . . . . Nov/Dec 94   2
PRESSURE-COOKED NORTH AFRICAN

LAMB STEW . . . . Jul/Aug 96   11
PRUNE CUSTARD PUDDING . Charter Issue   19
RAISIN COMPOTE WITH ROSEMARY AND
   THYME . . . . Jan/Feb 95   23
RICE PUDDING WITH CINNAMON AND
   DRIED FRUIT . . . . Sep/Oct 96   25
ROAST GOOSE WITH PRUNE AND APPLE
   STUFFING AND RED WINE GIBLET
   GRAVY . . . . Nov/Dec 94   7
Savory Dried Fruit Compotes . . . . . Jan/Feb 95   23
SPICED APPLE-RAISIN FILLING Nov/Dec 95   15
SWEET BREAD WITH ALMONDS AND
   DRIED CHERRIES . . . . May/Jun 94   29
WALNUT-RAISIN BAKED APPLES WITH
   MAPLE SYRUP . . . . Sep/Oct 95   13

Fruit, Fresh (See also Citrus Fruit; Cobblers; Pies and Tarts; specific kinds)

AMBROSIA . . . . Mar/Apr 94   21
ANY-FRUIT-WILL-DO MUFFINS WITH
   STREUSAL TOPPING . . . . Sep/Oct 93   8
BASIC BETTY, MASTER
   RECIPE FOR . . . . Sep/Oct 93   26
BRANDIED FALL FRUITS . . . . Sep/Oct 95   BC
Crisps and Betties . . . . Sep/Oct 93   26
CURRIED FRUIT CHUTNEY WITH LIME AND
   GINGER . . . . Jul/Aug 94   20
Exotic Produce by Mail (S&R) . . . . Nov/Dec 93   32
Exotic Tropical Jams (S&R) . . . . . . Sep/Oct 93   32
FREE-FORM FRUIT TART . . . . . . May/Jun 94   14
Free-Form Fruit Tart, Master
   Class . . . . May/Jun 94   14
FRUIT CRISP, MASTER
   RECIPE FOR . . . . Sep/Oct 93   26
FRUIT SORBETS, MASTER
   TECHNIQUE FOR . . . . Jul/Aug 95   25
GUBANA: ITALIAN EASTER BREAD FILLED
   WITH NUTS AND FRUIT . . . . . Mar/Apr 94   12
How to Poach Fruit . . . . May/Jun 93   24
How to Thicken Fruit Pies . . . . Jul/Aug 95   6
MANGO GRANITA, MASTER RECIPE FOR RAW
   FRUIT-BASED GRANITAS . . . . May/Jun 94   24
MIMOSA GRANITA, MASTER RECIPE FOR
   LIQUID-BASED GRANITAS . . . May/Jun 94   24
PLUM GRANITA, MASTER RECIPE FOR
   POACHED FRUIT-BASED
   GRANITAS . . . . May/Jun 94   24
Preparing Tropical Fruit . . . . Jan/Feb 94   16
Quick Granitas . . . . May/Jun 94   24

Secrets of Creamy Fruit Sorbets . . . Jul/Aug 95   24
Stone Fruit Relishes . . . . Jul/Aug 94   20
Winter Fruit Salads . . . . Nov/Dec 96   21

Garlic

BRAISED ARTICHOKE SAUCE WITH WHITE
   WINE, GARLIC, AND LEMON. . Mar/Apr 95   11
Blanching Garlic (QT) . . . . Jul/Aug 96   3
Blue Garlic (Notes). . . . . Mar/Apr 97   3
Chopping Garlic with Herbs (QT) . May/Jun 94   4
CLAM SAUCE WITH TOMATOES AND
   GARLIC . . . . Mar/Apr 96   9
Crushing Garlic and Spices (QT). . . Sep/Oct 94   5
Flavoring Roasts with Garlic (QT) . Nov/Dec 93   5
GARLIC AND BASIL ROAST CHICKEN WITH
   LEMON PAN SAUCE . . . . Sep/Oct 93   20
GARLIC AND SAGE SOUP . . . . . Mar/Apr 95   BC
GARLIC-GINGER MARINADE . . . Sep/Oct 93   12
GARLIC-HERB PIZZA CRUST, MASTER RECIPE
   FOR. May/Jun 93   8
Garlic Peeler . . . . Jul/Aug 96   16
Garlic Shoots (Notes) . . . . Mar/Apr 94   3
Garlic Slicer (Notes). . . . . May/Jun 95   3
GARLIC-STUDDED ROAST PORK
   LOIN. May/Jun 95   22
GRILLED BREAD WITH ROASTED GARLIC AND
   FRESH TOMATO SAUCE . . . . . Sep/Oct 93   19
GRILLED CHICKEN WITH OLIVES, ROSEMARY,
   AND GARLIC. . . . . Jul/Aug 93   12
GRILLED ITALIAN VEGETABLES WITH THYME
   AND GARLIC. . . . . Jul/Aug 96   8
GRILLED PORTOBELLO MUSHROOMS,
   RED PEPPER, AND GARLIC
   CROUTONS. . . . . Jul/Aug 96   9
GRILLED SHRIMP WITH SPICY GARLIC
   PASTE . . . . Jul/Aug 94   19
GRILLED TUNA WITH GINGER AND
   GARLIC . . . . Jul/Aug 93   12
Hand-Pureeing Garlic (QT). . . . . . Jan/Feb 97   4
LINGUINE WITH GARLIC CREAM
   SAUCE. . . . . Sep/Oct 93   20
LINGUINE WITH WALNUT, GARLIC, AND HERB
   SAUCE. . . . . Jan/Feb 96   21
MASHED POTATOES WITH POACHED GARLIC
   AND OLIVE OIL. . . . . Nov/Dec 93   11
Microwave Garlic Before Roasting
   (Notes) . . . . Sep/Oct 95   3
New Uses for Cheese Slicer (QT) . Jan/Feb 97   4
Peeling Garlic (QT), ... Sep/Oct 96   5

Pureeing Heads of Garlic (QT) . . . . Nov/Dec 95   5
PUREE OF BROCCOLI SOUP WITH GARLIC AND
   HOT RED PEPPER. . . . . Charter Issue   29
QUICK-COOKED GREENS WITH GARLIC AND
   RED PEPPER FLAKES . . . . Jan/Feb 95   13
Remedy for Garlic Odor (Notes) . . . Jul/Aug 94   3
ROASTED GARLIC PUREE, MASTER
   RECIPE FOR . . . . Sep/Oct 93   19
Roasting Garlic . . . . Sep/Oct 93   19
SAUTÉED BRUSSELS SPROUTS WITH GARLIC
   AND PINE NUTS . . . . Nov/Dec 95   21
SAUTÉED EGGPLANT IN SPICY GARLIC
   SAUCE. . . . . Jul/Aug 93   7
SAUTÉED FENNEL WITH GARLIC AND
   PARSLEY . . . . May/Jun 96   19
Separating and Peeling Large Amounts
   of Garlic (QT) . . . . Jan/Feb 95   5
SESAME GARLIC DRESSING . Charter Issue   30
SHREDDED ZUCCHINI AND CARROT SAUTÉ
   WITH GARLIC AND HERBS . . . Jul/Aug 95   9
SHREDDED ZUCCHINI SAUTÉ WITH
   GARLIC AND HERBS, MASTER
   RECIPE FOR . . . . Jul/Aug 95   9
THAI-STYLE ASPARAGUS WITH CHILES,
   GARLIC, AND BASIL. . . . . May/Jun 93   7
TOASTED BREAD CRUMBS WITH RED PEPPER
   FLAKES AND GARLIC . . . . May/Jun 95   25

Garnishes

Candied Violets (S&R) . . . . Nov/Dec 96   32
Simple Chocolate Decorations . . . . Mar/Apr 96   16

Gelatin

How Does Gelatin Work?. . . . . May/Jun 96   15
Sheet Gelatin (Notes) . . . . May/Jun 97   2
Sheet Gelatin (S&R) . . . . May/Jun 97   32

Genoise

Foolproof Genoise, Master Class. . . Nov/Dec 95   10
GRAND MARNIER CAKE WITH NEOCLASSIC
   ORANGE BUTTERCREAM . . . . Nov/Dec 95   11

Ginger

Crystallized Ginger (S&R) . . . . Nov/Dec 95   32
CURRIED FRUIT CHUTNEY WITH LIME AND
   GINGER. . . . . Jul/Aug 94   20
Extracting Ginger Juice (QT) . . . . . Jul/Aug 93   5
GARLIC-GINGER MARINADE . . . Sep/Oct 93   12
GINGER BEURRE BLANC. . . . . . May/Jun 93   28

Cook's Illustrated 1993–1997 Index

GINGER COOKIES . . . . Nov/Dec 96   20

GINGER POUND CAKE . . . . May/Jun 94   20

GINGER SAUCE . . . . Mar/Apr 96   20

GINGER WALNUT MISO
   DRESSING . . . . Charter Issue   30

GRILLED TUNA WITH GINGER AND
   GARLIC . . . . Jul/Aug 93   12

LIME-GINGER VINAIGRETTE . . May/Jun 94   13

MASHED BUTTERNUT SQUASH WITH
   GINGER . . . . Nov/Dec 94   15

Mincing Ginger (QT) . . . . May/Jun 96   4

MUNG BEAN SAUCE WITH GINGER,
   CILANTRO, AND SOY . . . . Sep/Oct 95   24

Peeling Ginger (QT) . . . . Sep/Oct 96   5

PIQUANT PLUM SAUCE WITH SESAME OIL
   AND GINGER . . . . Jul/Aug 94   20

PUREED BUTTERNUT SQUASH SOUP WITH
   GINGER . . . . Nov/Dec 96   23

QUICK-BRAISED BOK CHOY, TURNIPS,
   AND WATERCRESS WITH GINGER
   AND SOY . . . . Jan/Feb 96   26

SHRIMP FILLING WITH GINGER AND
   SESAME. . . . . Sep/Oct 94   14

SMOKED TURKEY BREAST WITH GINGER-
   CARDAMOM RUB . . . . Jul/Aug 95   20

SOY-GINGER DIPPING SAUCE . . Sep/Oct 94   15

SOY-GINGER SCALLOP
   CEVICHE. . . . . Jul/Aug 96   15

Gingerbread

APPLE UPSIDE-DOWN
   GINGERBREAD . . . . Nov/Dec 95   23

GINGERBREAD WITH DRIED
   FRUIT . . . . Nov/Dec 95   23

Old-Fashioned Gingerbread . . . . . . Nov/Dec 95   22

OLD-FASHIONED
   GINGERBREAD . . . . Nov/Dec 95   23

Gingerbread House

Constructing and Building a Gingerbread
   Alpine Cottage. . . . . Nov/Dec 97   16

CONSTRUCTION GINGERBREAD Nov/Dec 97   15

CONSTRUCTION MATERIALS . . Nov/Dec 97   15

Gingerbread Coiffure (QT) . . . . Nov/Dec 97   4

Gingerbread House Candies
   (S&R) . . . . Nov/Dec 97   32

Gingerbread House Landscaping . . Nov/Dec 97   BC

MULTI-PURPOSE ROYAL ICING Nov/Dec 97   15

Gnocchi

Forming Gnocchi (QT) . . . . Sep/Oct 95   5

Gnocchi Tools (S&R) . . . . Mar/Apr 95   32

MASTER RECIPE FOR POTATO
   GNOCCHI. . . . . Mar/Apr 95   10

POTATO GNOCCHI WITH BUTTER, SAGE,
   AND PARMESAN CHEESE . . . . Mar/Apr 95   10

POTATO GNOCCHI GRATINÉED WITH
   FONTINA CHEESE . . . . Mar/Apr 95   10

POTATO GNOCCHI WITH
   PESTO . . . . Mar/Apr 95   10

POTATO GNOCCHI WITH TOMATO-MINT
   SAUCE . . . . Mar/Apr 95   10

The Secrets of Gnocchi . . . . Mar/Apr 95   8

Goat Cheese

PROSCIUTTO AND GOAT CHEESE
   ROULADES . . . . May/Jun 96   16

Goose

The Best Way to Cook a Goose . . . . Nov/Dec 94   6

Geese by Mail (S&R) . . . . Nov/Dec 94   32

How to Carve Turkey and Goose . . Nov/Dec 94   16

ROAST GOOSE WITH PRUNE AND APPLE
   STUFFING AND RED WINE GIBLET
   GRAVY . . . . Nov/Dec 94   7

Gorgonzola

PEAR SALAD WITH ARUGULA, WALNUTS, AND
   GORGONZOLA . . . . Nov/Dec 96   21

POLENTA WITH GORGONZOLA . Jan/Feb 95   21

Grains (See also Rice; Wild Rice)

Grain Storage Containers (S&R) . . Nov/Dec 96   32

Rinsing Grains (QT) . . . . Mar/Apr 96   4

Granitas

MANGO GRANITA, MASTER RECIPE FOR RAW
   FRUIT-BASED GRANITAS . . . . May/Jun 94   24

MIMOSA GRANITA, MASTER RECIPE FOR
   LIQUID-BASED GRANITAS . . . May/Jun 94   24

PLUM GRANITA, MASTER RECIPE FOR
   POACHED FRUIT-BASED
   GRANITAS . . . . May/Jun 94   24

Quick Granitas. . . . . May/Jun 94   24

Granola

The Best Granola . . . . Jul/Aug 94   21

CLASSIC GRANOLA . . . . Jul/Aug 94   21

TOAST AND ROAST GRANOLA . . Jul/Aug 94   21

Grapefruit
CITRUS SALAD WITH BITTER GREENS AND
   PARMESAN SHAVINGS. . . . . . Nov/Dec 96   21
Fruit Sorbets at a Glance. . . . . Jul/Aug 95   25

Grapes
GRAPE AND FETA SALAD WITH
   ROSEMARY . . . . Nov/Dec 96   21

Grapeseed Oil
Grapeseed Oil (Notes). . . . . Nov/Dec 96   3
Grapeseed Oil (S&R) . . . . Nov/Dec 96   32

Gravlax
GRAVLAX . . . . Jan/Feb 96   13
Gravlax Made Easy, Master Class. . Jan/Feb 96   12

Gravy
BEST TURKEY GIBLET GRAVY . Nov/Dec 96   24
Make-Ahead Pan Gravy . . . . Nov/Dec 96   24
RED WINE GIBLET GRAVY . . . . . Nov/Dec 94   7
Separating Fat from Pan
   Drippings (QT) . . . . Sep/Oct 95   5

Green Beans
GREEN BEANS BRAISED IN
   TOMATOES . . . . Nov/Dec 96   7
GREEN BEANS AND MUSHROOMS BRAISED
   IN CREAM . . . . Nov/Dec 96   7
GREEN BEANS WITH BACON AND
   ONIONS . . . . Nov/Dec 96   7
GREEN BEANS WITH TOASTED WALNUTS
   AND TARRAGON . . . . Nov/Dec 96   7
PICKLED GREEN BEANS WITH
   DILL. . . . . Sep/Oct 94   19
Two Good Ways to Cook Green
   Beans. Nov/Dec 96   6

Green Bell Peppers (See Peppers, Bell)

Greens
BASIC SHALLOW-BLANCHED
   GREENS . . . . Jan/Feb 95   13
BRAISED FENNEL AND BITTER
   GREENS SAUCE WITH BALSAMIC
   VINEGAR . . . . Mar/Apr 95   11
BRAISED LAMB SHANKS WITH WHITE

BEANS, SWISS CHARD, AND
   MARJORAM . . . . Jan/Feb 95   19
BRAISED VEAL BREAST WITH SAUSAGE,
   OLIVE, AND SWISS CHARD
   STUFFING. . . . . Sep/Oct 93   22
CITRUS SALAD WITH BITTER GREENS AND
   PARMESAN SHAVINGS. . . . . . . Nov/Dec 96   21
Cooking Tender Greens . . . . Sep/Oct 94   20
COUNTRY HAM STUFFED WITH SPICY
   SOUTHERN GREENS . . . . Nov/Dec 93   12
Drying Cooked Greens (QT) . . . . . Mar/Apr 97   5
Drying Large Quantities of
   Greens (QT) . . . . Sep/Oct 95   4
ESCAROLE AND WHITE BEAN SAUCE WITH
   GARLIC AND OREGANO . . . . . Sep/Oct 94   22
Greens Nutrition (Notes). . . . . Jul/Aug 95   3
How to Quick-Cook Strong-Flavored
   Greens . . . . Jan/Feb 95   12
INDIAN-SPICED LENTILS WITH
   KALE . . . . Mar/Apr 95   25
Pea Shoots (S&R). . . . . May/Jun 93   32
PENNE WITH QUICK-COOKED GREENS AND
   PROSCIUTTO . . . . Jan/Feb 95   14
QUICK-COOKED GREENS WITH BACON AND
   BLACK-EYED PEAS . . . . Jan/Feb 95   14
QUICK-COOKED GREENS WITH BACON AND
   ONION. . . . . Jan/Feb 95   13
QUICK-COOKED GREENS WITH BLACK OLIVES
   AND LEMON ZEST. . . . . Jan/Feb 95   13
QUICK-COOKED GREENS WITH GARLIC AND
   RED PEPPER FLAKES. . . . . Jan/Feb 95   13
QUICK-COOKED GREENS WITH
   PROSCIUTTO . . . . Jan/Feb 95   13
QUICK-COOKED GREENS WITH RED BELL
   PEPPER. . . . . Jan/Feb 95   13
QUICK-COOKED GREENS WITH WHITE BEANS
   AND ROSEMARY . . . . Jan/Feb 95   14
Squeeze Water from Cooked
   Greens (QT) . . . . May/Jun 95   4
Stemming . . . . Jan/Feb 95   14
Stemming . . . . Sep/Oct 94   21
Stemming and Cutting Winter
   Greens (QT). . . . . Nov/Dec 93   4
Stir-Frying Kale (Notes) . . . . May/Jun 95   3
TENDER GREENS WITH ASIAN
   FLAVORINGS . . . . Sep/Oct 94   21
TENDER GREENS WITH CUMIN, TOMATOES,
   AND CILANTRO . . . . Sep/Oct 94   21
TENDER GREENS WITH INDIAN

SPICES. Sep/Oct 94   21
TENDER GREENS WITH RAISINS AND
    ALMONDS. . . . . Sep/Oct 94   21
WILTED AND SAUTÉED TENDER GREENS,
    MASTER RECIPE FOR. . . . . . . Sep/Oct 94   21

Grilling (*See* **also Barbecue; Smoke Cooking**)
    The Best Red Wines for Grilled
        Foods (BT) . . . . Jul/Aug 95   30
    Gather 'Round the Grill (BR) . . . . . Jul/Aug 95   31
    all-purpose tips
    Arranging the Fire . . . . Jul/Aug 97   16
    Building a Two-Level Fire. . . . . . May/Jun 96   23
    Checking the Fuel Level . . . . Jul/Aug 97   17
    Coating Grilled Food (QT). . . . . . Jan/Feb 97   5
    Dousing Flames. . . . . May/Jun 96   24
    Fuels . . . . Jul/Aug 97   16
    Grill Roasting . . . . Jul/Aug 93   18
    Grilling With Skewers . . . . Jul/Aug 97   17
    Grill-Roasting Over Charcoal . . . . Jul/Aug 93   19
    Grill-Roasting Over Gas . . . . Jul/Aug 93   20
    Maintaining (Grill) Temperature . . Jul/Aug 97   15
    Preventing Sticking . . . . Jul/Aug 97   17
    Smoke and Fire (hardwood charcoals)
        (S&R) . . . . Jul/Aug 97   32
    Starting the Fire . . . . Jul/Aug 97   16
    beef
    GRILLED PORTERHOUSE OR T-BONE
        STEAK . . . . May/Jun 96   25
    GRILLED STRIP SIRLOIN STEAK, MASTER
        RECIPE FOR . . . . May/Jun 96   25
    Grilling Steaks (on Cast-Iron Grate)
        (Notes) . . . . Jul/Aug 97   3
    GRILL-ROASTED BEEF
        TENDERLOIN. . . . . Jul/Aug 93   20
    How to Grill a Steak. . . . . May/Jun 96   23
    chicken
    GRILLED BONE-IN
    CHICKEN BREASTS, MASTER
        RECIPE FOR . . . . Jul/Aug 97   15
    GRILLED BONE-IN CHICKEN BREASTS
    WITH BARBECUE SAUCE . . . . . Jul/Aug 97   15
    GRILLED BUTTERFLIED CHICKEN WITH ROSE-
    MARY, LEMON, AND GARLIC . . Sep/Oct 94   24
    GRILLED CHICKEN WITH OLIVES, ROSEMARY,
    AND GARLIC. . . . . Jul/Aug 93   12
    Grilling Chicken Legs and Thighs. . Jul/Aug 96   22
    GRILL-ROASTED HICKORY
        CHICKEN . . . . Jul/Aug 93   20

MAHOGANY GRILLED CHICKEN THIGHS OR
    LEGS . . . . Jul/Aug 96   23
SPICE-RUBBED GRILLED BONE-IN CHICKEN
    BREASTS. . . . . Jul/Aug 97   15
fish (*See* **also specific kinds**)
fish . . . . Jul/Aug 97   17
lamb
GRILLED SHOULDER LAMB CHOPS WITH
    GARLIC-ROSEMARY MARINADE Mar/Apr 97   19
GRILLED SHOULDER LAMB CHOPS WITH
    SOY-SHALLOT MARINADE . . . Mar/Apr 97   19
GRILLED SKEWERED LAMB WITH YOGURT,
    CURRY, AND MINT. . . . . Jul/Aug 93   12
lobster
Lobster . . . . Jul/Aug 97   17
pizza
GRILLED SHRIMP PIZZA TOPPING WITH
    ROASTED TOMATOES AND FARMER'S
    CHEESE. . . . . May/Jun 93   9
Grilling Pizza. . . . . May/Jun 93   8
pork
GRILL-ROASTED SPARERIBS WITH BARBECUE
    SAUCE. Jul/Aug 93   20
salmon
GRILLED SALMON WITH INDIAN FLAVORS AND
    FRESH MANGO CHUTNEY . . . Jul/Aug 97   7
Grilling Salmon Fillets Another Way
    (Notes). Nov/Dec 97   3
GRILL-ROASTED SALMON WITH
    ALDERWOOD . . . . Jul/Aug 93   20
QUILTED GIRAFFE'S GRILLED SALMON WITH
    MUSTARD GLAZE . . . . Jul/Aug 97   7
SIMPLE GRILLED SALMON . . . . Jul/Aug 97   7
SPICE-RUBBED GRILLED BONE-IN CHICKEN
    BREASTS. . . . . Jul/Aug 97   15
SPICY CHILI RUB . . . . Jul/Aug 97   20
shrimp
GRILLED SHRIMP TOPPING WITH
    ROASTED TOMATOES AND FARMER'S
    CHEESE. . . . . May/Jun 93   9
GRILLED SHRIMP WITH SPICY GARLIC
    PASTE . . . . Jul/Aug 94   19
Preparing Shrimp for the Grill . . . . Jul/Aug 94   19
SKEWERED GRILLED SHRIMP WITH ARTI-
    CHOKE HEARTS . . . . Mar/Apr 94   BC
tools and accessories
Bamboo Skewers (S&R). . . . . Jul/Aug 96   32
Basic Tools . . . . Jul/Aug 97   16
Charcoal Baskets or Rails (S&R) . . Jul/Aug 97   32

Cook's Illustrated 1993–1997 Index

Chimney Starter (S&R) . . . . Jul/Aug 93   32
Chimney Starter (S&R) . . . . Jul/Aug 97   32
Coal Baskets . . . . Jul/Aug 97   16
Fire Fixin's (S&R) . . . . May/Jun 96   32
Grill Products (S&R) . . . . Jul/Aug 94   32
Grilling Rack (S&R), ... Jul/Aug 96   32
Hinged Grill Grids . . . . Jul/Aug 97   16
How to Check a Propane
    Tank (Notes) . . . . Jul/Aug 96   3
Oven Thermometer . . . . Jul/Aug 97   16
Rib Racks . . . . Jul/Aug 97   16
Tongs for Grilling (S&R) . . . . Jul/Aug 97   32
Wire "Fence" . . . . Jul/Aug 97   16

tuna
GRILLED TUNA WITH GINGER AND
    GARLIC . . . . Jul/Aug 93   12
SICILIAN GRILLED TUNA
    STEW . . . . Nov/Dec 94   21

vegetables and side dishes
ARUGULA SALAD WITH GRILLED FIGS
    AND ROASTED PEPPER
    VINAIGRETTE . . . . Sep/Oct 96   BC
BRUSCHETTA WITH GRILLED PORTOBELLO
    MUSHROOMS . . . . Sep/Oct 96   8
Great Grilled Vegetables . . . . Jul/Aug 96   8
GRILLED ASPARAGUS . . . . May/Jun 93   7
GRILLED BREAD WITH ROASTED GARLIC AND
    FRESH TOMATO SAUCE . . . . . Sep/Oct 93   19
GRILLED CORN ON THE COB . . . Jul/Aug 95   22
GRILLED ITALIAN VEGETABLES WITH THYME
    AND GARLIC . . . . Jul/Aug 96   8
GRILLED JALAPEÑO SALSA . . . . Jul/Aug 96   21
GRILLED LEEKS WITH ORANGE-CHIVE
    BUTTER . . . . Mar/Apr 95   15
GRILLED MOZZARELLA AND SUN-DRIED
    TOMATO SKEWERS . . . . May/Jun 96   17
GRILLED ZUCCHINI SALAD WITH TOMATOES
    AND BASIL . . . . Jul/Aug 95   9
Onions . . . . Jul/Aug 97   17
Vegetables . . . . Jul/Aug 97   17

Gruyère Cheese
ARUGULA SALAD WITH GARLIC
    CROUTONS, GRUYÈRE, AND HARD-BOILED
    EGGS . . . . May/Jun 95   23
BAKED LEEKS WITH BACON AND
    GRUYÈRE . . . . Mar/Apr 95   15

Guacamole

Preparing Guacamole Quickly (QT) May/Jun 96   5

Ham
Aged Country Ham Wins Tasting, But Young
    Hams Also Do Well (BT) . . . . . . Nov/Dec 96   26
ALFRED PORTALE'S JUMBO ASPARAGUS
    SALAD WITH PARMA HAM, PARMESAN, AND
    LEMON VINAIGRETTE . . . . . . May/Jun 93   7
Carve a Half-Ham (QT) . . . . Charter Issue   5
Carve a Whole Ham (QT) . . . . . Charter Issue   5
Country Ham (S&R) . . . . Nov/Dec 93   32
Country Ham Stuffed with Greens,
    Master Class . . . . Nov/Dec 93   12
COUNTRY HAM STUFFED WITH SPICY
    SOUTHERN GREENS . . . . Nov/Dec 93   12
How to Cook a Country Ham . . . . . Nov/Dec 96   12
POTATO, HAM, AND PARSLEY
    OMELET . . . . Sep/Oct 93   22
RISOTTO WITH CABBAGE AND COUNTRY
    HAM . . . . Mar/Apr 94   19
SIMMERED COUNTRY HAM . . . . Nov/Dec 96   12
SORGHUM-GLAZED COUNTRY
    HAM . . . . Nov/Dec 96   13

Hamburgers
A Better Burger . . . . Jul/Aug 95   14
A BETTER BURGER . . . . Jul/Aug 95   15
Burger Shaping . . . . Jul/Aug 95   15
Ice in Your Ground Beef (Notes) . . . Mar/Apr 96   2

Hazelnuts
Skinning Hazelnuts (Notes) . . . . . . Jul/Aug 93   3

Herbs (*See* also specific kinds)
Bouquet Garni (Notes) . . . . Sep/Oct 93   2
Bouquet Garni (QT) . . . . Nov/Dec 94   4
BREAD SALAD WITH TOMATOES, HERBS, AND
    RED ONIONS . . . . Sep/Oct 95   14
BROCCOLI WITH SPANISH GREEN HERB
    SAUCE . . . . Sep/Oct 97   8
BRUSCHETTA WITH FRESH
    HERBS . . . . Sep/Oct 96   8
BRUSCHETTA WITH RED ONIONS, HERBS, AND
    PARMESAN . . . . Sep/Oct 96   8
CHICKEN AND HERBED DUMPLINGS WITH
    AROMATIC VEGETABLES . . . . Mar/Apr 97   8
Chopping a Small Quantity of
    Herbs (QT) . . . . Nov/Dec 94   4
Chopping Garlic with Herbs (QT) . May/Jun 94   4

Cook's Illustrated 1993–1997 Index

Common Fresh Herbs . . . . Jul/Aug 93   13

CREAM BISCUITS WITH
   HERBS . . . . Nov/Dec 93   19

CREAMED ZUCCHINI WITH
   HERBS . . . . Jul/Aug 95   9

Drying Herbs (QT) . . . . Sep/Oct 94   5

FINE HERBS OMELET . . . . Sep/Oct 93   5

FRESH HERB PASTA . . . . Nov/Dec 95   27

FRITTATA WITH CHEESE AND FRESH
   HERBS . . . . Mar/Apr 96   11

GARLIC-HERB PIZZA CRUST, MASTER RECIPE
   FOR . . . . May/Jun 93   8

HERB AND MUSHROOM
   STUFFING . . . . Nov/Dec 95   26

HERBED ROESTI WITH SMOKED
   CHEDDAR . . . . Jan/Feb 95   22

HERB-POACHED SHRIMP . . . . . . Jul/Aug 97   13

Keeping Herbs Fresh (QT) . . . . Jul/Aug 96   3

Keeping Herbs Fresh (QT) . . . . . . Mar/Apr 96   5

LAMB SHANKS BRAISED IN RED WINE WITH
   HERBES DE PROVENCE . . . . . . Jan/Feb 95   19

LINGUINE WITH WALNUT, GARLIC, AND HERB
   SAUCE . . . . Jan/Feb 96   21

Make the Best Use of Dried
   Herbs (QT) . . . . May/Jun 95   5

Mesh Tea Balls (S&R) . . . . May/Jun 95   32

OVEN-ROASTED LOBSTER WITH HERBED
   BREAD CRUMBS . . . . May/Jun 97   15

PANFRIED SOFT-SHELL CRABS WITH LEMONS,
   CAPERS, AND HERBS . . . . May/Jun 95   7

PITA BREAD SALAD WITH CUCUMBERS,
   CHERRY TOMATOES, AND FRESH
   HERBS . . . . Sep/Oct 95   14

SAUTÉED ZUCCHINI WITH LEMON AND
   HERBS . . . . Jul/Aug 95   9

SAUTÉED ZUCCHINI WITH WALNUTS AND
   HERBS . . . . Jul/Aug 95   9

SHREDDED ZUCCHINI AND CARROT SAUTÉ
   WITH GARLIC AND HERBS . . . Jul/Aug 95   9

SHREDDED ZUCCHINI SAUTÉ WITH
   GARLIC AND HERBS, MASTER
   FOR . . . . Jul/Aug 95   9

ZUCCHINI FRITTATA WITH PARMESAN AND
   HERBS . . . . Jul/Aug 95   9

Honey

DRIED PEAR AND ORANGE COMPOTE WITH
   HONEY AND SAGE . . . . Jan/Feb 95   23

HONEY-BAKED APPLES WITH CRÈME

FRAÎCHE . . . . Sep/Oct 95   13

HONEY-LAVENDER BISCOTTI . . Jan/Feb 94   12

Measuring Honey (Notes) . . . . Mar/Apr 94   2

Honeydew

Carving a Honeydew to Resemble a Lotus
   Flower . . . . Jul/Aug 95   16

Horseradish

HORSERADISH AND CIDER CREAM
   SAUCE . . . . Sep/Oct 95   24

HORSERADISH CREAM . . . . May/Jun 97   9

Ice Cream (*See* also Sorbets)

ALMOND MERINGUE CAKE WITH
   STRAWBERRY AND VANILLA ICE
   CREAM . . . . May/Jun 95   13

The Best Homemade Vanilla Ice
   Cream . . . . Jul/Aug 93   26

CHOCOLATE ICE CREAM . . . . . . Jul/Aug 93   28

Choosing an Ice Cream Maker (ER) . Jul/Aug 93   28

COFFEE ICE CREAM . . . . Jul/Aug 93   28

Electric Ice Cream Machine (S&R) . . Jul/Aug 95   32

Electric Ice Cream
   Machine (S&R) . . . . May/Jun 96   32

Making a Low-Tech
   Milkshake (QT) . . . . May/Jun 97   4

Mini Ice Cream Scoop (S&R) . . . . Nov/Dec 97   32

Naturally Flavored Vanilla Ice Creams
   Win Tasting (BT) . . . . Jul/Aug 94   26

Professional Ice-Cream Scoops
   (S&R) . . . . Sep/Oct 93   32

STRAWBERRY ICE CREAM . . . . . Jul/Aug 93   28

VANILLA ICE CREAM, MASTER
   RECIPE FOR . . . . Jul/Aug 93   27

Irish Soda Bread

AMERICAN-STYLE SODA BREAD WITH RAISINS
   AND CARAWAY . . . . Mar/Apr 97   13

CLASSIC IRISH SODA BREAD . . Mar/Apr 97   13

Cream of Tartar (in) (Notes) . . . . . . Jul/Aug 97   2

Flour Flavor (Notes) . . . . Jul/Aug 97   2

IRISH BROWN SODA BREAD . . . Mar/Apr 97   13

OATMEAL-WALNUT SODA BREAD Mar/Apr 97   13

Proper Handling for a Proper Irish
   Bread . . . . Mar/Apr 97   13

Jalapeños (*See* also Chile Peppers)

GOLDEN CORNBREAD WITH

Cook's Illustrated 1993–1997 Index

JALAPEÑOS . . . . Sep/Oct 95 21
GRILLED JALAPEÑO SALSA . . . . Jul/Aug 96 21
JALAPEÑO PRESERVES . . . . May/Jun 93 23
ROAST LEG OF LAMB WITH RED CHILE CRUST
    AND JALAPEÑO PRESERVES . May/Jun 93 22

Jicama
APRICOT-JICAMA SALSA . . . . Jul/Aug 94 20
PICKLED JICAMA . . . . Sep/Oct 94 19
Preparing Jicama (QT) . . . . Jul/Aug 94 5

Juices
Culinary Uses for Homemade
    Juices . . . . Jan/Feb 94 27
Juicing Lemons (Notes) . . . . Mar/Apr 94 2
Mesh Skimmer (S&R) . . . . Jan/Feb 94 32
Rating Orange Juices (BT) . . . . . . May/Jun 97 29

Juniper Berries
DRIED APRICOT COMPOTE WITH
    BALSAMIC VINEGAR AND JUNIPER
    BERRIES . . . . Jan/Feb 95 23

Kale (*See* also Greens)
INDIAN-SPICED LENTILS WITH
    KALE . . . . Mar/Apr 95 25
Stir-Frying Kale (Notes) . . . . May/Jun 95 3

Kasha
ROASTED SALMON WITH SASHA AND LEEK
    STUFFING . . . . Jul/Aug 93 23
Keeping Food Warm (Notes) . . . . . Nov/Dec 94 2

Kiwi
Preparing Tropical Fruit . . . . Jan/Feb 94 16

Knife Sharpeners
Knife Sharpeners (S&R) . . . . Mar/Apr 97 32
Rating Electric Knife
    Sharpeners (ER) . . . . Mar/Apr 97 29
Will Electric Sharpeners Reduce the Life of Your
    Knives? . . . . Mar/Apr 97 28

Knives
Anatomy of the Knife . . . . Mar/Apr 97 27
Basic Knife Techniques . . . . Jan/Feb 96 16
Blade Guards (S&R) . . . . Sep/Oct 97 32
Carving a Rib Roast (QT) . . . . Nov/Dec 93 5
Chef's Knives at a Discount

(S&R) . . . . Mar/Apr 94 32
Chinese meat and vegetable
    cleavers . . . . Sep/Oct 97 16
Cleaver Quick Tips . . . . Sep/Oct 97 17
Meat Cleavers (S&R) . . . . Sep/Oct 97 32
Mincing With a Vegetable
    Cleaver . . . . Sep/Oct 97 17
Sharpening by Hand . . . . Mar/Apr 97 28
Slicing Through Knife Myths (ER) . Mar/Apr 94 27
Slicing With a Meat Cleaver . . . . . Sep/Oct 97 16
Slicing With a Vegetable Cleaver . . Sep/Oct 97 16
Vegetable Cleavers (S&R) . . . . Sep/Oct 97 32

Lamb
BRAISED LAMB SHANKS WITH LEMON
    AND MINT . . . . Jan/Feb 95 19
BRAISED LAMB SHANKS WITH NORTH
    AFRICAN SPICES . . . . Jan/Feb 95 19
BRAISED LAMB SHANKS WITH WHITE
    BEANS, SWISS CHARD, AND
    MARJORAM . . . . Jan/Feb 95 19
BRAISED LAMB SHOULDER CHOPS WITH
    TOMATOES AND RED WINE . Mar/Apr 97 18
BRAISED LAMB SHOULDER CHOPS WITH
    CAPERS, BALSAMIC VINEGAR, AND RED
    PEPPERS . . . . Mar/Apr 97 19
BRAISED SHOULDER CHOPS WITH
    TOMATOES, ROSEMARY, AND
    OLIVES . . . . Mar/Apr 97 19
BRAISED SHOULDER LAMB CHOPS WITH
    FIGS AND NORTH AFRICAN
    SPICES . . . . Mar/Apr 97 19
Braising Lamb Shanks . . . . Jan/Feb 95 18
Cleaning, Boning, and Carving a Leg of
    Lamb . . . . Mar/Apr 94 9
Comparing Shoulder, Rib, and Loin Lamb
    Chops . . . . Mar/Apr 97 19
GRILLED SHOULDER LAMB CHOPS WITH
    GARLIC-ROSEMARY MARINADE Mar/Apr 97 19
GRILLED SHOULDER LAMB CHOPS WITH
    SOY-SHALLOT MARINADE . . . Mar/Apr 97 19
GRILLED SKEWERED LAMB WITH YOGURT,
    CURRY, AND MINT . . . . Jul/Aug 93 12
LAMB CURRY WITH FIGS
    FENUGREEK . . . . Jan/Feb 97 9
LAMB CURRY WITH WHOLE
    SPICES . . . . Jan/Feb 97 9
LAMB SHANKS BRAISED IN RED WINE WITH
    HERBES DE PROVENCE . . . . . Jan/Feb 95 19

Cook's Illustrated 1993–1997 Index

Lamb Shank Tips (Notes) . . . . Nov/Dec 95   3

Leg of Lamb with Red Chile Crust and Jalepeño Preserves, Master Class . . . . May/Jun 93   22

MOROCCAN LAMB BROTH WITH CHICKPEAS AND VEGETABLES . . . . Mar/Apr 95   13

Moroccan Lamb Couscous, Master Class . . . . Mar/Apr 95   12

PRESSURE-COOKED NORTH AFRICAN LAMB STEW . . . . Jul/Aug 96   11

Roast Leg of Lamb Perfected . . . . . Mar/Apr 94   8

ROAST LEG OF LAMB WITH PIQUANT CAPER SAUCE . . . . Mar/Apr 94   10

ROAST LEG OF LAMB WITH RED CHILE CRUST AND JALAPEÑO PRESERVES . May/Jun 93   22

Which Chop's the Best? . . . . Mar/Apr 97   19

Lasagne

Classic Lasagne Made Easy . . . . . . Nov/Dec 94   10

LASAGNE WITH HERBED MEATBALLS, TOMATO SAUCE, AND MOZZARELLA . . . . Nov/Dec 94   11

MASTER RECIPE FOR VEGETABLE LASAGNE WITH TOMATO SAUCE . . . . Sep/Oct 97   6

No Boil Noodles (for Lasagne) . . . . Sep/Oct 97   6

No-Stick Lasagna Noodles (QT) . . . Nov/Dec 97   4

Preparing Vegetables for Lasagne . Sep/Oct 97   7

ROASTED ZUCCHINI AND EGGPLANT LASAGNE . . . . Sep/Oct 97   7

SPINACH AND MUSHROOM LASAGNE . . . . Sep/Oct 97   7

Latkes (See Potatoes, latkes)

Lavender

Dried Lavender (S&R) . . . . Jan/Feb 94   32

HONEY-LAVENDER BISCOTTI . . Jan/Feb 94   12

Leeks

BAKED LEEKS WITH BACON AND GRUYÈRE . . . . Mar/Apr 95   15

Cleaning Leeks (QT) . . . . Jul/Aug 93   4

FRITTATA WITH LEEKS AND POTATOES . . . . Mar/Apr 96   11

GRILLED LEEKS WITH ORANGE-CHIVE BUTTER . . . . Mar/Apr 95   15

HEARTY CHICKEN SOUP WITH LEEKS, WILD RICE, AND MUSHROOMS . . . . Mar/Apr 96   15

How to Cook Leeks . . . . Mar/Apr 95   14

ROASTED SALMON WITH KASHA AND LEEK

STUFFING . . . . Jul/Aug 93   23

SPINACH, LEEK, AND FETA FILLING . . . . Nov/Dec 95   15

STEAMED LEEKS GLAZED WITH CRUNCHY SEEDS . . . . Mar/Apr 95   15

STEAMED LEEKS, MASTER RECIPE FOR . . . . Mar/Apr 95   15

STEAMED LEEKS WITH MUSTARD VINAIGRETTE . . . . Mar/Apr 95   15

Legumes (See Beans, Dried; Lentils)

Lemongrass

Preparing Lemongrass (QT) . . . . . . Nov/Dec 93   4

Lemons (See also Citrus Fruit; Fruit, Fresh)

APPLE-CRANBERRY SALAD WITH CREAMY LEMON VINAIGRETTE . . . . Nov/Dec 96   21

BRAISED ARTICHOKE SAUCE WITH WHITE WINE, GARLIC, AND LEMON . . Mar/Apr 95   11

BRAISED LAMB SHANKS WITH LEMON AND MINT . . . . Jan/Feb 95   19

CORNMEAL-CITRUS COOKIES . . Nov/Dec 96   20

CREAM-BRAISED CABBAGE WITH LEMON AND SHALLOTS . . . . Sep/Oct 96   9

Fruit Sorbets at a Glance . . . . Jul/Aug 95   25

GARLIC AND BASIL ROAST CHICKEN WITH LEMON PAN SAUCE . . . . Sep/Oct 93   20

Get Quick, Seedless Lemon Juice (QT) May/Jun 95   5

Grating Lemon Peel (QT) . . . . May/Jun 93   5

GRILLED BUTTERFLIED CHICKEN WITH ROSE-MARY, LEMON, AND GARLIC . . Sep/Oct 94   24

Juicing Lemons (Notes) . . . . Mar/Apr 94   2

LEMON-ALMOND MACAROONS . Sep/Oct 96   7

LEMON-ANISE BISCOTTI . . . . . Jan/Feb 94   12

LEMON BUTTER COOKIES . . . . . Nov/Dec 96   20

LEMON-CAPER SAUCE . . . . Sep/Oct 93   10

LEMON CHIFFON CAKE . . . . . . May/Jun 96   8

LEMON-CHIVE VINAIGRETTE . . May/Jun 94   12

LEMON-COCONUT CHIFFON CAKE . . . . May/Jun 96   8

LEMON OR ORANGE MADELEINES . . . . Mar/Apr 96   21

LEMON, ORANGE, OR PLAIN GLAZE . . . . Nov/Dec 96   20

LEMON-POPPY SEED COOKIES . Nov/Dec 96   20

LEMON PUDDING CAKE . . . . Jan/Feb 95   24

LEMON SAUCE . . . . Mar/Apr 96   20

LEMON SAUCE . . . . May/Jun 93   19

LEMON WHIPPED CREAM . . . . . Nov/Dec 96   10
MASHED POTATOES WITH PARMESAN
    CHEESE AND LEMON . . . . Nov/Dec 93   11
No-Weep Lemon Meringue Pie . . . . Nov/Dec 94   22
PANFRIED SOFT-SHELL CRABS WITH LEMONS,
    CAPERS, AND HERBS. . . . . . . May/Jun 95   7
Preserved Lemons (Notes) . . . . Mar/Apr 95   2
SAUTÉED ZUCCHINI WITH LEMON AND
    HERBS. . . . . Jul/Aug 95   9
SAUTÉED ZUCCHINI WITH OLIVES AND
    LEMON . . . . Jul/Aug 95   9
SEARED SHRIMP WITH LEMON . Jul/Aug 94   19
STEAMED MUSSEL SAUCE WITH LEMON AND
    WHITE WINE. . . . . Mar/Apr 96   9
THE ULTIMATE LEMON MERINGUE
    PIE . . . . Nov/Dec 94   24

Lentils
Exotic Lentils (S&R) . . . . Mar/Apr 95   32
FRENCH LENTIL SALAD WITH CARAWAY
    AND RADISH . . . . Mar/Apr 95   25
How to Cook Lentils. . . . . Mar/Apr 95   25
INDIAN-SPICED LENTILS WITH
    KALE . . . . Mar/Apr 95   25
RED LENTIL PUREE WITH CUMIN AND
    ANISE. . . . . Mar/Apr 95   25

Lettuce
Coring and Washing Head
    Lettuce (QT) . . . . Jan/Feb 94   4

Lime (*See* also Citrus Fruit; Fruit, Fresh)
BROCCOLI WITH LIME-CUMIN
    DRESSING . . . . Sep/Oct 97   8
CURRIED FRUIT CHUTNEY WITH LIME AND
    GINGER. . . . . Jul/Aug 94   20
Kaffir Lime (S&R) . . . . Charter Issue   9
KEY LIME PIE . . . . Mar/Apr 97   23
LIME-GINGER VINAIGRETTE . . May/Jun 94   13
Real Key Lime Pie (Notes) . . . . Sep/Oct 97   2
True Key Limes vs. Supermarket
    (Persian) Limes . . . . Mar/Apr 97   23

Lobster
Approximate Steaming Times and Meat
    Yields . . . . May/Jun 97   14
Getting Lobster Straight (QT) . . . . Mar/Apr 94   5
Grilling a Lobster . . . . Jul/Aug 97   17
Hard or Soft Shell? . . . . May/Jun 97   17

How to Eat a Lobster . . . . May/Jun 97   17
How to Prepare Lobster . . . . Jul/Aug 93   16
If You Buy a Soft-Shell . . . . May/Jun 97   14
Lobster (S&R) . . . . May/Jun 97   32
Lobster Lore . . . . May/Jun 97   15
More Lobster Lore (Notes) . . . . Nov/Dec 97   3
OVEN-ROASTED LOBSTER WITH HERBED
    BREAD CRUMBS . . . . May/Jun 97   15
PAELLA, CRIOLLA'S STYLE . . . . . Jan/Feb 95   11
Prepare Lobster for Stew . . . . Nov/Dec 94   21
SPAGHETTI WITH ARTICHOKE-LOBSTER
    SAUCE . . . . May/Jun 94   12
STEAMED WHOLE LOBSTERS . May/Jun 97   14
To Kill a Lobster . . . . May/Jun 97   15
To Prepare a Lobster for Roasting   May/Jun 97   16

Macaroni and Cheese
BAKED MACARONI AND
    CHEESE . . . . Jan/Feb 97   21
CREAMY MACARONI AND
    CHEESE . . . . Jan/Feb 97   21
Packaged Versions . . . . Jan/Feb 97   21
STOVETOP MACARONI AND
    CHEESE . . . . Jan/Feb 97   21
Thickening Macaroni and
    Cheese (Notes) . . . . May/Jun 97   2

Macaroons
ALMOND MACAROONS. . . . . . . Sep/Oct 96   6
DELICATE COCONUT
    MACAROONS . . . . Sep/Oct 96   6
FUDGE-ALMOND MACAROONS. Sep/Oct 96   6
LEMON-ALMOND MACAROONS . Sep/Oct 96   7
Macaroons Six Ways . . . . Sep/Oct 96   6
PINE NUT-CRUSTED ALMOND
    MACAROONS . . . . Sep/Oct 96   7
PISTACHIO MACAROON
    BUTTONS . . . . Sep/Oct 96   7

Mace
PUREE OF CAULIFLOWER SOUP WITH
    CARDAMOM AND MACE. . . . Charter Issue   29

Madeleines
ALMOND MADELEINES . . . . Mar/Apr 96   21
CHOCOLATE MADELEINES . . . . Mar/Apr 96   21
LEMON OR ORANGE
    MADELEINES . . . . Mar/Apr 96   21
Madeleine Pans (S&R) . . . . Mar/Apr 96   32

Cook's Illustrated 1993–1997 Index

MADELEINES . . . . Mar/Apr 96   21

Magnificent Madeleines . . . . Mar/Apr 96   21

ROSEMARY MADELEINES . . . . Mar/Apr 96   21

Mail-Order Foods

Amaretti Cookies (S&R) . . . . Jul/Aug 97   32

American Pear Brandy (S&R) . . . . . Sep/Oct 94   32

Asian Ingredients (S&R) . . . . Sep/Oct 94   32

Asian Spices (S&R) . . . . Sep/Oct 95   32

Bakewell Cream (Notes) . . . . Jul/Aug 96   3

Barbecue Sauces (S&R) . . . . Jul/Aug 94   32

Boutique Apples (S&R) . . . . Sep/Oct 95   32

British Sweeteners (S&R) . . . . Mar/Apr 94   32

Brown Rices (S&R) . . . . Jan/Feb 94   32

Bulgur for Tabbooleh (S&R) . . . . . . Jul/Aug 94   32

California Artichokes (S&R) . . . . . May/Jun 94   32

California-Grown Dates (Notes) . . . Jan/Feb 97   3

Candied Fruit (S&R) . . . . Nov/Dec 94   32

Candied Violets (S&R) . . . . Nov/Dec 96   32

Caviar by Mail (S&R) . . . . Nov/Dec 93   32

Chinese Tea and Spices for

   Smoking (S&R) . . . . May/Jun 95   32

Chorizo Sausage (S&R) . . . . Jan/Feb 95   32

Citrus Oils (S&R) . . . . Nov/Dec 93   32

Cold-Pressed Peanut Oil (S&R) . . . May/Jun 93   32

Common Crackers (S&R) . . . . Jan/Feb 97   32

Cornmeal by Mail (S&R) . . . . Sep/Oct 95   32

Country Ham (S&R) . . . . Nov/Dec 93   32

Crystallized Ginger (S&R) . . . . Nov/Dec 95   32

Curry Spices and Ingredients

   (S&R) . . . . Jan/Feb 97   32

Discount Spices (S&R) . . . . Sep/Oct 94   32

Dried Chestnuts (S&R) . . . . Nov/Dec 95   32

Dried Chiles (S&R) . . . . May/Jun 93   32

Dried Cranberries (S&R) . . . . Nov/Dec 94   32

Dried Lavender (S&R) . . . . Jan/Feb 94   32

Dried Sweet Cherries (S&R) . . . . . . Sep/Oct 97   32

"Dry" Sea Scallops (S&R) . . . . Mar/Apr 96   32

Easter Bread Ingredients (S&R) . . Mar/Apr 94   32

Exotic Lentils (S&R) . . . . Mar/Apr 95   32

Exotic Produce by Mail (S&R) . . . . Nov/Dec 93   32

Exotic Teas by Mail (S&R) . . . . . . Mar/Apr 94   32

Exotic Tropical Jams (S&R) . . . . . . Sep/Oct 93   32

Extra-Virgin Olive Oils (S&R) . . . . Sep/Oct 96   32

The Fill of the Mill (S&R) . . . . Mar/Apr 96   32

Flavored Vinegars (S&R) . . . . Sep/Oct 96   32

Floral Waters (S&R) . . . . May/Jun 94   32

Fresh Crabmeat and

   Seasoning (S&R) . . . . Jul/Aug 95   32

Fresh Mozzarella (S&R) . . . . May/Jun 96   32

Fresh Phyllo (S&R) . . . . Nov/Dec 96   32

Fresh Raspberries (S&R) . . . . Nov/Dec 96   32

Geese by Mail (S&R) . . . . Nov/Dec 94   32

Genuine Saffron . . . . Nov/Dec 94   32

Glass Vinegar Flasks (S&R) . . . . . . Sep/Oct 93   32

Gingerbread House Candies

   (S&R) . . . . Nov/Dec 97   32

Grapeseed Oil (S&R) . . . . Nov/Dec 96   32

High-Gluten Flour (S&R) . . . . Sep/Oct 97   32

Hot Peppers (S&R) . . . . Jul/Aug 96   32

Instant Yeast (Notes) . . . . Mar/Apr 95   3

Instant Yeast (S&R) . . . . May/Jun 96   32

Italian Pancetta (S&R) . . . . Mar/Apr 94   32

Large Casserole Dish (S&R) . . . . . . Sep/Oct 95   32

Lobster (S&R) . . . . May/Jun 97   32

Mail-Order Cornmeal (S&R) . . . . . Nov/Dec 96   32

Mail-Order Duck (S&R) . . . . Sep/Oct 95   32

Mail-Order Gourmet (S&R) . . . . . . Jan/Feb 94   32

Malt Syrup (S&R) . . . . Sep/Oct 97   32

Meat Loaf Pan Update (S&R) . . . . Mar/Apr 97   32

Medjool Dates (S&R) . . . . May/Jun 96   32

Mexican Ingredients . . . . Jul/Aug 94   32

Muir Glen Diced Tomatoes (S&R) . May/Jun 97   32

Mushrooms by Mail (S&R) . . . . Sep/Oct 93   32

Mushrooms: Dried and

   Fresh (S&R) . . . . Jan/Feb 97   32

Mustard (S&R) . . . . Jan/Feb 94   32

Mustard Mecca (S&R) . . . . Jan/Feb 96   32

Nespresso (S&R) . . . . Nov/Dec 96   32

Nutmeg and Grinders (S&R) . . . . . Nov/Dec 95   32

Organic Meats (S&R) . . . . May/Jun 93   32

Ozark Trails Bacon (S&R) . . . . May/Jun 96   32

Pancetta (S&R) . . . . Jan/Feb 96   32

Panforte Essentials . . . . Nov/Dec 94   32

Pastas (S&R) . . . . Jan/Feb 94   32

Pea Shoots (S&R) . . . . May/Jun 93   32

Potatoes to Grow and Eat (S&R) . . Mar/Apr 97   32

Premium Potatoes (S&R) . . . . Mar/Apr 94   32

Purchasing Polenta (S&R) . . . . Jan/Feb 95   32

Real Maple Syrup (S&R) . . . . Jan/Feb 96   32

Sausage Casings (S&R) . . . . Mar/Apr 96   32

Seeds (S&R) . . . . Jan/Feb 94   32

Sheet Gelatin (S&R) . . . . May/Jun 97   32

Sorghum (S&R) . . . . Jan/Feb 97   32

Soy Sauces (S&R) . . . . May/Jun 93   32

Specialty Dried Pastas (S&R) . . . . . Sep/Oct 94   32

Specialty Flours and Baking

   Equipment (S&R) . . . . Jan/Feb 95   32

Specialty Teas (S&R) . . . . Mar/Apr 96   32

Spices for Rubs (S&R) . . . . Jul/Aug 95   32

Spicy Foods Catalog (S&R) . . . . Jul/Aug 93   32

Tasting Mail-Order Steaks (BT) . . May/Jun 96   26

Traditional Balsamic Vinegars
(S&R) . . . . Mar/Apr 95   32

Unique Sausages (S&R) . . . . Jul/Aug 93   32

West Coast Specialty Flours (S&R). Jan/Feb 95   32

Whole Wheat Graham Flour (S&R) Jan/Feb 97   32

Yukon Gold Potatoes (Notes) . . . . . . Sep/Oct 96   2

Malt Syrup

Malt Syrup (S&R) . . . . Sep/Oct 97   32

Mangoes

BLACK BEAN–MANGO SALSA. . . Jul/Aug 96   21

Cutting Mangoes (QT) . . . . Jul/Aug 93   4

Fruit Sorbets at a Glance . . . . Jul/Aug 95   25

GRILLED SALMON WITH INDIAN FLAVORS AND
FRESH MANGO CHUTNEY . . . . Jul/Aug 97   7

MANGO GRANITA, MASTER RECIPE FOR RAW
FRUIT-BASED GRANITAS . . . . May/Jun 94   24

SPINACH SALAD WITH SHRIMP, MANGO,
AND RED ONION . . . . Mar/Apr 97   9

Maple Syrup

MAPLE PECAN PIE . . . . Nov/Dec 95   8

Real Maple Syrup (S&R) . . . . Jan/Feb 96   32

WALNUT-RAISIN BAKED APPLES WITH MAPLE
SYRUP . . . . Sep/Oct 95   13

**Marinades and Marinating (*See* also specific fish,
meats, poultry, and vegetables)**

ASIAN MARINADE, MASTER RECIPE
FOR . . . . Jul/Aug 93   12

Do Marinades Work? . . . . Jul/Aug 93   11

GARLIC-GINGER MARINADE . . . Sep/Oct 93   12

Garlic-Rosemary . . . . Mar/Apr 97   19

Instant Marinating Needle (Notes) . Jul/Aug 93   3

Guide to Marinating for Flavor . . . . Jul/Aug 93   11

Instant Marinating Needle (Notes) . Jul/Aug 93   3

Marinating Needles (S&R) . . . . Jul/Aug 93   32

MEDITERRANEAN MARINADE, MASTER
RECIPE FOR . . . . Jul/Aug 93   12

RED CHILE MARINADE . . . . May/Jun 93   22

Soy-Shallot . . . . Mar/Apr 97   19

Margarine

MARGARINE. . . . . May/Jun 93   28

Marjoram

BRAISED LAMB SHANKS WITH WHITE
BEANS, SWISS CHARD, AND
MARJORAM . . . . Jan/Feb 95   19

TOASTED BREAD CRUMBS WITH MARJORAM,
THYME, AND LEMON ZEST . . May/Jun 95   25

Mascarpone

RUM-BAKED APPLES WITH MASCARPONE AND
ALMONDS . . . . Sep/Oct 95   13

Mayonnaise

Bring Out the Hellmans (BT) . . . . . Jul/Aug 94   7

DIJON MAYONNAISE . . . . Jul/Aug 97   10

Drizzling the Oil . . . . Jul/Aug 97   10

FOOD PROCESSOR MAYONNAISE Jul/Aug 97   10

LEMON MAYONNAISE . . . . Jul/Aug 97   10

HOMEMADE MAYONNAISE, MASTER
RECIPE FOR . . . . Jul/Aug 97   10

RASPBERRY MAYONNAISE . . . . May/Jun 93   28

ROASTED GARLIC MAYONNAISE Jul/Aug 97   10

TARRAGON MAYONNAISE . . . . . Jul/Aug 97   10

What Makes Mayo Thick? . . . . Jul/Aug 97   10

Whole-Egg Mayonnaise (Notes) . . . Nov/Dec 93   3

Meat (*See* also specific kinds)

Chinese Tip for Ribs (Notes) . . . . . . Jan/Feb 95   2

Cleaning Out a Meat
Grinder (QT) . . . . Jan/Feb 97   4

Do Marinades Work? . . . . Jul/Aug 93   10

Grinding Meat Without Mess (QT) Mar/Apr 96   4

Instant-Read Thermometer (S&R). May/Jun 95   32

MEAT AND RICOTTA FILLING WITH BASIL
FOR PASTA . . . . Sep/Oct 93   18

Meat Cleavers (S&R) . . . . Sep/Oct 97   32

Organic Meats (S&R) . . . . May/Jun 93   32

Parboiling Ribs (Notes) . . . . Jan/Feb 95   2

Reading a Meat Thermometer (QT) Jul/Aug 94   5

Slicing With a Meat Cleaver . . . . . Sep/Oct 97   16

STIR-FRY, MASTER
RECIPE FOR . . . . Mar/Apr 96   20

Test a Meat Thermometer (QT) . . . May/Jun 95   5

Meatballs

LASAGNE WITH HERBED MEATBALLS, TOMATO
SAUCE, AND MOZZARELLA. . . Nov/Dec 94   11

Meatloaf

BACON-WRAPPED MEAT LOAF WITH BROWN-

SUGAR KETCHUP GLAZE . . . . . Sep/Oct 96 22
LOAF PAN VARIATION FOR MEAT
    LOAF . . . . Sep/Oct 96 22
Meat Loaf Pan (S&R) . . . . Sep/Oct 96 32
Meat Loaf Pan Update (S&R) . . . . Mar/Apr 97 32
Memorable Meat Loaf . . . . Sep/Oct 96 22

Melon (See also specific kinds)
Decorative Melon Carving . . . . Jul/Aug 95 16
Melon Baller (S&R) . . . . Sep/Oct 95 32
Peeling and Seeding Melons (QT) . . Jul/Aug 94 4
V-shaped Melon Cutter (Notes) . . . . Jul/Aug 97 3

Meringues
ALMOND MERINGUE CAKE WITH
    STRAWBERRY AND VANILLA ICE
    CREAM . . . . May/Jun 95 13
CLASSIC MERINGUE . . . . May/Jun 95 12
FREE-FORM MERINGUE SHELLS FILLED
    WITH STRAWBERRIES AND
    PAPAYA . . . . May/Jun 95 13
No-Weep Lemon Meringue Pie . . . . Nov/Dec 94 22
REDUCED-GUILT CHOCOLATE LAYER CAKE
    WITH MERINGUE FROSTING . Jul/Aug 94 25
Shaping Foolproof Meringues,
    Master Class . . . . May/Jun 95 12
THE ULTIMATE LEMON MERINGUE
    PIE . . . . Nov/Dec 94 24
Mexican Ingredients (S&R) . . . . . . Jul/Aug 94 32

Microwaves
Lamb Shank Tips (Notes) . . . . Nov/Dec 95 3
Microwave Angel Food? . . . . Charter Issue 11
MICROWAVED CORN ON THE
    COB . . . . Jul/Aug 95 22
Microwave Garlic Before Roasting
    (Notes) . . . . Sep/Oct 95 3
Microwaving Corn (Notes) . . . . Jan/Feb 96 2
Proofing Bread (QT) . . . . Nov/Dec 96 4
Quicker Baked Potato . . . . Sep/Oct 95 25
Rising Bread in the Microwave
    (Notes) . . . . Nov/Dec 94 3

Milk
Clabbered Milk (Notes) . . . . Jul/Aug 96 2
Homemade Condensed
    Milk (Notes) . . . . Nov/Dec 94 2
Is Scalding Milk for Bread
    Essential? (Notes) . . . . Jan/Feb 94 2

Is Scalding Milk Necessary?
    (Notes) . . . . Charter Issue 2
Making a Low-Tech
    Milkshake (QT) . . . . May/Jun 97 4
More Details on Clabbered
    Milk (Notes) . . . . Nov/Dec 96 2
Preventing Milk Boil-Over (QT) . . . Nov/Dec 96 4
Scalding Milk (Notes) . . . . Sep/Oct 94 2
Scalding Milk for Bread (Notes) . . . Jul/Aug 94 2
The Science of Buttermilk . . . . Jul/Aug 93 1
Soured-Milk Substitute? . . . . Sep/Oct 93 7
What Is Evaporated Milk? . . . . Mar/Apr 96 24
Which Milk Is Best? . . . . Sep/Oct 93 27

Mint
ASPARAGUS FRITTATA WITH MINT AND
    PARMESAN . . . . Mar/Apr 96 11
BRAISED LAMB SHANKS WITH LEMON AND
    MINT . . . . Jan/Feb 95 19
DRIED PEACH COMPOTE WITH MINT AND
    WHISKEY . . . . Jan/Feb 95 23
FENNEL-ORANGE SALAD WITH BLACK OLIVES
    AND MINT . . . . May/Jun 96 19
GRILLED SKEWERED LAMB WITH YOGURT,
    CURRY, AND MINT . . . . Jul/Aug 93 12
POTATO GNOCCHI WITH TOMATO-MINT
    SAUCE . . . . Mar/Apr 95 10
SPRING VEGETABLE SOUP WITH EGG NOO-
    DLES AND MINT . . . . Charter Issue 29
WARM CUCUMBER/RED ONION RELISH WITH
    MINT . . . . May/Jun 94 13
YOGURT MINT CUCUMBER
    SALAD . . . . Jul/Aug 97 11
ZUCCHINI, RED PEPPER, AND TOMATO SAUCE
    WITH THYME AND MINT . . . . . Sep/Oct 94 22

Mirepoix
Mirepoix (Notes) . . . . May/Jun 94 2

Miso
GINGER WALNUT MISO
    DRESSING . . . . Charter Issue 30

Mousse
CHOCOLATE MOUSSE . . . . Jul/Aug 96 7
The Ultimate Chocolate Mousse . . . Jul/Aug 96 6

Mozzarella Cheese
Fresh Mozzarella (S&R) . . . . May/Jun 96 32

FRESH TOMATO PIZZA WITH ARUGULA AND
PROSCIUTTO .... May/Jun 95   11
GRILLED MOZZARELLA AND SUN-DRIED
TOMATO SKEWERS .... May/Jun 96   17
SAUSAGE AND BELL PEPPER PIZZA WITH
BASIL AND MOZZARELLA.... May/Jun 95   11

Muffins
ANY-FRUIT-WILL-DO MUFFINS WITH
STREUSAL TOPPING........ Sep/Oct 93   8
APRICOT ALMOND MUFFINS ... Jan/Feb 97   19
Avoiding Soggy Muffin
Bottoms (QT) .... Jan/Feb 97   5
BANANA WALNUT MUFFINS ... Jan/Feb 97   19
BIG BRAN MUFFINS WITH RAISINS AND
DATES .... Sep/Oct 93   7
Choosing Your Mixing Method .... Jan/Feb 97   19
Commercial Muffin Tins (S&R).... Sep/Oct 93   32
CRANBERRY-WALNUT-ORANGE
MUFFINS .... Jan/Feb 97   19
Do Muffin Papers Help? .... Jan/Feb 97   19
DOUBLE-CORN MUFFINS ...... Sep/Oct 93   7
How to Make Professional Muffins at
Home .... Sep/Oct 93   6
LEMON BLUEBERRY MUFFINS . Jan/Feb 97   19
LEMON POPPY SEED MUFFINS . Jan/Feb 97   19
MOCHA CHIP MUFFINS....... Jan/Feb 97   19
Muffin Tops (Notes)............ Jul/Aug 94   3
Quick Topping (QT) .... Mar/Apr 97   4
RASPBERRY ALMOND
MUFFINS .... Jan/Feb 97   19

Mushrooms
ASPARAGUS AND MUSHROOM SAUCE
WITH HERB AND MUSHROOM
STUFFING .... Nov/Dec 95   26
BEEF STEW WITH BACON, MUSHROOMS,
AND PEARL ONIONS........ Jan/Feb 96   20
BRUSCHETTA WITH GRILLED PORTOBELLO
MUSHROOMS.............. Sep/Oct 96   8
CARAMELIZED SHALLOTS..... Mar/Apr 95   11
CHICKEN IN THE POT WITH CARROTS,
MUSHROOMS, AND THYME ... Sep/Oct 95   19
Cleaning Cultivated
Mushrooms (QT) .... Jan/Feb 95   4
Fresh Mushrooms for Cooking .... Sep/Oct 93   14
GREEN BEANS AND MUSHROOMS BRAISED
IN CREAM .... Nov/Dec 96   7
GRILLED PORTOBELLO MUSHROOMS,

RED PEPPER, AND GARLIC
CROUTONS................. Jul/Aug 96   9
HEARTY CHICKEN SOUP WITH LEEKS, WILD
RICE, AND MUSHROOMS .... Mar/Apr 96   15
How to Rehydrate Porcini
Mushrooms................. Jan/Feb 97   15
Making Room in
Mushrooms (QT)............. Jul/Aug 97   4
Mushrooms by Mail (S&R) .... Sep/Oct 93   32
Mushrooms: Dried and
Fresh (S&R) .... Jan/Feb 97   32
POLENTA WITH WILD MUSHROOMS AND
ROSEMARY.............. Jan/Feb 95   21
PORCINI MUSHROOM SAUCE WITH
CREAM .... Jan/Feb 97   15
POT ROAST WITH PORCINI
MUSHROOMS............. Jan/Feb 94   9
Rehydrating Dried
Mushrooms (QT) .... Jan/Feb 97   4
Rehydrating Dried
Ingredients (QT) .... Nov/Dec 95   5
RISOTTO WITH ASPARAGUS AND WILD
MUSHROOMS .... Mar/Apr 94   19
SAUTÉED BUTTERFLIED CHICKEN
WITH MUSHROOM-SAGE PAN
SAUCE .... Sep/Oct 94   25
SHERRY-CREAM SAUCE WITH
MUSHROOMS............. Sep/Oct 93   10
SHIITAKE-STUFFED SALMON ROLLS WITH
TARRAGON-TOMATO SAUCE .. Jul/Aug 95   11
Slicing Mushrooms (QT)........ Nov/Dec 94   5
Submerging Rehydrated
Mushrooms (QT) .... Nov/Dec 97   5
TOMATO SAUCE WITH PORCINI
MUSHROOMS............. Jan/Feb 97   15
Truffle Slicer (Notes) .... May/Jun 94   3
Truffle Slicer (S&R) .... May/Jun 94   32
TWO MUSHROOM SAUCE WITH
ROSEMARY................. Jan/Feb 97   15
WILD MUSHROOM FILLING FOR
PASTA .... Sep/Oct 93   18
WILD MUSHROOM PIZZA WITH SAGE, FONTINA,
AND PARMESAN........... May/Jun 95   11

Mussels
The Key to Cooking Mussels ..... Nov/Dec 96   14
MUSSELS STEAMED IN WHITE WINE, MASTER
RECIPE FOR................ Nov/Dec 96   15
MUSSELS STEAMED IN WHITE WINE WITH

CURRY AND BASIL . . . . Nov/Dec 96   15

MUSSELS STEAMED IN WHITE WINE WITH
TOMATO AND BASIL . . . . Nov/Dec 96   15

PAELLA, CRIOLLA'S STYLE . . . . . Jan/Feb 95   11

STEAMED MUSSEL SAUCE WITH LEMON AND
WHITE WINE . . . . Mar/Apr 96   9

STEAMED MUSSELS WITH ASIAN
FLAVORS . . . . Nov/Dec 96   15

Mustard

BLACK PEPPER-MUSTARD
SAUCE . . . . Mar/Apr 95   20

BRAISED BRUSSELS SPROUTS WITH TAR-
RAGON-MUSTARD BUTTER. . . Nov/Dec 95   21

BROWN SUGAR AND HONEY MUSTARD
GLAZE. Nov/Dec 93   12

COUNTRY MUSTARD-SHALLOT SAUCE WITH
THYME. May/Jun 95   22

COUNTRY-STYLE MUSTARD . . . . Jan/Feb 94   18

Getting the Most Mustard (QT) . . . Jul/Aug 97   5

HOT-AND-SWEET CREAMY
MUSTARD . . . . Jan/Feb 94   18

HOT-AND-SWEET MUSTARD
VINAIGRETTE . . . . Jan/Feb 94   18

How to Make Mustard at Home . . . Jan/Feb 94   18

MID–SOUTH CAROLINA MUSTARD SAUCE
(for Barbecue). . . . . Jul/Aug 97   20

Mustard Mecca (S&R) . . . . Jan/Feb 96   32

MUSTARD SAUCE (for Steak) . . . May/Jun 97   9

Mustard Supplies (S&R) . . . . Jan/Feb 94   32

MUSTARD VINAIGRETTE . . . . . . Mar/Apr 95   15

QUICK-COOKED CARROTS WITH MUSTARD-
BROWN SUGAR GLAZE . . . . . . Mar/Apr 96   25

QUILTED GIRAFFE'S GRILLED SALMON
WITH MUSTARD GLAZE . . . . Jul/Aug 97   7

Rating Dijon Mustards (BT) . . . . . . Jan/Feb 96   24

ROAST CHICKEN WITH DIJON MUSTARD-
THYME SAUCE . . . . May/Jun 93   28

ROASTED BUTTERFLIED CHICKEN WITH
TARRAGON-MUSTARD PAN
SAUCE . . . . Sep/Oct 94   25

SAUTÉED PORK CHOPS WITH MUSTARD AND
CAPERS . . . . Sep/Oct 94   13

TWO-MUSTARD DRESSING WITH
CHIVES. . . . . Charter Issue   30

Natural Foods

Natural Foods Glossary . . . . Charter Issue   30

Nectarines

Crisps and Betties . . . . Sep/Oct 93   26

Noodles (See also Pasta)

HEARTY CHICKEN NOODLE SOUP, MASTER
RECIPE FOR . . . . Mar/Apr 96   15

SPRING VEGETABLE SOUP WITH EGG
NOODLES AND MINT . . . . . . Charter Issue   29

Nutmeg

BRAISED BRUSSELS SPROUTS WITH NUTMEG-
SCENTED WHITE SAUCE. . . . . Nov/Dec 95   21

Nutmeg and Grinders (S&R) . . . . . Nov/Dec 95   32

Nutmeg Grater . . . . Jul/Aug 96   16

PUREED CARROT SOUP WITH
NUTMEG . . . . Nov/Dec 96   23

Nuts (See also specific kinds)

Blanching Salted Nuts (QT) . . . . . . Sep/Oct 97   5

GUBANA: ITALIAN EASTER BREAD WITH
NUTS AND FRUIT . . . . Mar/Apr 94   12

NUT BUTTER COOKIE DOUGH. . Nov/Dec 93   7

Oatmeal

BIG CHEWY OATMEAL-RAISIN
COOKIES . . . . Jan/Feb 97   23

CHOCOLATE CHIP OATMEAL
COOKIES . . . . Jan/Feb 97   23

DATE OATMEAL COOKIES . . . . . Jan/Feb 97   23

GINGER OATMEAL COOKIES . . . Jan/Feb 97   23

NUT OATMEAL COOKIES . . . . . . Jan/Feb 97   23

Oatmeal Cookie Woes (Notes) . . . . Jul/Aug 97   2

OATMEAL LOAF BREAD . . . . May/Jun 96   11

OATMEAL-WALNUT SODA
BREAD . . . . Mar/Apr 97   13

ORANGE AND ALMOND OATMEAL
COOKIES . . . . Jan/Feb 97   23

Oats

YOGURT-CREAMED OATS WITH BERRIES AND
APPLES . . . . May/Jun 94   BC

Oils

Bottles for Infused Oils (S&R) . . . . . Jan/Feb 95   32

Citrus Oils (S&R) . . . . Nov/Dec 93   32

Cloudy Olive Oil (Notes) . . . . Jan/Feb 94   2

COLD OIL INFUSING, MASTER METHOD
FOR . . . . Jan/Feb 95   15

Cold-Pressed Peanut Oil (S&R) . . . May/Jun 93   32

Cook's Illustrated 1993–1997 Index

Extra-Virgin Olive Oils (S&R)..... Sep/Oct 96   32

Extra-Virgin Olive Oils Prove
Uniformly Good (BT) .... Sep/Oct 96   26

Grapeseed Oil (Notes).......... Nov/Dec 96   3

Grapeseed Oil (S&R) .... Nov/Dec 96   32

Light Olive Oil (Notes)......... May/Jun 93   2

MASHED POTATOES WITH POACHED
GARLIC AND OLIVE OIL ..... Nov/Dec 93   11

PIQUANT PLUM SAUCE WITH SESAME
OIL AND GINGER........... Jul/Aug 94   20

Recipes That Mix Oil and Other
Liquids (Notes) .... May/Jun 95   2

Spice-Infused Oils .... Jan/Feb 95   15

STEWED TOMATO SAUCE WITH BASIL AND
OLIVE OIL .... Mar/Apr 94   26

Taste-Testing Olive Oils (BT)... Charter Issue   13

WARM OIL INFUSING, MASTER
METHOD FOR.............. Jan/Feb 95   15

Which Oils Are Best for Your
Health? .... Charter Issue   20

Olives

BEEF STEW WITH TOMATOES, ORANGE
ZEST, AND OLIVES.......... Jan/Feb 96   20

BLACK OLIVE PASTE .... Mar/Apr 95   19

BRAISED VEAL BREAST WITH SAUSAGE,
OLIVE, AND SWISS CHARD
STUFFING (Notes) .... Sep/Oct 93   3

BREAD SALAD WITH ROASTED PEPPERS AND
SICILIAN OLIVES........... Sep/Oct 95   14

CARAMELIZED ONION PIZZA WITH OIL-CURED
OLIVES AND PARMESAN .... May/Jun 95   10

CHICKEN IN THE POT WITH TOMATOES,
BLACK OLIVES, AND CAPERS . Sep/Oct 95   19

FENNEL AND OLIVE SALAD WITH CREAMY
TARRAGON VINAIGRETTE ... May/Jun 95   23

FENNEL-ORANGE SALAD WITH BLACK OLIVES
AND MINT .... May/Jun 96   19

FETA CHEESE FRITTATA WITH OLIVES AND
SUN-DRIED TOMATOES...... Mar/Apr 96   11

GRILLED CHICKEN WITH OLIVES, ROSEMARY,
AND GARLIC............... Jul/Aug 93   12

MUFFULETTA .... Sep/Oct 96   21

Olive Picker (Notes)............ Sep/Oct 96   3

Olive Pitter .... Jul/Aug 96   16

ONION, BLACK OLIVE, AND CAPER
COMPOTE .... May/Jun 94   13

Pitting Olives (QT) .... Sep/Oct 93   5

QUICK-COOKED GREENS WITH BLACK OLIVES

AND LEMON ZEST .... Jan/Feb 95   13

SAUTÉED ZUCCHINI WITH OLIVES AND
LEMON .... Jul/Aug 95   9

TOMATO SAUCE WITH ARUGULA AND BLACK
OLIVES................... Mar/Apr 95   11

TOMATO SAUCE WITH TUNA AND GREEN
OLIVES................... Mar/Apr 96   9

Okra

PICKLED OKRA............... Sep/Oct 94   19

Onions

ASPARAGUS VINAIGRETTE WITH SIEVED
EGG AND PICKLED PINK
ONIONS .... May/Jun 95   23

BEEF STEW WITH BACON, MUSHROOMS, AND
PEARL ONIONS .... Jan/Feb 96   20

BRAISED ONIONS WITH RED WINE, THYME,
AND PANCETTA............. Jan/Feb 96   26

BREAD SALAD WITH TOMATOES, HERBS, AND
RED ONIONS .... Sep/Oct 95   14

BRUSCHETTA WITH RED ONIONS, HERBS, AND
PARMESAN .... Sep/Oct 96   8

CARAMELIZED ONION PIZZA WITH OIL-CURED
OLIVES AND PARMESAN .... May/Jun 95   10

CRANBERRY-ONION CONFIT... Nov/Dec 94   14

Dicing Onions (QT).......... Charter Issue   5

EASY ROASTED ONIONS ...... Nov/Dec 97   18

GLAZED ONIONS WITH
RAISINS .... Mar/Apr 95   13

GREEN BEANS WITH BACON AND
ONIONS .... Nov/Dec 96   7

LAMB BROTH, GLAZED ONIONS, AND FRIED
ALMONDS .... Mar/Apr 95   12

Making Scallion Brushes (QT) .... Sep/Oct 93   4

MASHED POTATOES AND APPLES WITH BACON
AND BROWNED ONIONS..... Nov/Dec 93   11

ONION RELISH .... Jan/Feb 96   13

ONION, BLACK OLIVE, AND CAPER
COMPOTE .... May/Jun 94   13

Onions' Sulfur Prevents Browning
(of Latkes) .... Nov/Dec 97   7

Peeling Onions (QT) .... Sep/Oct 96   4

PICKLED PURPLE ONIONS..... Sep/Oct 94   19

Preparing Pearl Onions (QT) ..... Mar/Apr 94   5

QUICK-COOKED GREENS WITH
BACON AND ONION .... Jan/Feb 95   13

ROASTED CARROTS AND RED ONION WITH
BALSAMIC VINEGAR......... Jan/Feb 94   11

ROASTED FENNEL WITH RED ONIONS AND
CARROTS . . . . May/Jun 96   19
ROASTED ONION AND BACON
DIP . . . . Nov/Dec 97   18
ROASTED POTATOES WITH ONION, BACON,
AND THYME . . . . Jan/Feb 94   11
ROASTED RED PEPPER SALAD WITH RED
ONIONS AND CUCUMBERS . . May/Jun 96   21
Store Vidalia Onions (QT) . . . . May/Jun 95   5
WARM CUCUMBER/RED ONION RELISH
WITH MINT . . . . May/Jun 94   13

Oranges (*See* also Citrus Fruit; Fruit, Fresh)
BEEF STEW WITH TOMATOES, ORANGE ZEST,
AND OLIVES, ... Jan/Feb 96   20
CITRUS SALAD WITH BITTER GREENS AND
PARMESAN SHAVINGS . . . . Nov/Dec 96   21
CORNMEAL-CITRUS COOKIES. . Nov/Dec 96   20
CRANBERRY-ORANGE CHIFFON
CAKE . . . . May/Jun 96   8
DRIED PEAR AND ORANGE COMPOTE WITH
HONEY AND SAGE . . . . Jan/Feb 95   23
FENNEL-ORANGE SALAD WITH BLACK
OLIVES AND MINT . . . . May/Jun 96   19
Fruit Sorbets at a Glance . . . . Jul/Aug 95   24
GRAND MARNIER CAKE WITH NEOCLASSIC
ORANGE BUTTERCREAM . . . . Nov/Dec 95   11
GRILLED LEEKS WITH ORANGE-CHIVE
BUTTER . . . . Mar/Apr 95   15
LEMON, ORANGE, OR PLAIN
GLAZE. . . . . Nov/Dec 96   20
NEAPOLITAN ORANGE CAKE Charter Issue   15
ORANGE-ALMOND BISCOTTI . . . Jan/Feb 94   12
ORANGE BUTTER COOKIES. . . . Nov/Dec 96   20
ORANGE CHIFFON CAKE . . . . . . May/Jun 96   8
ORANGE COMPOTE WITH STAR
ANISE . . . . Mar/Apr 96   BC
ORANGE MADELEINES . . . . Mar/Apr 96   21
ORANGE-NUT COOKIES . . . . Nov/Dec 96   20
ORANGE PUDDING CAKE . . . . . . Jan/Feb 95   25
ORANGE SAUCE. . . . . Mar/Apr 96   20
ORANGE SAUCE FOR
GINGERBREAD . . . . Nov/Dec 95   23
PICKLED BEETS WITH ORANGE &
ROSEMARY . . . . Mar/Apr 94   11
QUICK-COOKED CARROTS WITH ORANGE
AND PISTACHIO . . . . Mar/Apr 96   25
RICE PUDDING WITH ORANGE AND TOASTED
ALMONDS . . . . Sep/Oct 96   25

Segmenting Oranges (QT) . . . . . Charter Issue   4
STIR-FRIED BROCCOLI WITH ORANGE
SAUCE . . . . Sep/Oct 95   9
WATERCRESS SALAD WITH SEARED SCALLOPS
AND ORANGE VINAIGRETTE . Mar/Apr 96   8

Oregano (*See* also Herbs)
ESCAROLE AND WHITE BEAN SAUCE WITH
GARLIC AND OREGANO . . . . . . Sep/Oct 94   22

Oysters
BROILED OYSTERS TOPPED WITH ROASTED
CHILE-CILANTRO SAUCE . . . . Nov/Dec 94   BC
How to Shuck an Oyster (QT). . . Charter Issue   4
OYSTER FLAVORED SAUCE. . . . May/Jun 93   19
Oyster Varieties (Notes) . . . . Nov/Dec 93   2

Paella
Last-Minute Paella, Master Class. . Jan/Feb 95   10
PAELLA, CRIOLLA'S STYLE . . . . . Jan/Feb 95   11
Paella Pan (S&R). . . . . Jan/Feb 95   32

Pancakes (*See* also Crepes; Roesti)
BASIC BATTER . . . . Charter Issue   18
BLUEBERRY PANCAKES, ... Jan/Feb 96   8
FEATHERWEIGHT PANCAKES . . Jan/Feb 96   8
Griddles (S&R). . . . . Jan/Feb 96   32
Keeping Pancakes Warm (QT). . . . . Sep/Oct 96   4
Pancakes, wrapping to keep warm . Jan/Feb 96   8
LIGHT AND FLUFFY
PANCAKES . . . . Jan/Feb 96   8
One Batter, Many Desserts. . . . . Charter Issue   18
Perfect Pancakes . . . . Jan/Feb 96   6
Real Maple Syrup (S&R). . . . . Jan/Feb 96   32
REUBEN'S LEGENDARY APPLE
PANCAKE . . . . Charter Issue   19
SESAME CREPES (Notes) . . . . . . Jan/Feb 94   3
Swedish Pancake Pan (S&R) . . . . . Mar/Apr 94   32
TOASTED PECAN PANCAKES . . . Jan/Feb 96   8
WHOLE WHEAT PANCAKES . . . . Jan/Feb 96   8

Pancetta
BRAISED ONIONS WITH RED WINE, THYME,
AND PANCETTA. . . . . Jan/Feb 96   26
Italian Pancetta (S&R). . . . . Mar/Apr 94   32
OVEN-DRIED TOMATO SAUCE WITH
PANCETTA AND HOT PEPPER . Sep/Oct 96   21
Pancetta (S&R) . . . . Jan/Feb 96   32
Pancetta Substitutes (Notes) . . . . Mar/Apr 94   2

SAUTÉED ZUCCHINI WITH PANCETTA AND
PARSLEY . . . . Jul/Aug 95   9

Papaya
BANANA-PAPAYA FOOL . . . . Jan/Feb 95   BC
FREE-FORM MERINGUE SHELLS FILLED WITH
STRAWBERRIES AND PAPAYA May/Jun 95   13
Preparing Tropical Fruit . . . . Jan/Feb 94   16

Parmesan Cheese
ASPARAGUS FRITTATA WITH MINT AND
PARMESAN . . . . Mar/Apr 96   11
BRAISED FENNEL WITH WHITE WINE AND
PARMESAN . . . . May/Jun 96   18
BROILED BUTTERFLIED CHICKEN WITH
PARMESAN, LEMON, AND RED PEPPER
FLAKES . . . . Sep/Oct 94   25
BRUSCHETTA WITH RED ONIONS, HERBS,
AND PARMESAN . . . . Sep/Oct 96   8
CARAMELIZED ONION PIZZA WITH OIL-CURED
OLIVES AND PARMESAN . . . . May/Jun 95   10
CITRUS SALAD WITH BITTER GREENS AND
PARMESAN SHAVINGS . . . . . . Nov/Dec 96   21
CRISPY CHEESE WAFERS . . . . . May/Jun 96   17
Grated Parmesan (Notes) . . . . Nov/Dec 93   3
MARINATED ZUCCHINI WITH
PARMESAN . . . . May/Jun 96   16
PARMESAN WITH DATES . . . . . . May/Jun 96   16
MASHED POTATOES WITH PARMESAN
CHEESE AND LEMON . . . . Nov/Dec 93   11
Parmesan Cheese Debate . . . . May/Jun 94   3
POLENTA WITH PARMESAN AND
BUTTER . . . . Jan/Feb 95   21
POTATO GNOCCHI WITH BUTTER, SAGE,
AND PARMESAN CHEESE . . . . Mar/Apr 95   10
POTATO GRATIN WITH BROTH AND
PARMESAN . . . . Nov/Dec 95   19
WILD MUSHROOM PIZZA WITH SAGE, FONTINA,
AND PARMESAN . . . . May/Jun 95   11
ZUCCHINI FRITTATA WITH PARMESAN AND
HERBS . . . . Jul/Aug 95   9

Parsley
BRAISED CABBAGE WITH PARSLEY AND
THYME . . . . Sep/Oct 96   9
CELERY ROOT AND POTATO ROESTI WITH
LEMON AND PARSLEY . . . . Jan/Feb 95   22
POTATO, HAM, AND PARSLEY
OMELET . . . . Sep/Oct 93   22

QUICK-COOKED CARROTS WITH BUTTER
AND PARSLEY . . . . Mar/Apr 96   25
ROASTED CARROTS AND PARSLEY
ROOTS . . . . Jul/Aug 93   25
SAUTÉED FENNEL WITH GARLIC AND
PARSLEY, ... May/Jun 96   19
SAUTÉED ZUCCHINI WITH PANCETTA
AND PARSLEY . . . . Jul/Aug 95   9

Parsnips
CORN AND CLAM CHOWDER WITH ROASTED
PARSNIPS . . . . Jul/Aug 93   9
CREAMY PARSNIP PUREE WITH
SHALLOTS . . . . Sep/Oct 94   9
PAN-BRAISED ROOT VEGETABLES WITH RED
CABBAGE AND ROSEMARY . . . Jan/Feb 96   26
Pureed Is Best for Parsnips . . . . . . Sep/Oct 94   9
ROASTED PARSNIPS . . . . Sep/Oct 94   9
SIMPLE PUREED PARSNIPS . . . . Sep/Oct 94   9

Passion Fruit
Preparing Tropical Fruit . . . . Jan/Feb 94   16

Pasta (See also Lasagne)
American Spaghetti Tops
Tasting (BT) . . . . May/Jun 94   21
BROCCOLI-ANCHOVY SAUCE WITH
ZITI . . . . Sep/Oct 94   22
CAVATELLI WITH WHITE BEANS AND
CLAMS . . . . Jan/Feb 94   19
Classic Lasagne Made Easy . . . . . . Nov/Dec 94   10
DURUM WHEAT PASTA . . . . Nov/Dec 95   27
EGG PASTA, MASTER
RECIPE FOR . . . . Nov/Dec 95   27
Foaming Pasta Water (Notes) . . . . May/Jun 96   3
FRESH HERB PASTA . . . . Nov/Dec 95   27
FUSILLI WITH ARUGULA AND TOMATO
SAUCE . . . . Jan/Feb 94   21
HEARTY CHICKEN SOUP WITH ORZO AND
SPRING VEGETABLES . . . . Mar/Apr 96   15
HEARTY CHICKEN SOUP WITH SHELLS, TOMA-
TOES, AND ZUCCHINI . . . . . . Mar/Apr 96   15
Heating a Pasta Bowl (QT) . . . . . . Nov/Dec 94   4
How to Cook Dried Pasta . . . . May/Jun 94   23
LASAGNE WITH HERBED MEATBALLS,
TOMATO SAUCE, AND
MOZZARELLA . . . . Nov/Dec 94   11
LINGUINE WITH GARLIC CREAM
SAUCE . . . . Sep/Oct 93   20

Cook's Illustrated 1993–1997 Index

LINGUINE WITH WALNUT, GARLIC, AND HERB SAUCE . . . . Jan/Feb 96 21

Making Pasta Machines Work . . . . Nov/Dec 95 27

ORECCHIETTE WITH BROCCOLI RABE . . . . Jan/Feb 94 21

ORECCHIETTE WITH CAULIFLOWER AND BACON . . . . Jan/Feb 94 21

PENNE WITH QUICK-COOKED GREENS AND PROSCIUTTO . . . . Jan/Feb 95 14

RAVIOLI . . . . Sep/Oct 93 16

RICK MOONEN'S ANGEL HAIR PASTA WITH SEARED SCALLOPS . . . . Mar/Apr 96 8

SEMOLINA DOUGH . . . . Jan/Feb 94 19

Semolina Flour (S&R) . . . . Jan/Feb 94 32

SPAGHETTI WITH ARTICHOKE-LOBSTER SAUCE . . . . May/Jun 94 12

SPAGHETTI WITH FENNEL AND BREAD CRUMBS . . . . May/Jun 95 25

SPINACH PASTA. . . . . Nov/Dec 95 27

Specialty Dried Pastas (S&R) . . . . . Sep/Oct 94 32

Three Filled Pastas . . . . Sep/Oct 93 15

Three Hand-Formed Pastas. . . . . . Jan/Feb 94 19

TORTELLINI . . . . Sep/Oct 93 15

TWISTED TORTELLINI. . . . . Sep/Oct 93 16

WHOLE WHEAT DOUGH . . . . Jan/Feb 94 19

equipment

Electric Pasta Machines (S&R). . . . Nov/Dec 95 32

Pasta Machine (S&R) . . . . Sep/Oct 93 32

Pasta Partitioner (Notes) . . . . Sep/Oct 97 3

Rating Electric Pasta Makers (ER) Nov/Dec 95 28

Ravioli Cutters (S&R) . . . . Sep/Oct 93 32

fillings

Filling Stuffed Manicotti (QT) . . . . Nov/Dec 95 4

MEAT AND RICOTTA FILLING WITH BASIL FOR PASTA . . . . Sep/Oct 93 18

SPINACH AND RICOTTA FILLING FOR PASTA . . . . Sep/Oct 93 18

SQUASH, PROSCIUTTO, AND PARMESAN FILLING FOR PASTA . . . . Sep/Oct 93 18

WILD MUSHROOM FILLING FOR PASTA . . . . Sep/Oct 93 18

sauces

ALL-PURPOSE TOMATO SAUCE . . . . Mar/Apr 94 26

AROMATIC TOMATO SAUCE . . . Mar/Apr 94 26

ASPARAGUS AND MUSHROOM SAUCE WITH CARAMELIZED SHALLOTS . . . Mar/Apr 95 11

BASIL SAUCE WITH SAUTÉED SHRIMP . . . . Mar/Apr 96 9

BRAISED ARTICHOKE SAUCE WITH WHITE WINE, GARLIC, AND LEMON. . Mar/Apr 95 11

BRAISED FENNEL AND BITTER GREENS SAUCE WITH BALSAMIC VINEGAR . . . . Mar/Apr 95 11

BROWN BUTTER AND PINE NUT SAUCE . . . . Sep/Oct 93 18

CLAM SAUCE WITH TOMATOES AND GARLIC . . . . Mar/Apr 96 9

Country Italian Vegetable Pasta Sauces . . . . Mar/Apr 95 11

ESCAROLE AND WHITE BEAN SAUCE WITH GARLIC AND OREGANO . . . . . Sep/Oct 94 22

FRESH TOMATO-HERB SAUCE, MASTER RECIPE FOR . . . . Jul/Aug 93 14

GARDEN TOMATO SAUCE . . . . . Sep/Oct 93 18

OVEN-DRIED TOMATO SAUCE WITH PANCETTA AND HOT PEPPER . . . . Sep/Oct 96 21

PASTA AND SIMPLE TOMATO SAUCE, MASTER RECIPE FOR . . . . May/Jun 97 9

PASTA AND TOMATO SAUCE WITH ANCHOVIES AND OLIVES . . . . May/Jun 97 11

PASTA AND TOMATO SAUCE WITH BACON AND PARSLEY . . . . May/Jun 97 11

PASTA AND TOMATO SAUCE WITH VODKA AND CREAM . . . . May/Jun 97 11

PASTA WITH FRESH CLAM SAUCE Nov/Dec 97 14

PORCINI MUSHROOM SAUCE WITH CREAM . . . . Jan/Feb 97 15

Quick Seafood Pasta Sauces . . . . . Mar/Apr 96 9

QUICK-COOKED TOMATOES WITH OLIVE OIL . . . . Mar/Apr 94 26

ROASTED RED AND YELLOW PEPPER SAUCE WITH GARLIC . . . . Sep/Oct 94 22

STEAMED MUSSEL SAUCE WITH LEMON AND WHITE WINE . . . . Mar/Apr 96 9

STEWED TOMATO SAUCE WITH BASIL AND OLIVE OIL . . . . Mar/Apr 94 26

Testing Pasta Doneness . . . . May/Jun 97 5

Tomato Sauces for Pasta . . . . Mar/Apr 94 26

TOMATO SAUCE WITH ARUGULA AND BLACK OLIVES. . . . . Mar/Apr 95 11

TOMATO SAUCE WITH PORCINI MUSHROOMS. . . . . Jan/Feb 97 15

TOMATO SAUCE WITH TUNA AND GREEN OLIVES. . . . . Mar/Apr 96 9

TWO MUSHROOM SAUCE WITH ROSEMARY. . . . . Jan/Feb 97 15

Vegetable Pasta Sauces . . . . Sep/Oct 94 22

ZUCCHINI, RED PEPPER, AND TOMATO SAUCE
WITH THYME AND MINT . . . . . Sep/Oct 94   22

Pastries (*See* also Brioche; Doughs; Pies and Tarts)
Blind-Baking Different (Pastry)
    Doughs . . . . Sep/Oct 97   11
CINNAMON-NUT SEASONING
    FOR PASTRY . . . . Mar/Apr 94   15
CLASSIC BAKLAVA FILLING . . . Nov/Dec 95   15
Cotton Pastry Cloth (S&R) . . . . Jan/Feb 95   32
Cutting Butter for Pastry (QT) . . . May/Jun 94   5
EASY PASTRY CREAM . . . . May/Jun 94   14
Egg (Pastry) Doughs Lift Off . . . . . Sep/Oct 97   11
Fearless Phyllo . . . . Nov/Dec 95   15
Filling and holding pastry bags . . . May/Jun 95   16
Filling a Pastry Bag (QT) . . . . May/Jun 97   5
Filling Pastry Bags (QT) . . . . Sep/Oct 96   5
Fitting Pastry into Pie Dishes . . . . Sep/Oct 97   10
FLAKY PASTRY SHELL . . . . Nov/Dec 93   23
FLAKY PASTRY TOPPING . . . . . . Jul/Aug 96   20
FREE-FORM PASTRY SHELL . . . May/Jun 94   14
Free-Form Pastry Shells, Making . . May/Jun 94   15
Freezing Pie Pastry (QT) . . . . Nov/Dec 97   4
Fresh Phyllo (S&R) . . . . Nov/Dec 96   32
LADY FINGERS . . . . Jan/Feb 94   2
Loading a Pastry Bag (QT) . . . . Jan/Feb 95   4
Making Phyllo Pastries . . . . Nov/Dec 95   16
Making Puff Pastries . . . . Mar/Apr 94   16
Moving Pie Pastry (QT) . . . . May/Jun 94   4
Palmiers . . . . Mar/Apr 94   16
PARMESAN-PAPRIKA
    PALMIERS . . . . Mar/Apr 94   16
PARMESAN-PAPRIKA PASTRY
    STRAWS . . . . Mar/Apr 94   16
PARMESAN-PAPRIKA SEASONING
    FOR PASTRY . . . . Mar/Apr 94   15
Pastry Board (S&R) . . . . Jul/Aug 95   32
PEAR AND DRIED FRUIT
    STRUDEL . . . . Sep/Oct 94   10
Pie Pastry Revisited . . . . Sep/Oct 96   24
PUFF PASTRY TARTLETS . . . . . Mar/Apr 94   17
Quickest Puff Pastry . . . . Mar/Apr 94   14
QUICKEST PUFF PASTRY . . . . . Mar/Apr 94   15
The Secrets of Pie Pastry . . . . . . Charter Issue   16
SMOKED SALMON AND CHIVE
    MILLE FEUILLE . . . . Mar/Apr 94   17
SOUR CREAM FLAKY PASTRY
    DOUGH . . . . Sep/Oct 94   10

Sour Cream Flaky Pastry Dough . . Sep/Oct 94   10
Sour Cream Pastry Strudel . . . . Sep/Oct 94   10
Sour Cream Pastry Strudel,
    Master Class . . . . Sep/Oct 94   10
Straws . . . . Mar/Apr 94   16

Peaches
BAKED PEACH BRUSCHETTA . . . Sep/Oct 97   BC
BAKED PEACHES WITH AMARETTI
    COOKIES . . . . Jul/Aug 94   BC
Crisps and Betties . . . . Sep/Oct 93   26
DRIED PEACH AND APPLE SALAD WITH
    ALMONDS AND CUMIN . . . . . . Jul/Aug 94   20
DRIED PEACH COMPOTE WITH MINT AND
    WHISKEY . . . . Jan/Feb 95   23
Fruit Sorbets at a Glance . . . . Jul/Aug 95   25
How to Poach Fruit . . . . May/Jun 93   24
PEACHES AND CHERRIES POACHED IN
    SPICED RED WINE . . . . May/Jun 93   26
PEACH PIE . . . . Jul/Aug 95   7
PEACH SALSA . . . . Sep/Oct 93   11
SIMPLE PEACH SALSA . . . . Jul/Aug 96   21
SPICED PEACHES . . . . Nov/Dec 93   13

Peanut Butter
PEANUT BUTTER COOKIES . . . . Nov/Dec 96   20

Pears
American Pear Brandy (S&R) . . . . . Sep/Oct 94   32
BAKED PEAR PUDDING . . . . . Charter Issue   18
BRANDIED FALL FRUIT . . . . Sep/Oct 95   BC
Core a Pear . . . . May/Jun 93   25
Coring Hook (Notes) . . . . Jan/Feb 96   3
CRANBERRY-PEAR BUTTER . . . . Nov/Dec 94   14
CRANBERRY-PEAR SALSA IN PEAR
    SHELLS . . . . Nov/Dec 96   BC
Crisps and Betties . . . . Sep/Oct 93   26
DRIED PEAR AND ORANGE COMPOTE WITH
    HONEY AND SAGE . . . . Jan/Feb 95   23
How to Poach Fruit . . . . May/Jun 93   24
PEAR AND DRIED FRUIT
    STRUDEL . . . . Sep/Oct 94   10
PEAR BRANDY CUSTARD
    SAUCE . . . . Sep/Oct 94   11
PEAR SALAD WITH ARUGULA, WALNUTS, AND
    GORGONZOLA . . . . Nov/Dec 96   21
POACHED PEARS ON SALAD GREENS WITH
    WALNUTS AND STILTON . . . . . Jan/Feb 94   BC
POACHED PEARS WITH STAR

Cook's Illustrated 1993–1997 Index

ANISE . . . . May/Jun 93   25
SAUSAGE AND PEAR STUFFING WITH CHEST-
NUTS AND PRUNES . . . . Nov/Dec 95   26

Peas (*See* also Sugar Snap Peas)
HEARTY CHICKEN SOUP WITH ORZO AND
SPRING VEGETABLES . . . . . . Mar/Apr 96   15
SHRIMP CURRY WITH YOGURT AND
PEAS . . . . Jan/Feb 97   9

Pea Shoots
LYNNE ARONSON'S SEARED SNAPPER WITH
PEA SHOOTS AND COCONUT CURRY
SAUCE (Notes) . . . . May/Jun 93   2
Pea Shoots (Notes) . . . . May/Jun 93   2

Pecans
The Best Pecan Pie . . . . Nov/Dec 95   6
BUTTERMILK PECAN PIE WITH
RAISINS . . . . Nov/Dec 95   8
GERMAN CHOCOLATE-STYLE LAYER CAKE
WITH COCONUT-PECAN
FILLING . . . . Jul/Aug 94   25
MAPLE PECAN PIE . . . . Nov/Dec 95   8
Pecan Pie and Its Kin (Notes) . . . . May/Jun 96   3
PERFECT PECAN PIE . . . . Nov/Dec 95   8
STRAWBERRY AND RHUBARB COMPOTES
WITH SUGARED PECANS . . . . May/Jun 93   25
TOASTED PECAN PANCAKES . . . Jan/Feb 96   8
TRIPLE CHOCOLATE CHUNK
PECAN PIE . . . . Nov/Dec 95   8

Pepper, Black
BLACK PEPPER-MUSTARD
SAUCE . . . . Mar/Apr 95   20
The Fill of the Mill (S&R) . . . . . . Mar/Apr 96   32
Pepper Mills (S&R) . . . . Mar/Apr 96   32
TOASTED BREAD CRUMBS WITH CRACKED
BLACK PEPPER . . . . May/Jun 95   25
Traditional Designs Score Well in Pepper Mill
Testing (ER) . . . . Mar/Apr 96   28

Peppers, Bell
ARUGULA SALAD WITH GRILLED FIGS
AND ROASTED PEPPER
VINAIGRETTE . . . . Sep/Oct 96   BC
BASIL AND MOZZARELLA . . . . . May/Jun 95   11
Bell-Pepper Tricks (Notes) . . . . Nov/Dec 93   3
Blistering Pepper Skins Quickly

(Notes) . . . . Sep/Oct 96   2
BREAD SALAD WITH ROASTED PEPPERS AND
SICILIAN OLIVES . . . . Sep/Oct 95   14
CHICKEN ROASTED IN RED
PEPPERS . . . . Sep/Oct 93   BC
CRANBERRY-RED PEPPER
RELISH . . . . Nov/Dec 94   14
GRILLED PORTOBELLO MUSHROOMS,
RED PEPPER, AND GARLIC
CROUTONS . . . . Jul/Aug 96   9
How to Roast a Bell Pepper . . . . . . May/Jun 96   20
Peeling and Seeding Roasted
Peppers (QT) . . . . Jul/Aug 93   5
PICKLED BELL PEPPERS . . . . . Sep/Oct 94   19
POTATO GRATIN WITH SWEET PEPPERS
AND TOMATOES . . . . Nov/Dec 95   19
Preparing Peppers for
Stuffing (QT) . . . . Jan/Feb 97   5
QUICK-COOKED GREENS WITH RED
BELL PEPPER . . . . Jan/Feb 95   13
RED PEPPER-BASIL SAUCE WITH BALSAMIC
VINEGAR . . . . May/Jun 95   22
Roast Bell Peppers Easily (QT) . . . May/Jun 95   4
ROASTED RED AND YELLOW PEPPER SAUCE
WITH GARLIC . . . . Sep/Oct 94   22
ROASTED RED BELL PEPPERS . May/Jun 96   21
ROASTED RED PEPPER
ROUILLE . . . . Nov/Dec 94   21
ROASTED RED PEPPER SALAD WITH RED
ONIONS AND CUCUMBERS . . May/Jun 96   21
SAUSAGE AND BELL PEPPER PIZZA WITH
SCALLOP CEVICHE WITH SWEET PEPPER
CONFETTI . . . . Jul/Aug 96   15
SPICY RED PEPPER BUTTER . . . Mar/Apr 95   20
Storing Roasted Peppers (Notes) . . May/Jun 95   3
SWEET AND SPICY ROASTED RED
PEPPER DIP . . . . May/Jun 96   21
TOMATO SAUCE WITH BELL PEPPERS AND
BALSAMIC VINEGAR . . . . Mar/Apr 95   20
Trimming Bell Peppers (QT) . . . . . May/Jun 93   4
ZUCCHINI, RED PEPPER, AND TOMATO SAUCE
WITH THYME AND MINT . . . . . Sep/Oct 94   22

Persimmons
Preparing Persimmons (QT) . . . . . . Nov/Dec 94   5

Pesto
CILANTRO PESTO . . . . May/Jun 93   22
ED BROWN'S SEARED SCALLOPS WITH

CILANTRO PESTO .... Mar/Apr 96   8
PESTO....................... Jul/Aug 96   29
Pesto at Its Best .... Jul/Aug 96   29
POTATO GNOCCHI WITH
    PESTO .... Mar/Apr 95   10

Phyllo Dough
Fearless Phyllo .... Nov/Dec 95   15
Fresh Phyllo (S&R)............. Nov/Dec 96   32
Making Phyllo Pastries .... Nov/Dec 95   16
Working with Dough (QT) .... Mar/Apr 97   4

Pickles
AMERICAN-STYLE POTATO SALAD WITH EGGS
    AND SWEET PICKLES........ Jul/Aug 94   8
BASIC PICKLING LIQUID ...... Sep/Oct 94   18
BREAD AND BUTTER PICKLES. . Sep/Oct 94   19
PICKLED BEETS WITH ORANGE AND ROSE-
    MARY .... Mar/Apr 94   11
PICKLED BELL PEPPERS ...... Sep/Oct 94   19
PICKLED CUCUMBER SPEARS . . Sep/Oct 94   19
PICKLED CURRIED
    CAULIFLOWER............. Sep/Oct 94   19
PICKLED FENNEL .... Sep/Oct 94   19
PICKLED GREEN BEANS WITH
    DILL..................... Sep/Oct 94   19
PICKLED JICAMA .... Sep/Oct 94   19
PICKLED OKRA.............. Sep/Oct 94   19
PICKLED PURPLE ONIONS..... Sep/Oct 94   19
PICKLED TURNIPS .... Sep/Oct 94   19
Pickle Jars (S&R) .... Sep/Oct 94   32
Quick Homemade Pickles .... Sep/Oct 94   18
QUICK PICKLE RECIPES .... Sep/Oct 94   19

Pies and Tarts
cream
BANANA CREAM PIE......... Mar/Apr 96   24
BUTTERSCOTCH CREAM PIE .. Mar/Apr 96   24
CHOCOLATE CREAM PIE ..... Mar/Apr 96   24
Classic Cream Pies............ Mar/Apr 96   22
COCONUT CREAM PIE .... Mar/Apr 96   24
VANILLA CREAM PIE .... Mar/Apr 96   24
crusts
AMERICAN PIE DOUGH, MASTER
    RECIPE FOR .... Sep/Oct 96   24
THE BEST PIE DOUGH......... Sep/Oct 94   8
Blind-Baking Different Doughs ... Sep/Oct 97   11
Easy Decorative Pie Edgings...... Sep/Oct 96   16
Egg Doughs Lift Off .... Sep/Oct 97   11

FIRM CRUST VARIATION FOR AMERICAN PIE
    DOUGH .... Sep/Oct 96   24
FLAKY PASTRY SHELL .... Nov/Dec 93   23
FLAKY PASTRY TOPPING...... Jul/Aug 96   20
Freezing Pie Pastry (QT) .... Nov/Dec 97   4
GRAHAM CRACKER-COATED PIE
    SHELL .... Mar/Apr 96   23
GRAHAM CRACKER CRUST .... Mar/Apr 97   23
Make Working With Pie Crust
    Easier (QT)................ May/Jun 95   5
Making a Foil Cover for Pie
    Crusts (QT) .... Jan/Feb 95   4
Moistening Pie Dough (QT)...... Jul/Aug 95   5
Moving Pie Pastry (QT) .... May/Jun 94   4
Pastry Board (S&R)............ Jul/Aug 95   32
Perfect Pie Crust .... Sep/Oct 94   7
Pie Pastry Revisited .... Sep/Oct 96   24
PIE SHELL FOR PECAN PIE .... Nov/Dec 95   7
PREBAKED PIE SHELL, MASTER
    RECIPE FOR .... Sep/Oct 97   11
Pressing Crumb Crusts (QT)..... Jan/Feb 95   4
Protecting Pie Crust Rims (QT) ... Jul/Aug 95   4
RICH, FLAKY PIE DOUGH ..... May/Jun 96   13
Rolling and Transferring Pie
    Dough (QT)................ Jul/Aug 96   4
Rolling Out Perfect Cookie (or Pie)
    Dough (QT)................ Jan/Feb 96   5
The Secrets of Pie Pastry ...... Charter Issue   16
SOUR CREAM VARIATION FOR AMERICAN PIE
    DOUGH .... Sep/Oct 96   24
Transferring Pie Crust (QT)...... Nov/Dec 95   5
equipment
Dark-Finished Tart Pans (S&R) ... Sep/Oct 97   32
Pie Marker (Notes)............. May/Jun 97   3
Pie Weights (S&R).............. Sep/Oct 97   32
fruit
APPLE PIE WITH CRYSTALLIZED
    GINGER .... Nov/Dec 97   22
APPLE PIE WITH DRIED FRUIT Nov/Dec 97   22
APPLE PIE WITH FRESH
    CRANBERRIES .... Nov/Dec 97   22
Apple Tartlets................ Mar/Apr 94   17
THE BEST APPLE PIE......... Sep/Oct 94   8
BISTRO APPLE TART.......... Mar/Apr 94   17
BLUEBERRY PIE............. Jul/Aug 95   6
BRIOCHE PLUM TART .... Sep/Oct 95   16
CHERRY PIE .... Jul/Aug 95   7
CLASSIC APPLE PIE, MASTER
    RECIPE FOR .... Nov/Dec 97   21

Cook's Illustrated 1993–1997 Index

Do-Ahead Fresh Baked
Apple Pie . . . . Nov/Dec 97   19
FREE-FORM FRUIT TART . . . . . . May/Jun 94   14
Free-Form Fruit Tart, Master
Class . . . . May/Jun 94   14
How to Thicken Fruit Pies . . . . Jul/Aug 95   6
Is a Lower Fat (Key Lime) Pie Really
Worth It? . . . . Mar/Apr 97   22
KEY LIME PIE . . . . Mar/Apr 97   23
Lemon Meringue Tips . . . . Nov/Dec 94   24
PEACH PIE . . . . Jul/Aug 95   7
Potato Starch in Pies (Notes) . . . . . Jan/Feb 96   3
Real Key Lime Pie (Notes) . . . . Sep/Oct 97   2
Sealing the Pie in the Pastry . . . . . Nov/Dec 97   20
STRAWBERRY-RHUBARB PIE . . . Jul/Aug 95   7
TARTE TATIN . . . . Jan/Feb 96   15
Thickening Fruit Pies (Notes) . . . . Jul/Aug 96   2
True Key Limes vs. Supermarket
(Persian) Limes . . . . Mar/Apr 97   23
THE ULTIMATE LEMON MERINGUE
PIE . . . . Nov/Dec 94   24
Glass Pie Plate (S&R) . . . . Sep/Oct 94   32
Ladyfingers for Lemon Meringue
Pie (Notes) . . . . Jan/Feb 94   2

pecan
The Best Pecan Pie . . . . Nov/Dec 95   6
BUTTERMILK PECAN PIE WITH
RAISINS . . . . Nov/Dec 95   8
MAPLE PECAN PIE . . . . Nov/Dec 95   8
Pecan Pie and Its Kin (Notes) . . . . May/Jun 96   3
PERFECT PECAN PIE . . . . Nov/Dec 95   8
TRIPLE CHOCOLATE CHUNK
PECAN PIE . . . . Nov/Dec 95   8

pumpkin
THE BEST PUMPKIN PIE . . . . . . Nov/Dec 93   22
The Only Pumpkin Pie Recipe You'll Ever
Need . . . . Nov/Dec 93   32

Pineapple
Fruit Sorbets at a Glance . . . . Jul/Aug 95   25
How to Poach Fruit . . . . May/Jun 93   24
SAUTÉED PORK CHOPS WITH PINEAPPLE
SALSA . . . . Sep/Oct 94   13
Slicing Pineapple . . . . May/Jun 93   25

Pine Nuts
BROWN BUTTER AND PINE NUT
SAUCE . . . . Sep/Oct 93   18
PESTO . . . . Jul/Aug 96   29

PINE NUT–CRUSTED ALMOND
MACAROONS . . . . Sep/Oct 96   7
SAUTÉED BRUSSELS SPROUTS WITH GARLIC
AND PINE NUTS . . . . Nov/Dec 95   21

Pistachios
CLASSIC BAKLAVA FILLING . . . Nov/Dec 95   15
PISTACHIO MACAROON
BUTTONS . . . . Sep/Oct 96   7
QUICK-COOKED CARROTS WITH ORANGE
AND PISTACHIO . . . . Mar/Apr 96   25

Pita Bread
PITA BREAD SALAD WITH CUCUMBERS,
CHERRY TOMATOES, AND FRESH
HERBS . . . . Sep/Oct 95   14

Pita Chips
Seasoning (QT) . . . . Mar/Apr 97   5

Pizza
CARAMELIZED ONION PIZZA WITH OIL-CURED
OLIVES AND PARMESAN . . . . May/Jun 95   10
EIGHT-HOUR PIZZA DOUGH . . . May/Jun 95   10
FRESH TOMATO PIZZA WITH ARUGULA AND
PROSCIUTTO . . . . May/Jun 95   11
GARLIC-HERB PIZZA CRUST, MASTER RECIPE
FOR . . . . May/Jun 93   8
Getting Pizza into the Oven (QT) . May/Jun 97   5
GRILLED SHRIMP TOPPING WITH
ROASTED TOMATOES AND FARMER'S
CHEESE . . . . May/Jun 93   9
Grilling Pizza . . . . May/Jun 93   8
Overcoming the Obstacles of Homemade
Pizza . . . . May/Jun 95   8
PIZZA DOUGH, MASTER RECIPE
FOR . . . . May/Jun 95   10
Pizza Tools (S&R) . . . . May/Jun 95   32
QUICK TOMATO SAUCE FOR
PIZZA . . . . May/Jun 95   10
ROASTED TOMATO TOPPING WITH FENNEL
AND ASIAGO . . . . May/Jun 93   9
SAUSAGE AND BELL PEPPER PIZZA WITH
BASIL AND MOZZARELLA . . . May/Jun 95   11
75-MINUTE PIZZA DOUGH . . . . May/Jun 95   10
Simple Toppings . . . . May/Jun 93   9
WILD MUSHROOM PIZZA WITH SAGE,
FONTINA, AND PARMESAN . . May/Jun 95   11

Cook's Illustrated 1993–1997 Index

Plantains

More Plantain Tips (Notes) . . . . . . May/Jun 94   3

Preparing Tropical Fruit . . . . Jan/Feb 94   17

Plums (*See also* Fruits, Fresh)

BRIOCHE PLUM TART . . . . Sep/Oct 95   16

Crisps and Betties . . . . Sep/Oct 93   26

How to Poach Fruit . . . . May/Jun 93   24

PIQUANT PLUM SAUCE WITH SESAME

   OIL AND GINGER. . . . . Jul/Aug 94   20

PLUM GRANITA, MASTER RECIPE

   FOR POACHED FRUIT-BASED

   GRANITAS . . . . May/Jun 94   24

POACHED PLUM AND RASPBERRY COMPOTE

   IN SWEET WINE SYRUP . . . . . Jul/Aug 96   BC

Poblano Chiles (*See also* Chile Peppers)

TOMATO BASE WITH POBLANOS AND

   CILANTRO. . . . . Jan/Feb 95   11

Polenta

Another Way to Cook Polenta

   (Notes). . . . . Nov/Dec 95   2

DOUBLE-BOILER POLENTA . . . . Jan/Feb 95   21

Foolproof Polenta. . . . . Jan/Feb 95   20

Polenta vs. Cornmeal (Notes) . . . . . Mar/Apr 96   2

POLENTA WITH GORGONZOLA . Jan/Feb 95   21

POLENTA WITH ITALIAN SAUSAGES AND

   TOMATO SAUCE . . . . Jan/Feb 95   21

POLENTA WITH PARMESAN AND

   BUTTER. . . . . Jan/Feb 95   21

POLENTA WITH WILD MUSHROOMS AND

   ROSEMARY. . . . . Jan/Feb 95   21

Purchasing Polenta (S&R). . . . . . . Jan/Feb 95   32

Slow-Cooking Polenta (Notes) . . . . . Jul/Aug 95   3

Pomegranates (*See also* Fruits, Fresh)

Extracting Pomegranate

   Seeds (QT) . . . . Nov/Dec 93   4

Juicing a Pomegranate (QT) . . . . . . Jan/Feb 95   5

Popovers

BANANA BERRY POPOVER. . . Charter Issue   18

THE BEST POPOVERS . . . . Nov/Dec 94   9

Popover Pan (S&R). . . . . Nov/Dec 94   32

Popovers Perfected . . . . Nov/Dec 94   9

Poppy *Seeds*

LEMON–POPPY SEED COOKIES Nov/Dec 96   20

LEMON–POPPY SEED MUFFINS Jan/Feb 97   19

Pork

BACON-WRAPPED MEAT LOAF WITH BROWN-

   SUGAR KETCHUP GLAZE . . . . . Sep/Oct 96   22

Cooking Pork Safely (Notes) . . . . . May/Jun 95   2

CREAM PAN SAUCE WITH APPLES AND

   SAGE . . . . Jul/Aug 97   19

Cuts of Pork for Barbecue . . . . Jul/Aug 97   19

Essential Steps to Homemade Pork

   Barbecue . . . . Jul/Aug 97   20

Flavor Injector (for Roast Pork)

   (S&R). Nov/Dec 97   32

GARLIC-STUDDED ROAST

   PORK LOIN . . . . May/Jun 95   22

GRILL-ROASTED SPARERIBS WITH

   BARBECUE SAUCE . . . . Jul/Aug 93   20

LOAF PAN VARIATION FOR MEAT

   LOAF . . . . Sep/Oct 96   22

MIXED HERB AND SPICE RUB FOR SAUTÉED

   PORK CHOPS . . . . Sep/Oct 94   13

ORANGE PAN SAUCE WITH FENNEL AND

   GREEN OLIVES . . . . Jul/Aug 97   19

Perfect Pork Roast . . . . May/Jun 95   20

PORT PAN SAUCE WITH CHERRIES AND

   ROSEMARY . . . . Sep/Oct 97   19

Preparing the Roast (Rack of Pork) Nov/Dec 97   13

Preparing the Tenderloin . . . . Jul/Aug 97   19

PULLED PORK, MASTER

   RECIPE FOR . . . . Jul/Aug 97   19

ROAST CURED RACK OF PORK Nov/Dec 97   13

ROAST MARINATED RACK OF

   PORK . . . . Nov/Dec 97   13

SAUTÉED PORK CHOPS WITH MUSTARD AND

   CAPERS. . . . . Sep/Oct 94   13

SAUTÉED PORK CHOPS WITH PINEAPPLE

   SALSA . . . . Sep/Oct 94   13

SAUTÉED PORK CHOPS WITH WHITE

   WINE PAN SAUCE, MASTER

   RECIPE FOR . . . . Sep/Oct 94   13

SAUTÉED PORK TENDERLOIN, MASTER

   RECIPE FOR . . . . Sep/Oct 97   18

Smoke-Cooking Times . . . . Jul/Aug 95   20

SMOKED PORK CHOPS WITH FENNEL-

   MUSTARD RUB. . . . . Jul/Aug 95   20

SPICE RUB FOR PORK . . . . Jul/Aug 95   21

The Way to Cook Pork Chops . . . . . Sep/Oct 94   12

WINE VINEGAR PAN SAUCE WITH WARM

   SPICES AND RAISINS . . . . Jul/Aug 97   19

Portobello Mushrooms

BRUSCHETTA WITH GRILLED PORTOBELLO
MUSHROOMS . . . . Sep/Oct 96   8
GRILLED PORTOBELLO MUSHROOMS,
RED PEPPER, AND GARLIC
CROUTONS . . . . Jul/Aug 96   9

Potatoes

BOILED POTATOES, MASTER
RECIPE FOR . . . . Jul/Aug 94   7
CHICKEN IN THE POT WITH POTATOES AND
INDIAN SPICES . . . . Sep/Oct 95   19
CREAMY POTATO SOUP WITH
CHIVES. . . . . Nov/Dec 96   23
Drying Grated Potatoes (QT). . . . . Sep/Oct 96   5
FRITTATA WITH LEEKS AND
POTATOES. . . . . Mar/Apr 96   11
POTATO, HAM, AND PARSLEY
OMELET . . . . Sep/Oct 93   22
Potatoes to Grow and Eat (S&R) . . Mar/Apr 97   32
Potato Starch (Notes) . . . . Jan/Feb 95   2
Premium Potatoes (S&R) . . . . Mar/Apr 94   32
Select a Spud (S&R) . . . . Nov/Dec 95   32
Slice a Spud (S&R) . . . . Nov/Dec 95   32
Yukon Gold Potatoes (Notes) . . . . . Sep/Oct 96   2

baked

The Best Baked Potato . . . . Sep/Oct 95   25
OVEN-BAKED POTATO, MASTER
RECIPE FOR . . . . Sep/Oct 95   25
Retrieving Baked Potatoes (QT) . . May/Jun 96   5

chips

Making Herbed Potato
Chips (QT). . . . . Mar/Apr 94   5

French fries

Better French Fries (Notes) . . . . . . Jan/Feb 95   3
CLASSIC FRENCH FRIES. . . . . . . Jul/Aug 96   13
Make Perfect French Fries at
Home. Jul/Aug 96   12

gnocchi

Forming Gnocchi (QT). . . . . Sep/Oct 95   5
Gnocchi Tools (S&R). . . . . Mar/Apr 95   32
POTATO GNOCCHI, MASTER
RECIPE FOR . . . . Mar/Apr 95   10
POTATO GNOCCHI GRATINÉED WITH FONTINA
CHEESE. . . . . Mar/Apr 95   10
POTATO GNOCCHI WITH BUTTER, SAGE, AND
PARMESAN CHEESE . . . . Mar/Apr 95   10
POTATO GNOCCHI WITH
PESTO . . . . Mar/Apr 95   10

POTATO GNOCCHI WITH TOMATO-MINT
SAUCE . . . . Mar/Apr 95   10
The Secrets of Gnocchi . . . . Mar/Apr 95   8

gratin

CLASSIC POTATO GRATIN . . . . . Nov/Dec 95   19
How to Make Potato Gratin . . . . . . Nov/Dec 95   18
POTATO GRATIN WITH BROTH AND
PARMESAN . . . . Nov/Dec 95   19
POTATO GRATIN WITH SWEET PEPPERS AND
TOMATOES . . . . Nov/Dec 95   19

latkes

Onions' Sulfur Prevents Browning Nov/Dec 97   7
Preparing the Potatoes . . . . Nov/Dec 97   7
THICK AND CREAMY POTATO
LATKES . . . . Nov/Dec 97   7

mashed

Italian Potato Masher (S&R) . . . . . Nov/Dec 93   32
Making the Perfect Mashed
Potatoes. . . . . Nov/Dec 93   10
MASHED POTATOES, MASTER
RECIPE FOR. . . . . Nov/Dec 93   11
MASHED POTATOES AND APPLES WITH BACON
AND BROWNED ONIONS . . . . . Nov/Dec 93   11
MASHED POTATOES WITH PARMESAN CHEESE
AND LEMON . . . . Nov/Dec 93   11
MASHED POTATOES WITH POACHED GARLIC
AND OLIVE OIL. . . . . Nov/Dec 93   11

roasted

BAY-SCENTED ROASTED
POTATOES . . . . Jul/Aug 95   BC
ROASTED POTATOES WITH ONION, BACON,
AND THYME . . . . Jan/Feb 94   11

roesti

BEET AND POTATO ROESTI WITH
CHIVES . . . . Jan/Feb 95   22
CELERY ROOT AND POTATO ROESTI WITH
LEMON AND PARSLEY . . . . Jan/Feb 95   22
HERBED ROESTI WITH SMOKED
CHEDDAR . . . . Jan/Feb 95   22
How to Make Roesti . . . . Jan/Feb 95   22
ROESTI, MASTER RECIPE FOR. . Jan/Feb 95   22
Traditional Roesti (Notes) . . . . Nov/Dec 95   2

salad

AMERICAN-STYLE POTATO SALAD WITH EGGS
AND SWEET PICKLES. . . . . Jul/Aug 94   8
FRENCH-STYLE POTATO SALAD WITH TAR-
RAGON VINAIGRETTE . . . . Jul/Aug 94   7
GERMAN-STYLE POTATO SALAD WITH BACON
AND BALSAMIC VINEGAR . . . . Jul/Aug 94   8

Perfect Potato Salad . . . . Jul/Aug 94   6

Pot Roast
MASTER RECIPE FOR POT
   ROAST . . . . Jan/Feb 94   9
POT ROAST IN RED WINE . . . . . . Jan/Feb 94   9
Pot Roast Perfected . . . . Jan/Feb 94   6
POT ROAST WITH PORCINI
   MUSHROOMS . . . . Jan/Feb 94   9
PRESSURE-COOKED POT
   ROAST . . . . Jul/Aug 96   11
SOUTHWESTERN POT ROAST . . Jan/Feb 94   9

Poultry (See also Chicken; Stuffings; Turkey)
Cutting Up Poultry, Step by Step . . May/Jun 93   16
A Different Take on Vertical
   Roasters . . . . May/Jun 97   2
Poultry Lacers (S&R) . . . . Nov/Dec 97   32
Poultry Stuffing Bag (S&R) . . . . . . Jul/Aug 95   32
Rating Roasting Racks for Poultry . Jan/Feb 97   28
Removing Boneless Breast Meat . . May/Jun 93   17
Removing Stuffing Easily (QT) . . . . Jul/Aug 95   4
roast/turkey lifters . . . . Nov/Dec 97   9
Smoke-Cooking Times . . . . Jul/Aug 95   20
"Stuff" the Skin Before Roasting . . May/Jun 93   17
Taking Poultry Temperature (QT) . May/Jun 94   5
Trussing Needles (S&R) . . . . Nov/Dec 94   32
We're Not High on Vertical
   Roasters . . . . Jan/Feb 97   28

Preservatives
Preservatives in Dried
   Fruits (Notes) . . . . Nov/Dec 94   2

Preserves
CRANBERRY-PEAR BUTTER . . . . Nov/Dec 94   14
Exotic Tropical Jams (S&R) . . . . . . Sep/Oct 93   32
JALAPEÑO PRESERVES . . . . May/Jun 93   23

Pressure Cooking
PRESSURE-COOKED NORTH AFRICAN LAMB
   STEW . . . . Jul/Aug 96   11
PRESSURE-COOKED POT
   ROAST . . . . Jul/Aug 96   11
PRESSURE COOKER RISOTTO . . Jul/Aug 96   10
Pressure Cookers (S&R) . . . . Jul/Aug 96   32
PRESSURE-STEAMED
   ARTICHOKES . . . . Jul/Aug 96   11
Spring-Valve Pressure Cookers Top

Testing (ER) . . . . Jul/Aug 96   26
The Truth About Pressure Cookers   Jul/Aug 96   10

Prickly Pear
Preparing Tropical Fruit . . . . Jan/Feb 94   17

Prosciutto
FRESH TOMATO PIZZA WITH ARUGULA AND
   PROSCIUTTO . . . . May/Jun 95   11
PENNE WITH QUICK-COOKED GREENS AND
   PROSCIUTTO . . . . Jan/Feb 95   14
PROSCIUTTO AND GOAT CHEESE
   ROULADES . . . . May/Jun 96   16
QUICK-COOKED GREENS WITH
   PROSCIUTTO . . . . Jan/Feb 95   13
SQUASH, PROSCIUTTO, AND PARMESAN
   FILLING FOR PASTA . . . . Sep/Oct 93   18

Prunes
PRUNE CUSTARD PUDDING . Charter Issue   19
ROAST GOOSE WITH PRUNE AND APPLE
   STUFFING AND RED WINE GIBLET
   GRAVY . . . . Nov/Dec 94   7
SAUSAGE AND PEAR STUFFING WITH
   CHESTNUTS AND PRUNES . . . Nov/Dec 95   26

Pudding
BAKED PEAR PUDDING . . . . . Charter Issue   18
BASIC BATTER . . . . Charter Issue   18
FRESH RASPBERRY SUMMER
   BREAD PUDDING . . . . Jul/Aug 93   BC
PRUNE CUSTARD PUDDING . Charter Issue   19
RICE PUDDING WITH CINNAMON AND
   DRIED FRUIT . . . . Sep/Oct 96   25
RICE PUDDING WITH ORANGE AND
   TOASTED ALMONDS . . . . Sep/Oct 96   25
SHAKER-STYLE CREAMY CORN
   PUDDING . . . . Jul/Aug 93   9
SIMPLE STOVETOP RICE
   PUDDING . . . . Sep/Oct 96   25
SOUFFLÉED BATTER
   PUDDING . . . . Charter Issue   18

Pudding Cakes
CHOCOLATE PUDDING CAKE . . Jan/Feb 95   25
COFFEE PUDDING CAKE . . . . . . Jan/Feb 95   25
LEMON PUDDING CAKE . . . . Jan/Feb 95   24
The Magic of Pudding Cakes . . . . . Jan/Feb 95   24
ORANGE PUDDING CAKE . . . . . . Jan/Feb 95   25

Cook's Illustrated 1993–1997 Index

Pudding Cake Ramekins (S&R) . . . Jan/Feb 95   32
VANILLA-BOURBON PUDDING
    CAKE . . . . Jan/Feb 95   25

Pumpkin
THE BEST PUMPKIN PIE . . . . . . Nov/Dec 93   22
Cleaning Pumpkins and Winter
    Squash (QT) . . . . Sep/Oct 96   4
The Only Pumpkin Pie Recipe You'll Ever
    Need . . . . Nov/Dec 93   22

Quiche
CRABMEAT QUICHE . . . . Sep/Oct 97   12
HAM AND ASPARAGUS QUICHE Sep/Oct 97   12
LEEK AND GOAT CHEESE
    QUICHE . . . . Sep/Oct 97   12
MASTER RECIPE FOR QUICHE
    LORRAINE . . . . Sep/Oct 97   12
Porcelain Quiche Dishes (S&R) . . . . Sep/Oct 97   32

Radishes
FRENCH LENTIL SALAD WITH CARAWAY
    AND RADISH . . . . Mar/Apr 95   25

Raisins (See also Fruits, Dried)
BIG BRAN MUFFINS WITH RAISINS AND
    DATES . . . . Sep/Oct 93   7
BRAISED BUTTERNUT SQUASH WITH
    DRIED APRICOTS, RAISINS, AND MADRAS
    SPICES . . . . Jan/Feb 96   26
BUTTERMILK PECAN PIE WITH
    RAISINS . . . . Nov/Dec 95   8
CURRIED COLESLAW WITH APPLES AND
    RAISINS. . . . . Jul/Aug 95   13
GLAZED ONIONS WITH
    RAISINS . . . . Mar/Apr 95   13
RAISIN COMPOTE WITH ROSEMARY AND
    THYME . . . . Jan/Feb 95   23
RAISIN-SPICE COOKIES . . . . Nov/Dec 96   20
SPICED APPLE-RAISIN FILLING Nov/Dec 95   15
WALNUT-RAISIN BAKED APPLES WITH
    MAPLE SYRUP . . . . Sep/Oct 95   13

Raspberries
Fresh Raspberries (S&R) . . . . Nov/Dec 96   32
FRESH RASPBERRY PUREE . . . . Nov/Dec 96   9
FRESH RASPBERRY SUMMER BREAD
    PUDDING . . . . Jul/Aug 93   BC
Fruit Sorbets at a Glance . . . . Jul/Aug 95   25

POACHED PLUM AND RASPBERRY COMPOTE
    IN SWEET WINE SYRUP . . . . . Jul/Aug 96   BC
RASPBERRY-ALMOND COFFEE
    CAKE . . . . Mar/Apr 95   21
RASPBERRY-ALMOND FILLING May/Jun 95   19
RASPBERRY BRIOCHE
    SHORTCAKE . . . . Sep/Oct 95   17
RASPBERRY CHARLOTTE
    ROYALE. . . . . Jan/Feb 94   14
RASPBERRY FROZEN YOGURT . May/Jun 96   15
RASPBERRY SPRITZER . . . . Jul/Aug 97   BC

Red Bell Peppers (See Peppers, Bell)

Red Wine (See also Wines)
Acceptable Cheap Reds (BT) . . . . . . Sep/Oct 96   30
American Pinot Noirs Eclipse French
    Burgundies (BT). . . . . Sep/Oct 93   30
American "Rhone" Wine Wins
    Tasting (BT) . . . . Mar/Apr 95   30
The Best Red Wines for Grilled
    Foods (BT) . . . . Jul/Aug 95   30
Bordeaux (BT) . . . . Sep/Oct 97   30
Burgundies (BT) . . . . Jan/Feb 97   30
BRAISED LAMB SHOULDER CHOPS WITH
    TOMATOES AND RED WINE   . Mar/Apr 97   18
BRAISED ONIONS WITH RED WINE, THYME,
    AND PANCETTA. . . . . Jan/Feb 96   26
Inexpensive Chianti Wins Blind
    Tasting (BT). . . . . Charter Issue   32
Inexpensive Pinot Noirs
    Disappoint (BT) . . . . Sep/Oct 94   30
Judging Merlots (Notes). . . . . Mar/Apr 96   2
LAMB SHANKS BRAISED IN RED WINE WITH
    HERBES DE PROVENCE . . . . . Jan/Feb 95   19
PEACHES AND CHERRIES POACHED IN SPICED
    RED WINE . . . . May/Jun 93   26
POT ROAST IN RED WINE . . . . . Jan/Feb 94   9
Rating California's Best
    Reds (BT) . . . . Jan/Feb 95   30
Ranking Inexpensive
    Bordeaux (BT) . . . . Jan/Feb 96   30
Ranking Inexpensive Merlots (BT) . Sep/Oct 95   30
Rating Tuscan Wines (BT) . . . . . . Mar/Apr 96   30
RED WINE GIBLET GRAVY . . . . Nov/Dec 94   7
SLOW-ROASTED BEEF WITH RED WINE PAN
    JUICES . . . . Sep/Oct 96   13
Wine for the Stew . . . . Jan/Feb 96   20

Cook's Illustrated 1993–1997 Index

Relishes

ONION RELISH . . . . Jan/Feb 96   13
PEPPERED OVEN-DRIED TOMATO
RELISH . . . . Sep/Oct 96   21

Rhubarb

How to Poach Fruit . . . . May/Jun 93   24
STRAWBERRY AND RHUBARD COMPOTES
WITH SUGARED PECANS . . . . May/Jun 93   25
STRAWBERRY-RHUBARB PIE . . . Jul/Aug 95   7
Stringing Rhubarb (QT) . . . . May/Jun 93   4

Rice

The Best Way to Cook Long-Grain
White Rice . . . . May/Jun 96   22
Converted Rice (Notes) . . . . Nov/Dec 93   3
Cooling Sushi Rice (QT) . . . . Sep/Oct 95   5
Last-Minute Paella, Master
Class . . . . Jan/Feb 95   10
MASTER RECIPE FOR FLUFFY
WHITE RICE . . . . May/Jun 96   22
PAELLA, CRIOLLA'S STYLE . . . . . Jan/Feb 95   11
Paella Pan (S&R) . . . . Jan/Feb 95   32
PAR-COOKED ARBORIO RICE . . . Jan/Feb 95   11
PRESSURE COOKER RISOTTO . . Jul/Aug 96   10
Rating Rice Cookers (ER) . . . . Mar/Apr 95   28
Rice Cookers (S&R) . . . . Jan/Feb 94   32
Rice Cookers (S&R) . . . . Mar/Apr 95   32
Rinsing Rice (Notes) . . . . Jan/Feb 95   3
The Secret to Perfect Rice . . . . . . Charter Issue   7
SUMMER VEGETABLE AND RICE
STUFFING . . . . Jul/Aug 93   25
BASMATI RICE, PILAF-STYLE . . . Jan/Feb 97   10
Easy Rice Handling and
Storage (QT) . . . . Sep/Oct 97   4
WILD RICE STUFFING WITH CARROTS, MUSH-
ROOMS, AND THYME . . . . Jul/Aug 97   21
WILD RICE STUFFING WITH CRANBERRIES
AND TOASTED PECANS . . . . . Jul/Aug 97   21

Rice Pudding

RICE PUDDING WITH CINNAMON AND DRIED
FRUIT . . . . Sep/Oct 96   25
RICE PUDDING WITH ORANGE AND TOASTED
ALMONDS . . . . Sep/Oct 96   25
Simple Stovetop Rice Pudding . . . . Sep/Oct 96   25
SIMPLE STOVETOP RICE
PUDDING . . . . Sep/Oct 96   25

Risotto

BASIC RISOTTO, MASTER
RECIPE FOR . . . . Mar/Apr 94   19
PRESSURE COOKER RISOTTO . . Jul/Aug 96   10
Risotto Rules . . . . Mar/Apr 94   18
RISOTTO WITH ASPARAGUS AND
WILD MUSHROOMS . . . . Mar/Apr 94   19
RISOTTO WITH CABBAGE AND COUNTRY
HAM . . . . Mar/Apr 94   19
RISOTTO WITH TOMATOES AND
BASIL . . . . Mar/Apr 94   19
VEGETABLE RISOTTO IN CARROT AND
CELERY BROTH . . . . Jan/Feb 94   27

Roasting (See also Beef; Chicken; Cornish Hens; Pork; Turkey)

A Different Take on Vertical
Roasters . . . . May/Jun 97   2
Adapting Your Carving Board
(to Collect Juices) (QT) . . . . Jul/Aug 97   5
Adjustable Roasting Rack (S&R) . . Nov/Dec 93   32
Basket Roasting Rack (S&R) . . . . . Jan/Feb 97   32
Clay Roasters (Notes) . . . . May/Jun 94   2
Clay Roasters Revisited (Notes) . . . Nov/Dec 94   3
Customizing a Roasting Pan . . . . Charter Issue   27
Flavoring Roasts with Garlic (QT) . Nov/Dec 93   4
Grill Roasting . . . . Jul/Aug 93   18
How to Roast a Bell Pepper . . . . . May/Jun 96   20
How to Roast a Cheap Cut of Beef . Sep/Oct 96   10
How to Roast Root Vegetables . . . . Jan/Feb 94   10
Important Steps in Roasting Hens . Jul/Aug 97   21
Instant-Read Thermometer (S&R) . May/Jun 95   32
Kitchen Twine (S&R) . . . . May/Jun 95   32
Mesh Roasting Rack (S&R) . . . . . . Mar/Apr 94   32
Perfect Pork Roast . . . . May/Jun 95   20
Perfect Prime Rib . . . . Nov/Dec 95   12
Preparing a Lobster for Roasting . May/Jun 97   16
Preparing a Turkey Breast for
Roasting . . . . Jan/Feb 97   25
Preparing the Roast (Rack of Pork) Nov/Dec 97   13
Rating Roasting Racks for
Poultry (ER) . . . . Jan/Feb 97   28
Roast Turkey Revisited . . . . Nov/Dec 95   9
Roast/Turkey Lifters . . . . Nov/Dec 97   9
ROASTED ROOT VEGETABLES, MASTER
RECIPE FOR . . . . Jan/Feb 94   10
Roasting Chicken 14 Ways . . . . . . Jan/Feb 96   9
Roasting Pan (S&R) . . . . Mar/Apr 95   32
Roasting Racks (S&R) . . . . Jan/Feb 96   32

Cook's Illustrated 1993–1997 Index

Slow-Roast Safety (Notes) . . . . Jan/Feb 96   3
Stuffing and Roasting the
    Big Bird (the Turkey) . . . . Nov/Dec 97   9
Trussing Needles (S&R) . . . . Sep/Oct 94   32
Vertical Roasters (Notes) . . . . May/Jun 95   3
The Way to Roast Chicken . . . . . Charter Issue   27
We're Not High on Vertical
    Roasters . . . . Jan/Feb 97   28

Roesti
BEET AND POTATO ROESTI WITH
    CHIVES . . . . Jan/Feb 95   22
CELERY ROOT AND POTATO ROESTI WITH
    LEMON AND PARSLEY . . . . Jan/Feb 95   22
HERBED ROESTI WITH SMOKED
    CHEDDAR . . . . Jan/Feb 95   22
How to Make Roesti . . . . Jan/Feb 95   22
MASTER RECIPE FOR ROESTI . . Jan/Feb 95   22
Traditional Roesti (Notes) . . . . Nov/Dec 95   2

Root Vegetables (*See* also specific kinds)
How to Roast Root Vegetables . . . . . Jan/Feb 94   10
PAN-BRAISED ROOT VEGETABLES WITH RED
    CABBAGE AND ROSEMARY . . . Jan/Feb 96   26
ROASTED ROOT VEGETABLES, MASTER
    RECIPE FOR . . . . Jan/Feb 94   10
Slicing Oval Root Vegetables (QT) . May/Jun 94   5

Rosemary
BRAISED SHOULDER CHOPS WITH TOMATOES,
ROSEMARY, AND OLIVES . . . . . Mar/Apr 97   19
Garlic-Rosemary Marinade . . . . . . Mar/Apr 97   19
GRAPE AND FETA SALAD WITH
    ROSEMARY . . . . Nov/Dec 96   21
GRILLED BUTTERFLIED CHICKEN WITH
    ROSEMARY, LEMON,
    AND GARLIC . . . . Sep/Oct 94   24
GRILLED CHICKEN WITH OLIVES, ROSEMARY,
    AND GARLIC . . . . Jul/Aug 93   12
GRILLED SHOULDER LAMB CHOPS
WITH GARLIC-ROSEMARY
    MARINADE . . . . Mar/Apr 97   19
PAN-BRAISED ROOT VEGETABLES WITH RED
    CABBAGE AND ROSEMARY . . . Jan/Feb 96   26
PICKLED BEETS WITH ORANGE
    AND ROSEMARY . . . . Mar/Apr 94   11
POLENTA WITH WILD MUSHROOMS AND
    ROSEMARY . . . . Jan/Feb 95   21
PORT PAN SAUCE WITH CHERRIES AND ROSE-

MARY . . . . Sep/Oct 97   19
QUICK-COOKED GREENS WITH WHITE BEANS
    AND ROSEMARY . . . . Jan/Feb 95   14
RAISIN COMPOTE WITH ROSEMARY AND
    THYME . . . . Jan/Feb 95   23
ROASTED TURNIPS, SHALLOTS, AND GARLIC
    WITH ROSEMARY . . . . Jan/Feb 94   11
ROSEMARY MADELEINES . . . . . Mar/Apr 96   21
ROSEMARY-SAGE SALT . . . . Sep/Oct 95   11
TOMATO-ROSEMARY CREAM
    SAUCE . . . . May/Jun 95   22
TWO MUSHROOM SAUCE WITH
    ROSEMARY . . . . Jan/Feb 97   15

Rosé Wine (*See* also Wines)
Rating Pink Sparklers (BT) . . . . . . Nov/Dec 95   30

Rouille
ROASTED RED PEPPER
    ROUILLE . . . . Nov/Dec 94   21

Rugelach
Filling and Forming Rugelach . . . . Sep/Oct 97   25
Freeze-and-Bake Rugelach . . . . . . Sep/Oct 97   25
MASTER RECIPE FOR CRESCENT-SHAPED
    RUGELACH WITH RAISIN-WALNUT
    FILLING . . . . Sep/Oct 97   24
ROULADE-SHAPED RUGELACH   Sep/Oct 97   25
RUGELACH WITH CHOCOLATE-WALNUT
    FILLING . . . . Sep/Oct 97   25

Rubs (*See* Spice Rubs and Pastes)

Rum
RUM-BAKED APPLES WITH MASCARPONE AND
    ALMONDS . . . . Sep/Oct 95   13

Saffron
Genuine Saffron (S&R) . . . . Nov/Dec 94   32
Pulverize Saffron (QT) . . . . May/Jun 95   5

Sage
CHICKEN SAUSAGE WITH APPLES AND
    SAGE . . . . Mar/Apr 96   12
CREAM PAN SAUCE WITH APPLES AND
    SAGE . . . . Jul/Aug 97   19
DRIED PEAR AND ORANGE COMPOTE WITH
    HONEY AND SAGE . . . . Jan/Feb 95   23
GARLIC AND SAGE SOUP . . . . . . Mar/Apr 95   BC

Cook's Illustrated 1993–1997 Index

POTATO GNOCCHI WITH BUTTER, SAGE, AND
PARMESAN CHEESE . . . . Mar/Apr 95 10
ROSEMARY-SAGE SALT . . . . Sep/Oct 95 11
SAGE FOCACCIA . . . . May/Jun 97 7
SAUTÉED BUTTERFLIED CHICKEN
WITH MUSHROOM-SAGE PAN
SAUCE . . . . Sep/Oct 94 25
TUSCAN BEANS WITH
SAGE (Notes) . . . . Charter Issue 2
WILD MUSHROOM PIZZA WITH SAGE,
FONTINA, AND PARMESAN . . May/Jun 95 11

Salad Dressings (*See* also Mayonnaise; Vinaigrettes)

AVOCADO BASIL DRESSING. . Charter Issue 30
BASIL-CURRY DRESSING . . . . . . Jan/Feb 94 23
BEST CAESAR SALAD. . . . . Sep/Oct 97 23
GINGER WALNUT MISO
DRESSING . . . . Charter Issue 30
Natural Salad Dressings . . . . . . Charter Issue 30
Salad Dressing 101 . . . . Jul/Aug 96 14
SESAME GARLIC DRESSING . Charter Issue 30
TWO-MUSTARD DRESSING WITH
CHIVES. . . . . Charter Issue 30

Salads

SALAD WITH PARMA HAM, PARMESAN, AND
LEMON VINAIGRETTE . . . . . . May/Jun 93 7
AMBROSIA . . . . Mar/Apr 94 21
APPLE-BEET SALAD WITH CREAMY DILL
DRESSING . . . . Nov/Dec 96 21
APPLE-CRANBERRY SALAD WITH CREAMY
LEMON VINAIGRETTE. . . . . . . Nov/Dec 96 21
ARTICHOKE CUPS WITH SEAFOOD SALAD
AND HERB VINAIGRETTE. . . . May/Jun 93 BC
Attractive Vegetable Salads (QT). . May/Jun 96 5
BROCCOFLOWER AND CELERY
SALAD . . . . May/Jun 95 23
BROWN RICE AND CHICKPEA
SALAD . . . . Jan/Feb 94 23
CITRUS SALAD WITH BITTER GREENS AND
PARMESAN SHAVINGS. . . . . . . Nov/Dec 96 21
DRIED PEACH AND APPLE SALAD WITH
ALMONDS AND CUMIN. . . . . . Jul/Aug 94 20
ESCAROLE SALAD WITH BACON AND
POACHED EGG. . . . . May/Jun 97 24
FENNEL AND OLIVE SALAD WITH CREAMY
TARRAGON VINAIGRETTE . . . May/Jun 95 23
FENNEL-ORANGE SALAD WITH BLACK
OLIVES AND MINT. . . . . May/Jun 96 19
FRENCH LENTIL SALAD WITH CARAWAY
AND RADISH . . . . Mar/Apr 95 25
GRAPE AND FETA SALAD WITH
ROSEMARY . . . . Nov/Dec 96 21
GRILLED ZUCCHINI SALAD WITH TOMATOES
AND BASIL . . . . Jul/Aug 95 9
MIXED GREEN SALAD WITH CLASSIC FRENCH
DRESSING. . . . . Jul/Aug 96 14
POACHED PEARS ON SALAD GREENS WITH
WALNUTS AND STILTON . . . . . Jan/Feb 94 BC
Real Tabbooleh . . . . Jul/Aug 94 9
ROASTED RED PEPPER SALAD WITH RED
ONIONS AND CUCUMBERS . . May/Jun 96 21
Salad Without the Bowl (Notes) . . . Jul/Aug 97 3
Spring Vegetable Salads . . . . May/Jun 95 23
TABBOOLEH . . . . Jul/Aug 94 9
WATERCRESS SALAD WITH SEARED SCALLOPS
AND ORANGE VINAIGRETTE . Mar/Apr 96 8
WATERCRESS, ENDIVE, AND RADICCHIO
SALAD . . . . May/Jun 97 BC
Winter Fruit Salads . . . . Nov/Dec 96 21

arugula

ARUGULA SALAD WITH GARLIC
CROUTONS, GRUYÈRE, AND HARD-BOILED
EGGS . . . . May/Jun 95 23
ARUGULA SALAD WITH GRILLED FIGS
AND ROASTED PEPPER
VINAIGRETTE . . . . Sep/Oct 96 BC
PEAR SALAD WITH ARUGULA, WALNUTS,
AND GORGONZOLA . . . . Nov/Dec 96 21

asparagus

ALFRED PORTALE'S JUMBO ASPARAGUS
ASPARAGUS VINAIGRETTE WITH
SIEVED EGG AND PICKLED PINK
ONIONS . . . . May/Jun 95 23

bread salads

Bread Salads . . . . Sep/Oct 95 14
BREAD SALAD WITH ROASTED PEPPERS
AND SICILIAN OLIVES . . . . . . Sep/Oct 95 14
BREAD SALAD WITH TOMATOES, HERBS,
AND RED ONIONS . . . . Sep/Oct 95 14
PITA BREAD SALAD WITH CUCUMBERS,
CHERRY TOMATOES, AND FRESH
HERBS. . . . . Sep/Oct 95 14

Caesar

BEST CAESAR SALAD. . . . . Sep/Oct 97 23
CAESAR SALAD WITH TOFU
DRESSING. . . . . Sep/Oct 97 23

Cook's Illustrated 1993–1997 Index

chicken

CHICKEN SALAD WITH HOISIN
DRESSING .... Jul/Aug 97   8

CLASSIC CREAMY CHICKEN
SALAD .... Jul/Aug 97   8

CURRIED CHICKEN SALAD WITH RAISINS
AND HONEY .... Jul/Aug 97   8

Preparing the Chicken .... Jul/Aug 97   8

SIMPLE ROAST CHICKEN
BREASTS .... Jul/Aug 97   8

WALDORF CHICKEN SALAD ... Jul/Aug 97   8

cucumber

CREAMY DILL CUCUMBER
SALAD .... Jul/Aug 97   11

How to Salt and Drain
Cucumbers .... Jul/Aug 97   11

SESAME LEMON CUCUMBER
SALAD .... Jul/Aug 97   11

SWEET-AND-TART CUCUMBER
SALAD .... Jul/Aug 97   11

YOGURT MINT CUCUMBER
SALAD .... Jul/Aug 97   11

potato

AMERICAN-STYLE POTATO SALAD WITH EGGS
AND SWEET PICKLES........ Jul/Aug 94   8

FRENCH-STYLE POTATO SALAD WITH
TARRAGON VINAIGRETTE.... Jul/Aug 94   7

GERMAN-STYLE POTATO SALAD WITH BACON
AND BALSAMIC VINEGAR .... Jul/Aug 94   8

Perfect Potato Salad .... Jul/Aug 94   6

spinach

SPINACH AND AVOCADO SALAD WITH CHILI-
FLAVORED CHICKEN .... Mar/Apr 97   9

SPINACH SALAD WITH MUSHROOMS,
CROUTONS, AND WARM LEMON
DRESSING .... Mar/Apr 97   9

SPINACH SALAD WITH SHRIMP, MANGO,
AND RED ONION .... Mar/Apr 97   9

Salmon

Boning the Whole Salmon .... Jul/Aug 93   24

FAST SALMON CARPACCIO..... Jul/Aug 95   11

Gravlax Made Easy, Master Class.. Jan/Feb 96   12

GRAVLAX .... Jan/Feb 96   13

GRILLED SALMON WITH INDIAN FLAVORS AND
FRESH MANGO CHUTNEY ... Jul/Aug 97   7

Grilling Salmon Fillets Another
Way (Notes)................. Nov/Dec 97   3

GRILL-ROASTED SALMON WITH

ALDERWOOD .... Jul/Aug 93   20

QUICK SALMON BROTH .... Jul/Aug 93   25

QUILTED GIRAFFE'S GRILLED SALMON WITH
MUSTARD GLAZE .... Jul/Aug 97   7

Removing Pin Bones from Salmon . Jul/Aug 97   6

ROASTED SALMON WITH KASHA AND LEEK
STUFFING................. Jul/Aug 93   23

Roasted Salmon with Kasha and Leek Stuffing,
Master Class............... Jul/Aug 93   23

SHIITAKE-STUFFED SALMON ROLLS WITH
TARRAGON-TOMATO SAUCE.. Jul/Aug 95   11

SIMPLE GRILLED SALMON .... Jul/Aug 97   7

Steaming Times for Fish Fillets and
Steaks .... Mar/Apr 95   20

Tasting Farmed Salmon .... Jul/Aug 97   7

Thin-Sliced Salmon Rolls with Couscous Filling,
Master Class................ Jul/Aug 95   10

smoked

SALMON AND CHIVE MILLE
FEUILLE .... Mar/Apr 94   17

SMOKED SALMON OMELET .... Sep/Oct 93   22

Smoked Salmon Slicer (Notes,
What Is It?) .... Nov/Dec 95   3

Smoked Salmon Tasting (BT)..... Nov/Dec 95   24

SMOKED SALMON WITH CORIANDER-
PEPPER RUB .... Jul/Aug 95   20

SMOKED SALMON–FILLED BELGIAN
ENDIVE .... Nov/Dec 95   BC

Salsa

APRICOT-JICAMA SALSA .... Jul/Aug 94   20

AVOCADO-CORN SALSA........ Jul/Aug 96   21

BLACK BEAN–MANGO SALSA... Jul/Aug 96   21

CLASSIC RED TABLE SALSA.... Jul/Aug 96   21

CRANBERRY-PEAR SALSA IN PEAR
SHELLS .... Nov/Dec 96   BC

Easy Summer Salsas............ Jul/Aug 96   21

GRILLED JALAPEÑO SALSA ... Jul/Aug 96   21

MEXICAN-STYLE SALSA
CRUDA.................... Jul/Aug 93   14

PEACH SALSA .... Sep/Oct 93   11

PINEAPPLE SALSA .... Sep/Oct 94   13

PLUM TOMATO SALSA WITH SHERRY
VINEGAR................. May/Jun 94   13

ROASTED CORN SALSA .... Jul/Aug 93   8

SIMPLE PEACH SALSA........ Jul/Aug 96   21

Rating Salsas (BT)............. Jul/Aug 97   26

SALSA TASTING RECIPE
(Notes)..................... Nov/Dec 97   2

Sandwiches

MUFFULETTA . . . . Sep/Oct 96   21

Sauces (*See* also Chutneys; Condiments; Gravy; Salsa; Vinaigrettes)

ASIAN-STYLE SWEET AND SOUR
PAN SAUCE . . . . Sep/Oct 93   11

BLACK PEPPER–MUSTARD
SAUCE . . . . Mar/Apr 95   20

CILANTRO CREAM . . . . Jan/Feb 96   13

COUNTRY MUSTARD–SHALLOT SAUCE WITH
THYME. . . . . May/Jun 95   22

Emulsifying Sauces (Notes). . . . . . . Jan/Feb 94   3

GINGER BUERRE BLANC. . . . . . May/Jun 93   28

HOISIN-SESAME SAUCE . . . . . . May/Jun 94   13

LEMON-CAPER SAUCE. . . . . Sep/Oct 93   10

MUNG BEAN SAUCE WITH GINGER, CILANTRO,
AND SOY . . . . Sep/Oct 95   24

OAXACAN-STYLE SAUCE WITH CLOVES AND
CINNAMON. . . . . Sep/Oct 93   10

PIQUANT CAPER SAUCE . . . . . . Mar/Apr 94   10

QUICK-COOKED TOMATILLO-CHILE
SAUCE . . . . Jul/Aug 94   14

RED PEPPER-BASIL SAUCE WITH BALSAMIC
VINEGAR . . . . May/Jun 95   22

ROASTED RED PEPPER
ROUILLE . . . . Nov/Dec 94   21

Save "Broken" Hollandaise (QT) . . May/Jun 95   4

SHERRY-CREAM SAUCE WITH
MUSHROOMS . . . . Sep/Oct 93   10

Spiral Sauce Whisk (Notes) . . . . . . Mar/Apr 95   3

WARM BALSAMIC VINEGAR SAUCE WITH
BACON. . . . . Jul/Aug 93   25

WHITE WINE-BUTTER SAUCE WITH
CAPERS . . . . Mar/Apr 95   19

barbecue

BARBECUE SAUCE, MASTER
RECIPE FOR . . . . Jul/Aug 94   13

Barbecue Sauces (S&R). . . . . Jul/Aug 94   32

BARBECUE SAUCE WITH ASIAN
FLAVORS . . . . Jul/Aug 97   15

BARBECUE SAUCE WITH MEXICAN
FLAVORS. . . . . Jul/Aug 97   15

BASIC BARBECUE SAUCE . . . . . Jul/Aug 97   15

EASTERN NORTH CAROLINA–STYLE
BARBECUE SAUCE . . . . Jul/Aug 97   20

KENTUCKY SMOKED BARBECUE
SAUCE . . . . Jul/Aug 94   13

LOUISIANA SWEET BARBECUE
SAUCE . . . . Jul/Aug 94   13

MID–SOUTH CAROLINA MUSTARD
SAUCE . . . . Jul/Aug 97   20

SPICY RIO GRANDE BARBECUE
SAUCE. . . . . Jul/Aug 94   13

Tasting Barbecue Sauces (BT). . . . . Jul/Aug 95   26

WESTERN SOUTH CAROLINA–STYLE
BARBECUE SAUCE . . . . Jul/Aug 97   20

dessert

BOURBON BUTTER SAUCE . . . . . Jan/Feb 95   25

DESSERT SAUCES. . . . . May/Jun 93   28

ORANGE SAUCE FOR
GINGERBREAD . . . . Nov/Dec 95   23

PEAR BRANDY CUSTARD
SAUCE. . . . . Sep/Oct 94   11

RASPBERRY SAUCE . . . . Jan/Feb 94   14

dipping

CHILE DIPPING SAUCE . . . . Sep/Oct 94   15

CREAMY DIPPING SAUCE . . . . . Jul/Aug 95   23

PIQUANT PLUM SAUCE WITH SESAME OIL
AND GINGER . . . . Jul/Aug 94   20

SOY-GINGER DIPPING SAUCE . . Sep/Oct 94   15

horseradish

HORSERADISH AND CIDER CREAM
SAUCE. . . . . Sep/Oct 95   24

HORSERADISH CREAM . . . . May/Jun 97   9

pasta

ALL PURPOSE TOMATO
SAUCE . . . . Mar/Apr 94   26

AROMATIC TOMATO SAUCE . . . Mar/Apr 94   26

ARTICHOKE-LOBSTER SAUCE . Mar/Apr 94   12

ASPARAGUS AND MUSHROOM SAUCE WITH
CARAMELIZED SHALLOTS . . . Mar/Apr 95   11

BASIL SAUCE WITH SAUTÉED
SHRIMP . . . . Mar/Apr 96   9

BRAISED ARTICHOKE SAUCE WITH WHITE
WINE, GARLIC, AND LEMON . Mar/Apr 95   11

BRAISED FENNEL AND BITTER
GREENS SAUCE WITH BALSAMIC
VINEGAR . . . . Mar/Apr 95   11

BROWN BUTTER AND PINE NUT
SAUCE. . . . . Sep/Oct 93   18

CLAM SAUCE WITH TOMATOES AND
GARLIC . . . . Mar/Apr 96   9

Country Italian Vegetable Pasta
Sauces . . . . Mar/Apr 95   11

ESCAROLE AND WHITE BEAN SAUCE WITH
GARLIC AND OREGANO . . . . . . Sep/Oct 94   22

FRESH CLAM SAUCE. . . . . Nov/Dec 97   14

FRESH TOMATO-HERB SAUCE, MASTER
RECIPE FOR . . . . Jul/Aug 93   14

GARDEN TOMATO SAUCE . . . . . . Sep/Oct 93   18

The Happy Marriage of Sweet and Tart (in Tomato
Sauce) . . . . May/Jun 97   11

OVEN-DRIED TOMATO SAUCE WITH PANCETTA
AND HOT PEPPER . . . . Sep/Oct 96   21

PASTA AND SIMPLE TOMATO SAUCE, MASTER
RECIPE FOR . . . . May/Jun 97   11

PORCINI MUSHROOM SAUCE WITH
CREAM . . . . Jan/Feb 97   15

QUICK-COOKED TOMATOES WITH
OLIVE OIL . . . . Mar/Apr 94   26

Quick Seafood Pasta Sauces . . . . . . Mar/Apr 96   9

ROASTED RED AND YELLOW PEPPER SAUCE
WITH GARLIC . . . . Sep/Oct 94   22

STEAMED MUSSEL SAUCE WITH LEMON
AND WHITE WINE . . . . Mar/Apr 96   9

STEWED TOMATOES WITH BASIL AND OLIVE
OIL . . . . Mar/Apr 94   26

Tomato Sauces for Pasta . . . . . . Mar/Apr 94   26

TOMATO SAUCE WITH ANCHOVIES AND
OLIVES . . . . May/Jun 97   11

TOMATO SAUCE WITH ARUGULA AND BLACK
OLIVES . . . . Mar/Apr 95   11

TOMATO SAUCE WITH BACON AND
PARSLEY . . . . May/Jun 97   11

TOMATO SAUCE WITH PORCINI
MUSHROOMS . . . . Jan/Feb 97   15

TOMATO SAUCE WITH TUNA AND GREEN
OLIVES . . . . Mar/Apr 96   9

TOMATO SAUCE WITH VODKA AND
CREAM . . . . May/Jun 97   11

TWO MUSHROOM SAUCE WITH
ROSEMARY . . . . Jan/Feb 97   15

Vegetable Pasta Sauces . . . . Sep/Oct 94   22

ZUCCHINI, RED PEPPER, AND TOMATO SAUCE
WITH THYME AND MINT . . . . . Sep/Oct 94   22

pork

CREAM PAN SAUCE WITH APPLES AND
SAGE . . . . Jul/Aug 97   19

ORANGE PAN SAUCE WITH FENNEL AND
GREEN OLIVES . . . . Jul/Aug 97   19

PORT PAN SAUCE WITH CHERRIES AND
ROSEMARY . . . . Sep/Oct 97   19

WINE VINEGAR PAN SAUCE WITH WARM
SPICES AND RAISINS . . . . Jul/Aug 97   19

seafood

COCKTAIL SAUCE . . . . Jul/Aug 97   13

Five Easy Sauces for Fish . . . . May/Jun 94   13

HOISIN-SESAME SAUCE . . . . . . May/Jun 94   13

LIME-GINGER VINAIGRETTE . . May/Jun 94   13

ONION, BLACK OLIVE, AND CAPER
COMPOTE . . . . May/Jun 94   13

Quick Pan Sauces for Sautéed
Fish . . . . Sep/Oct 95   24

Quick Seafood Pasta Sauces . . . . . . Mar/Apr 96   9

TARTAR SAUCE . . . . Jul/Aug 97   10

WARM CUCUMBER/RED ONION RELISH
WITH MINT . . . . May/Jun 94   13

steak

HORSERADISH CREAM . . . . May/Jun 97   9

MUSTARD SAUCE . . . . May/Jun 97   9

ROQUEFORT BUTTER . . . . May/Jun 97   9

stir-fry

BLACK BEAN SAUCE . . . . May/Jun 93   19

Chinese Flavoring Sauces . . . . May/Jun 93   19

COCONUT CURRY SAUCE . . . . . May/Jun 93   19

CURRY SAUCE . . . . Mar/Apr 96   20

GINGER SAUCE . . . . Mar/Apr 96   20

HOT-AND-SOUR SAUCE . . . . Mar/Apr 96   20

LEMON SAUCE . . . . Mar/Apr 96   20

LEMON SAUCE . . . . May/Jun 93   19

ORANGE SAUCE . . . . Mar/Apr 96   20

OYSTER FLAVORED SAUCE . . . . May/Jun 93   19

SPICY TANGERINE SAUCE . . . . May/Jun 93   19

SWEET AND SOUR SAUCE . . . . . May/Jun 93   19

SZECHUAN CHILI SAUCE . . . . . May/Jun 93   19

TOMATO FIREWORKS SAUCE . . May/Jun 93   19

tomato

ALL-PURPOSE TOMATO
SAUCE . . . . Mar/Apr 94   26

AROMATIC TOMATO SAUCE . . . Mar/Apr 94   26

CLAM SAUCE WITH TOMATOES AND
GARLIC . . . . Mar/Apr 96   9

FRESH TOMATO-HERB SAUCE, MASTER
RECIPE FOR . . . . Jul/Aug 93   14

GARDEN TOMATO SAUCE . . . . . . Sep/Oct 93   18

The Happy Marriage of Sweet and Tart
(in Tomato Sauce) . . . . May/Jun 97   11

LASAGNE WITH HERBED MEATBALLS,
TOMATO SAUCE, AND
MOZZARELLA . . . . Nov/Dec 94   11

POLENTA WITH ITALIAN SAUSAGES AND
TOMATO SAUCE . . . . Jan/Feb 95   21

POTATO GNOCCHI WITH TOMATO-MINT
SAUCE . . . . Mar/Apr 95   10

POTATO GRATIN WITH SWEET PEPPERS AND

TOMATOES . . . . Nov/Dec 95   19

PROVENÇAL TOMATO SAUCE WITH BASIL
AND ORANGE . . . . Sep/Oct 95   24

QUICK-COOKED TOMATOES WITH
OLIVE OIL . . . . Mar/Apr 94   26

QUICK TOMATO SAUCE FOR
PIZZA . . . . May/Jun 95   10

Raw Tomato Sauces . . . . Jul/Aug 93   14

SAUTÉED EGGPLANT IN TOMATO SAUCE
WITH BASIL . . . . Jul/Aug 93   7

SHIITAKE-STUFFED SALMON ROLLS WITH
SIMPLE TOMATO SAUCE . . . . . Nov/Dec 94   11

STEWED TOMATO SAUCE WITH BASIL AND
OLIVE OIL . . . . Mar/Apr 94   26

TARRAGON-TOMATO SAUCE . . . Jul/Aug 95   11

TOMATO-BASIL SAUCE WITH
CAPERS . . . . Sep/Oct 93   11

TOMATO FIREWORKS SAUCE . . May/Jun 93   19

TOMATO-ROSEMARY CREAM
SAUCE . . . . May/Jun 95   22

Tomato Sauces for Pasta . . . . Mar/Apr 94   26

TOMATO SAUCE WITH ANCHOVIES AND
OLIVES . . . . May/Jun 97   11

TOMATO SAUCE WITH ARUGULA AND BLACK
OLIVES . . . . Mar/Apr 95   11

TOMATO SAUCE WITH BACON AND
PARSLEY . . . . May/Jun 97   11

TOMATO SAUCE WITH BELL PEPPERS AND
BALSAMIC VINEGAR . . . . Mar/Apr 95   20

TOMATO SAUCE WITH PORCINI
MUSHROOMS . . . . Jan/Feb 97   15

TOMATO SAUCE WITH TUNA AND GREEN
OLIVES . . . . Mar/Apr 96   9

TOMATO SAUCE WITH VODKA AND
CREAM . . . . May/Jun 97   11

TOMATO YOGURT SAUCE . . . . . Jul/Aug 93   14

ZUCCHINI, RED PEPPER AND TOMATO SAUCE
WITH THYME AND MINT . . . . . Sep/Oct 94   22

Sausages

BRAISED VEAL BREAST WITH SAUSAGE,
OLIVE, AND SWISS CHARD
STUFFING (Notes) . . . . Sep/Oct 93   3

CHICKEN SAUSAGE WITH APPLES AND
SAGE . . . . Mar/Apr 96   12

CHICKEN SAUSAGE WITH MEDITERRANEAN
FLAVORS . . . . Mar/Apr 96   12

Chorizo Sausage (S&R) . . . . Jan/Feb 95   32

Food Processor Sausage, Master

Class . . . . Mar/Apr 96   12

PAELLA, CRIOLLA'S STYLE . . . . . Jan/Feb 95   11

POLENTA WITH ITALIAN SAUSAGES AND
TOMATO SAUCE . . . . Jan/Feb 95   21

SAUSAGE AND BELL PEPPER PIZZA WITH
BASIL AND MOZZARELLA . . . . May/Jun 95   11

SAUSAGE AND PEAR STUFFING WITH
CHESTNUTS AND PRUNES . . . Nov/Dec 95   26

Sausage Casings (S&R) . . . . Mar/Apr 96   32

Unique Sausages (S&R) . . . . Jul/Aug 93   32

Scallops

BASIC CEVICHE . . . . Jul/Aug 96   15

Crisp, Sweet Sea Scallops . . . . . . Mar/Apr 96   6

"Dry" Sea Scallops (S&R) . . . . Mar/Apr 96   32

ED BROWN'S SEARED SCALLOPS WITH
CILANTRO PESTO . . . . Mar/Apr 96   8

RICK MOONEN'S ANGEL HAIR PASTA WITH
SEARED SCALLOPS . . . . Mar/Apr 96   8

SCALLOP CEVICHE WITH SWEET PEPPER
CONFETTI . . . . Jul/Aug 96   15

Scallop Cooking . . . . Mar/Apr 96   7

Scallop Muscle Removal . . . . Mar/Apr 96   6

SEARED SCALLOPS, MASTER
RECIPE FOR . . . . Mar/Apr 96   8

Simple Scallop Ceviche . . . . Jul/Aug 96   15

SOY-GINGER SCALLOP
CEVICHE . . . . Jul/Aug 96   15

WATERCRESS SALAD WITH SEARED SCALLOPS
AND ORANGE VINAIGRETTE . Mar/Apr 96   8

Science of Cooking

Cookware Reactivity (Notes) . . . . . . Sep/Oct 96   2

How Does Gelatin Work? . . . . May/Jun 96   15

The Incredible Shrinking Flank
Steak . . . . Sep/Oct 96   12

The Science of Brewing . . . . Jan/Feb 96   29

The Science of Brining Turkey . . . . Nov/Dec 93   19

The Science of Butter (Notes) . . . Charter Issue   2

The Science of Buttermilk . . . . Jul/Aug 93   1

The Science of Custard . . . . Nov/Dec 96   9

The Science of Egg Whites . . . . . Charter Issue   11

The Science of Roasting . . . . Sep/Oct 96   12

Scones

CITRUS HONEY-NUT SCONES . . Mar/Apr 94   7

CREAM AND CURRANT
SCONES . . . . Mar/Apr 94   7

Scones in 20 Minutes . . . . Mar/Apr 94   6

SWEET-MILK SCONES, MASTER
RECIPE FOR . . . . Mar/Apr 94   7

Seafood (See also Fish and specific kinds)
ARTICHOKE CUPS WITH SEAFOOD SALAD AND
HERB VINAIGRETTE . . . . May/Jun 93   BC
Cleaning Shrimp, Squid, and Soft-Shell
Crab . . . . May/Jun 94   16
SEAFOOD CABBAGE
CASSEROLE . . . . Charter Issue   6
Smoke-Cooking Times . . . . Jul/Aug 95   20

Seasonings and Spices (See also Spice Rubs and Pastes)
ALL-PURPOSE BARBECUE RUB . Jul/Aug 95   21
Asian Spices (S&R) . . . . Sep/Oct 95   32
BLACK OLIVE PASTE . . . . Mar/Apr 95   19
Chinese Tea and Spices for
Smoking (S&R) . . . . May/Jun 95   32
Chop Fennel Seeds (QT) . . . . Mar/Apr 95   4
COLD OIL INFUSING, MASTER
METHOD FOR . . . . Jan/Feb 95   15
Cooking Spices: A Matter of
Temperature . . . . Jan/Feb 97   7
Cracking Peppercorns
Neatly (QT) . . . . Jul/Aug 97   4
Crystallized Ginger (S&R) . . . . Nov/Dec 95   32
Curry Spices and
Ingredients (S&R) . . . . Jan/Feb 97   32
Grinding Spices . . . . Jan/Feb 97   7
Nutmeg and Grinders (S&R) . . . . . Nov/Dec 95   32
Pulverize Saffron (QT) . . . . May/Jun 95   5
RAS AL HANOUT . . . . Jan/Feb 95   19
Remove Spices Easily (QT) . . . . . . May/Jun 95   4
ROSEMARY-SAGE SALT . . . . Sep/Oct 95   11
Spice Funnel (QT) . . . . Mar/Apr 97   5
Spice Grinder (Notes) . . . . Sep/Oct 95   2
SPICE RUB FOR CHICKEN . . . . . Jul/Aug 95   21
SPICE RUB FOR OILY FISH . . . . . Jul/Aug 95   21
SPICE RUB FOR PORK . . . . Jul/Aug 95   21
SPICE RUB FOR STEAKS AND
CHOPS . . . . Jul/Aug 95   21
Spice Rubs . . . . Jul/Aug 95   21
Spice-Infused Oils . . . . Jan/Feb 95   15
Spices for Rubs (S&R) . . . . Jul/Aug 95   32
SPICY CHILI RUB . . . . Jul/Aug 97   20
Taming Toasted Seeds (QT) . . . . . . Nov/Dec 97   5
THREE-SEED SALT . . . . Sep/Oct 95   11
TOMATO BASE WITH POBLANOS AND

CILANTRO . . . . Jan/Feb 95   11
WARM OIL INFUSING, MASTER
METHOD FOR . . . . Jan/Feb 95   15

Semifreddo
CHOCOLATE ORANGE
SEMIFREDDO . . . . Jul/Aug 97   23
MASTER RECIPE FOR CAPPUCCINO SEMIFRED-
DO WITH ALMOND BISCOTTI . Jul/Aug 97   23
VANILLA SEMIFREDDO WITH ALMONDS AND
AMARETTI . . . . Jul/Aug 97   23
WARM BITTERSWEET CHOCOLATE
SAUCE . . . . Jul/Aug 97   23
What Is Semifreddo? . . . . Jul/Aug 97   23

Semolina
SEMOLINA DOUGH . . . . Jan/Feb 94   32
Semolina Flour (S&R) . . . . Jan/Feb 94   32

Sesame
PIQUANT PLUM SAUCE WITH SESAME
OIL AND GINGER . . . . Jul/Aug 94   20
SESAME CREPES (Notes) . . . . Jan/Feb 94   3
SESAME GARLIC DRESSING . Charter Issue   30
SHRIMP FILLING WITH GINGER AND
SESAME . . . . Sep/Oct 94   14
Taming Toasted Seeds (QT) . . . . . . Nov/Dec 97   5

Shallots
ASPARAGUS AND MUSHROOM SAUCE WITH
CARAMELIZED SHALLOTS . . . Mar/Apr 95   11
COUNTRY MUSTARD–SHALLOT SAUCE WITH
THYME . . . . May/Jun 95   22
CREAM-BRAISED CABBAGE WITH LEMON AND
SHALLOTS . . . . Sep/Oct 96   9
CREAMY PARSNIP PUREE WITH
SHALLOTS . . . . Sep/Oct 94   9
Dicing a Shallot (QT) . . . . Jan/Feb 94   5
GRILLED SHOULDER LAMB CHOPS WITH SOY-
SHALLOT MARINADE . . . . Mar/Apr 97   19
ROASTED BUTTERNUT SQUASH WITH SHAL-
LOTS AND THYME . . . . Nov/Dec 94   15
ROASTED TURNIPS, SHALLOTS, AND GARLIC
WITH ROSEMARY . . . . Jan/Feb 94   11

Sherry
SHERRY-CREAM SAUCE WITH
MUSHROOMS . . . . Sep/Oct 93   10

Shiitake Mushrooms
SHIITAKE-STUFFED SALMON ROLLS WITH
TARRAGON-TOMATO SAUCE . . Jul/Aug 95   11

Shortening
Measuring Shortening (Notes) . . . . Sep/Oct 94   2
Measuring Shortening (Notes). . . . May/Jun 95   2

Shrimp
BASIL SAUCE WITH SAUTÉED
SHRIMP . . . . Mar/Apr 96   9
BRINED SHRIMP, MASTER
RECIPE FOR . . . . Jul/Aug 94   19
Brining Thawed Shrimp (Notes) . . May/Jun 95   2
Cleaning Shrimp, Squid, and Soft-Shell
Crab . . . . May/Jun 94   16
COCKTAIL SAUCE . . . . Jul/Aug 97   13
GRILLED SHRIMP PIZZA TOPPING WITH
ROASTED TOMATOES AND FARMER'S
CHEESE. . . . . May/Jun 93   9
GRILLED SHRIMP WITH SPICY
GARLIC PASTE . . . . Jul/Aug 94   19
HERB-POACHED SHRIMP . . . . . Jul/Aug 97   13
How to Peel and Devein Shrimp . . May/Jun 94   17
Making Steamed Shrimp Go
Further (QT). . . . . Jul/Aug 95   4
A New Way to Prepare Shrimp . . . . Jul/Aug 94   18
PAELLA, CRIOLLA'S STYLE . . . . . Jan/Feb 95   11
Preparing Shrimp for the Grill . . . . Jul/Aug 94   19
SEARED SHRIMP WITH LEMON . Jul/Aug 94   19
A Shrimp-Buying Guide . . . . Jul/Aug 97   13
SHRIMP CURRY WITH YOGURT AND
PEAS . . . . Jan/Feb 97   9
SHRIMP FILLING WITH GINGER AND
SESAME. . . . . Sep/Oct 94   14
SKEWERED GRILLED SHRIMP WITH ARTI-
CHOKE HEARTS . . . . Mar/Apr 94   BC
SPINACH SALAD WITH SHRIMP, MANGO,
AND RED ONION . . . . Mar/Apr 97   9
Fry in a Skillet (Notes) . . . . Sep/Oct 93   2

Smoke Cooking
Cast-Iron Pot for Smoking (S&R) . May/Jun 95   32
Chinese Tea and Spices for
Smoking (S&R) . . . . May/Jun 95   32
How to Smoke-Cook With a Kettle-Style
Grill . . . . Jul/Aug 95   19
How to Smoke-Cook With a Water
Smoker . . . . Jul/Aug 95   19

Smoke Cooking . . . . Jul/Aug 95   18
SMOKED PORK CHOPS WITH FENNEL-
MUSTARD RUB. . . . . Jul/Aug 95   20
SMOKED SALMON WITH CORIANDER-PEPPER
RUB . . . . Jul/Aug 95   20
SMOKED TURKEY BREAST WITH GINGER-
CARDAMOM RUB . . . . Jul/Aug 95   20
Smoking Equipment (S&R) . . . . . . Jul/Aug 95   32
STOVE-TOP TEA-SMOKED
CHICKEN. . . . . May/Jun 95   15
Tea-Smoked Chicken . . . . May/Jun 95   14
Twice-Cooked Duck, Master Class . Sep/Oct 95   10

Sorbets (See also Ice Cream)
MASTER TECHNIQUE FOR FRUIT
SORBETS. . . . . Jul/Aug 95   25
Secrets of Creamy Fruit Sorbets . . . Jul/Aug 95   24

Soufflés
CHOCOLATE SOUFFLÉ . . . . Sep/Oct 96   19
MAKE-AHEAD CHOCOLATE
SOUFFLÉ. . . . . Sep/Oct 96   19
Mastering the Chocolate Soufflé . . . Sep/Oct 96   18

Soup (See also Broth; Stock)
Clarifying Broth (Notes). . . . . Nov/Dec 96   3
CORN AND CLAM CHOWDER WITH ROASTED
PARSNIPS . . . . Jul/Aug 93   9
CREAMY POTATO SOUP WITH
CHIVES. . . . . Nov/Dec 96   23
Culinary Uses for Homemade
Juices . . . . Jan/Feb 94   27
GARLIC AND SAGE SOUP . . . . . Mar/Apr 95   BC
GAZPACHO . . . . May/Jun 93   28
HEARTY CHICKEN NOODLE SOUP, MASTER
RECIPE FOR . . . . Mar/Apr 96   15
HEARTY CHICKEN SOUP WITH LEEKS, WILD
RICE, AND MUSHROOMS . . . . Mar/Apr 96   15
HEARTY CHICKEN SOUP WITH ORZO AND
SPRING VEGETABLES . . . . Mar/Apr 96   15
HEARTY CHICKEN SOUP WITH SHELLS,
TOMATOES, AND ZUCCHINI . . Mar/Apr 96   15
Improving Vegetable Soups . . . . Charter Issue   28
No-Cream Cream Soups . . . . Nov/Dec 96   22
PUREE OF BROCCOLI SOUP WITH GARLIC
AND HOT RED PEPPER . . . . Charter Issue   29
PUREE OF CAULIFLOWER SOUP WITH
CARDAMOM AND MACE. . . . Charter Issue   29
PUREED BROCCOLI SOUP WITH

Cook's Illustrated 1993–1997 Index

BASIL . . . . Nov/Dec 96   23
PUREED BUTTERNUT SQUASH SOUP WITH
   GINGER . . . . Nov/Dec 96   23
PUREED CARROT SOUP WITH
   NUTMEG . . . . Nov/Dec 96   23
PUREED CAULIFLOWER SOUP WITH
   CORIANDER. . . . . Nov/Dec 96   23
PUREED VEGETABLE SOUP, MASTER RECIPE
   FOR . . . . Nov/Dec 96   23
Quick Homemade Chicken Soup . . Mar/Apr 96   14
SPRING VEGETABLE SOUP WITH EGG
   NOODLES AND MINT . . . . . . Charter Issue   29
SUMMER HARVEST SOUP WITH
   BASIL . . . . Charter Issue   29

Sour Cream
   BRAISED CARROTS WITH SOUR CREAM-
      CILANTRO SAUCE . . . . Jan/Feb 96   BC
   Sour Cream Flaky Pastry Dough . . Sep/Oct 94   10
   SOUR CREAM FLAKY PASTRY
      DOUGH . . . . Sep/Oct 94   10
   SOUR CREAM-FUDGE LAYER CAKE WITH
      CHOCOLATE BUTTER ICING . . Jul/Aug 94   25
   Sour Cream Pastry Strudel. . . . . . Sep/Oct 94   10
   Sour Cream Pastry Strudel, Master
      Class. . . . . Sep/Oct 94   10
   SOUR CREAM VARIATION FOR AMERICAN
      PIE DOUGH. . . . . Sep/Oct 96   24

Soy Sauce
   QUICK-BRAISED BOK CHOY, TURNIPS, AND
      WATERCRESS WITH GINGER AND
      SOY . . . . Jan/Feb 96   26
   Secrets of Soy Sauce (BT) . . . . May/Jun 93   13
   SOY-GINGER DIPPING SAUCE . . Sep/Oct 94   15
   SOY-GINGER SCALLOP
      CEVICHE. . . . . Jul/Aug 96   15
   Soy Sauces (S&R). . . . . May/Jun 93   32

Spatzle
   BUTTERED SPATZLE (Notes) . . . May/Jun 93   2
   Making Spatzle (QT). . . . . Jan/Feb 96   5
   Spatzle Machine (Notes) . . . . May/Jun 93   2
   Spatzle Machine (S&R) . . . . May/Jun 93   32

Spice Rubs and Pastes
   Achiote Paste (Notes). . . . . Sep/Oct 94   3
   ALL-PURPOSE BARBECUE RUB . Jul/Aug 95   21
   ASIAN SPICE PASTE. . . . . Jul/Aug 96   23

BARBECUE-STYLE DRY RUB . . . Jul/Aug 94   13
CHILI SPICE PASTE WITH CITRUS AND
   CILANTRO. . . . . Jul/Aug 96   23
Dry Rubs . . . . Jul/Aug 94   13
MEDITERRANEAN SPICE PASTE Jul/Aug 96   23
MIXED HERB AND SPICE RUB FOR SAUTÉED
   PORK CHOPS . . . . Sep/Oct 94   13
SPICE RUB FOR CHICKEN . . . . . Jul/Aug 95   21
SPICE RUB FOR OILY FISH . . . . . Jul/Aug 95   21
SPICE RUB FOR PORK . . . . Jul/Aug 95   21
SPICE RUB FOR STEAKS AND
   CHOPS. . . . . Jul/Aug 95   21
SPICY CHILI RUB . . . . Jul/Aug 97   20
Spice Rubs. . . . . Jul/Aug 95   21
SWEET-AND-SOUR CURRY
   SPICE RUB . . . . Jul/Aug 96   23

Spinach (*See also* Greens)
   PANFRIED SOFT-SHELL CRABS ON A BED OF
      SPINACH . . . . May/Jun 95   7
   SPINACH AND AVOCADO SALAD WITH CHILI-
      FLAVORED CHICKEN . . . . Mar/Apr 97   9
   SPINACH AND RICOTTA FILLING
      FOR PASTA . . . . Sep/Oct 93   18
   SPINACH, LEEK, AND FETA
      FILLING . . . . Nov/Dec 95   15
   SPINACH PASTA. . . . . Nov/Dec 95   27
   SPINACH SALAD WITH MUSHROOMS,
      CROUTONS, AND WARM LEMON
      DRESSING . . . . Mar/Apr 97   9
   SPINACH SALAD WITH SHRIMP, MANGO, AND
      RED ONION . . . . Mar/Apr 97   9

Spoon Bread
   Southern Spoon Bread . . . . Nov/Dec 96   25
   SOUTHERN SPOON BREAD . . . . Nov/Dec 96   25
   SPOON BREAD WITH CHEDDAR
      CHEESE . . . . Nov/Dec 96   25

Spring Rolls
   Assembling Spring Rolls
      Quickly (QT). . . . . May/Jun 96   5

Squash
   Autumn and Winter Squashes . . . . Nov/Dec 93   14
   BRAISED BUTTERNUT SQUASH WITH
      DRIED APRICOTS, RAISINS, AND MADRAS
      SPICES . . . . Jan/Feb 96   26
   Cleaning Pumpkins and Winter

Cook's Illustrated 1993–1997 Index

Squash (QT) . . . . Sep/Oct 96   4

How to Cook Butternut Squash . . . Nov/Dec 94   15

MASHED BUTTERNUT SQUASH WITH
GINGER . . . . Nov/Dec 94   15

PUREED BUTTERNUT SQUASH SOUP WITH
GINGER . . . . Nov/Dec 96   23

ROASTED BUTTERNUT SQUASH WITH SHAL-
LOTS AND THYME . . . . Nov/Dec 94   15

Slicing Hard Winter Squash (QT) . May/Jun 96   4

SQUASH, PROSCIUTTO, AND PARMESAN FILL-
ING FOR PASTA . . . . Sep/Oct 93   18

Squid

Cleaning Shrimp, Squid, and Soft-Shell
Crab . . . . May/Jun 94   16

PAELLA, CRIOLLA'S STYLE . . . . . Jan/Feb 95   11

Star Anise

ORANGE COMPOTE WITH STAR
ANISE. . . . . Mar/Apr 96   BC

POACHED PEARS WITH STAR
ANISE. . . . . May/Jun 93   25

Steaming

Setting Up a Simple Steamer (QT) . Jan/Feb 96   5

Steamer, Simple (QT) . . . . Jan/Feb 96   5

Steaming Equipment . . . . Mar/Apr 95   19

Steaming Fish Fillets and Steaks . Mar/Apr 95   18

Steak

GRILLED PORTERHOUSE OR T-BONE
STEAK . . . . May/Jun 96   25

GRILLED STRIP SIRLOIN STEAK, MASTER
RECIPE FOR . . . . May/Jun 96   25

Grilling Steaks (on Cast-Iron Grate)
(Notes) . . . . Jul/Aug 97   3

GRILL-ROASTED BEEF
TENDERLOIN . . . . Jul/Aug 93   20

How to Grill a Steak . . . . May/Jun 96   23

PANFRIED STEAKS, MASTER
RECIPE FOR . . . . May/Jun 97   9

SPICE RUB FOR STEAKS AND
CHOPS. . . . . Jul/Aug 95   21

SPICY SOUTHWESTERN FLANK
STEAK . . . . Jul/Aug 93   12

Tasting Mail-Order Steaks (BT) . . May/Jun 96   26

Two-Part Steaks. . . . . May/Jun 96   24

sauces

HORSERADISH CREAM . . . . May/Jun 97   9

MUSTARD SAUCE . . . . May/Jun 97   9

ROQUEFORT BUTTER . . . . May/Jun 97   9

Stew

BEEF STEW WITH BACON, MUSHROOMS, AND
PEARL ONIONS . . . . Jan/Feb 96   20

BEEF STEW WITH TOMATOES, CINNAMON,
AND CLOVES . . . . Jan/Feb 96   20

BEEF STEW WITH TOMATOES, ORANGE ZEST,
AND OLIVES. . . . . Jan/Feb 96   20

BOUILLABAISE . . . . Nov/Dec 94   20

Fish Stew Basics. . . . . Nov/Dec 94   18

FISH STEW FLAVORING BASE,
MASTER RECIPE FOR . . . . Nov/Dec 94   20

FISH STEW, MASTER RECIPE
FOR. . . . . Nov/Dec 94   20

HEARTY BEEF STEW . . . . Jan/Feb 96   19

PRESSURE-COOKED NORTH AFRICAN LAMB
STEW. Jul/Aug 96   11

SICILIAN GRILLED TUNA
STEW . . . . Nov/Dec 94   21

Simple, Satisfying Beef Stew. . . . . Jan/Feb 96   18

ZARZUELA. . . . . Nov/Dec 94   20

Sticky Buns

THE BEST STICKY BUNS. . . . . . . Jan/Feb 94   26

Making Bakery-Style Sticky Buns . Jan/Feb 94   26

Stir-Frying

STIR-FRIED BROCCOLI WITH ORANGE
SAUCE . . . . Sep/Oct 95   9

STIR-FRIED CABBAGE. . . . . Charter Issue   7

STIR-FRIED SHANGHAI BOK CHOY WITH
CRABMEAT . . . . Charter Issue   7

MASTER RECIPE FOR
STIR-FRY . . . . Mar/Apr 96   20

Stir-Fry in a Skillet (Notes). . . . . . Sep/Oct 93   2

Stir-Frying Comes Home . . . . May/Jun 93   18

Stir-Frying Kale (Notes) . . . . May/Jun 95   3

Throw Out Your Wok!. . . . . Mar/Apr 96   18

sauces

BLACK BEAN SAUCE . . . . May/Jun 93   19

Chinese Flavoring Sauces . . . . . . May/Jun 93   19

COCONUT CURRY SAUCE . . . . . May/Jun 93   19

CURRY SAUCE . . . . Mar/Apr 96   20

GINGER SAUCE . . . . Mar/Apr 96   20

HOT-AND-SOUR SAUCE . . . . . . Mar/Apr 96   20

LEMON SAUCE. . . . . Mar/Apr 96   20

LEMON SAUCE . . . . May/Jun 93   19

Cook's Illustrated 1993–1997 Index

ORANGE SAUCE . . . . Mar/Apr 96   20
OYSTER FLAVORED SAUCE . . . . May/Jun 93   19
SPICY TANGERINE SAUCE . . . . May/Jun 93   19
SWEET AND SOUR SAUCE . . . . May/Jun 93   19
SZECHUAN CHILI SAUCE . . . . . May/Jun 93   19
TOMATO FIREWORKS SAUCE . . May/Jun 93   19

Stock (See also Broth; Soup)
BROWN GOOSE STOCK . . . . Nov/Dec 94   7
CHEATER'S FISH STOCK . . . . . . Nov/Dec 94   21
Clarifying Broth (Notes) . . . . Nov/Dec 96   3
FISH STOCK, MASTER
    RECIPE FOR . . . . Nov/Dec 94   20
Foam on Beans and Stock (Notes) . May/Jun 94   2
Freezing Stock (QT) . . . . Jul/Aug 96   3
Freezing Stock in Convenient
    Portions (QT) . . . . Nov/Dec 95   4
LONG-COOKED STOCK . . . . . . Charter Issue   29
QUICK BROTH . . . . Charter Issue   28
Removing Fat from Stock (QT) . . . . Sep/Oct 94   4
ROASTED STOCK . . . . Charter Issue   29
SHORT-COOKED STOCK . . . . . Charter Issue   29
Simple Veal Stock (Notes) . . . . Sep/Oct 93   3
SLOW-COOKED BROTH . . . . . . Charter Issue   29
SOUP BASE . . . . Charter Issue   28
Stock for Soup: A Kitchen Test . . Charter Issue   29
VEGETABLE BROTH . . . . Charter Issue   29
What's the Difference Between Broth and
    Stock? . . . . Charter Issue   28

Strawberries (See also Berries; Fruits)
Elegant Dipped Strawberries (QT) . Jul/Aug 97   5
FREE-FORM MERINGUE SHELLS FILLED WITH
    STRAWBERRIES AND PAPAYA May/Jun 95   13
Fruit Sorbets at a Glance . . . . Jul/Aug 95   25
How to Poach Fruit . . . . May/Jun 93   24
Keeping Strawberries Fresh (QT) . . Jul/Aug 96   3
Making Perfect Dipped
    Berries (QT) . . . . Mar/Apr 96   5
RICH AND TENDER SHORTCAKES WITH
    STRAWBERRIES AND WHIPPED
    CREAM . . . . May/Jun 97   19
STRAWBERRY FROZEN YOGURT May/Jun 96   15
STRAWBERRY-RHUBARB PIE . . . Jul/Aug 95   7
STRAWBERRY SHORTCAKE . . . . May/Jun 93   12

Strudel
PEAR AND DRIED FRUIT
    STRUDEL . . . . Sep/Oct 94   10

Sour Cream Pastry Strudel . . . . Sep/Oct 94   10
Sour Cream Pastry Strudel, Master
    Class . . . . Sep/Oct 94   11

Stuffing
BACON AND APPLE STUFFING, MASTER
    RECIPE FOR . . . . Nov/Dec 97   9
CHESTNUTS AND PRUNES . . . . . Nov/Dec 95   26
CORNBREAD-APPLE STUFFING Nov/Dec 95   26
CORNBREAD STUFFING WITH SAUSAGE AND
    PECANS . . . . Nov/Dec 97   9
COUSCOUS STUFFING WITH CURRANTS,
    APRICOTS, AND PISTACHIOS . . Jul/Aug 97   21
HERB AND MUSHROOM
    STUFFING . . . . Nov/Dec 95   26
Homemade Stuffing Bag (QT) . . . . Nov/Dec 97   4
KASHA AND LEEK STUFFING . . Jul/Aug 93   23
Poultry Stuffing Bag (S&R) . . . . . . Jul/Aug 95   32
PRUNE AND APPLE STUFFING . Nov/Dec 94   7
Removing Stuffing Easily (QT) . . . . Jul/Aug 95   4
Rustic Holiday Stuffings . . . . Nov/Dec 95   26
SAUSAGE AND PEAR STUFFING WITH
    CHESTNUTS AND PRUNES . . . Nov/Dec 95   26
SAUSAGE, OLIVE, AND SWISS CHARD
    STUFFING (Notes) . . . . Sep/Oct 93   3
SHIITAKE STUFFING . . . . Jul/Aug 95   11
SPICY GREENS STUFFING . . . . . Nov/Dec 93   12
SUMMER VEGETABLE AND RICE
    STUFFING . . . . Jul/Aug 93   25
WILD RICE STUFFING WITH CARROTS,
    MUSHROOMS, AND THYME . . . Jul/Aug 97   21
WILD RICE STUFFING WITH CRANBERRIES
    AND TOASTED PECANS . . . . . . Jul/Aug 97   21

Sugar
BROWN SUGAR AND HONEY MUSTARD
    GLAZE . . . . Nov/Dec 93   12
QUICK-COOKED CARROTS WITH MUSTARD-
    BROWN SUGAR GLAZE . . . . . . Mar/Apr 96   25
Castor Sugar (Notes) . . . . Nov/Dec 96   2
Confectioners' Sugar (Notes) . . . . . Mar/Apr 95   3
Nonmelting Sugar (S&R) . . . . Mar/Apr 97   32
Packed Brown Sugar (QT) . . . . Mar/Apr 97   5
Softening Brown Sugar (Notes) . . . . Sep/Oct 94   3
Superfine Sugar (Notes) . . . . Jul/Aug 93   3

Sugar Snap Peas
BLANCHED SUGAR SNAP
    PEAS . . . . May/Jun 97   12

Cook's Illustrated 1993–1997 Index

SUGAR SNAP PEAS WITH ASIAN
DRESSING . . . . May/Jun 97   12
SUGAR SNAP PEAS WITH HAM AND
MINT . . . . May/Jun 97   12
SUGAR SNAP PEAS WITH HAZELNUT
BUTTER . . . . May/Jun 97   12
SUGAR SNAP PEAS WITH LEMON, GARLIC,
AND BASIL . . . . May/Jun 97   12

Sun-Dried Tomatoes
FETA CHEESE FRITTATA WITH OLIVES AND
SUN-DRIED TOMATOES. . . . . . Mar/Apr 96   11
GRILLED MOZZARELLA AND SUN-DRIED
TOMATO SKEWERS . . . . May/Jun 96   17
Homemade Oven-Dried Tomatoes . . Sep/Oct 96   20
MUFFULETTA . . . . Sep/Oct 96   21
OVEN-DRIED TOMATOES . . . . . . Sep/Oct 96   21
OVEN-DRIED TOMATO SAUCE WITH PANCETTA
AND HOT PEPPER . . . . Sep/Oct 96   21
PEPPERED OVEN-DRIED TOMATO
RELISH . . . . Sep/Oct 96   21

Sushi
Cooling Sushi Rice (QT) . . . . Sep/Oct 95   5

Sweet Potatoes
BAKED SWEET POTATOES . . . . . Nov/Dec 96   11
The Best Baked Sweet Potato . . . . . Nov/Dec 96   11
ROASTED SWEET POTATOES WITH
CHIVES . . . . Jan/Feb 94   11
SAVORY MASHED SWEET
POTATOES . . . . Nov/Dec 96   11

Sweeteners (See also Honey; Sugar)
British Sweeteners (S&R) . . . . Mar/Apr 94   32

Swiss Chard (See also Greens)
BRAISED LAMB SHANKS WITH WHITE
BEANS, SWISS CHARD, AND
MARJORAM . . . . Jan/Feb 95   19
BRAISED VEAL BREAST WITH SAUSAGE,
OLIVE, AND SWISS CHARD
STUFFING (Notes) . . . . Sep/Oct 93   3

Syrups (See Malt Syrup; Maple Syrup)

Tabbooleh
Bulgur for Tabbooleh (S&R) . . . . . . Jul/Aug 94   32
Real Tabbooleh . . . . Jul/Aug 94   9

TABBOOLEH . . . . Jul/Aug 94   9

Tamales
FRESH CORN TAMALES WITH TOMATILLO-
CHILE SAUCE . . . . Jul/Aug 94   14
SUBSTITUTE MASA FOR
TAMALES . . . . Jul/Aug 94   15
Tamales, Making . . . . Jul/Aug 94   15

Tamari (See Soy Sauce)

Tangerines
SPICY TANGERINE SAUCE . . . . May/Jun 93   19

Tapenade
BLACK OLIVE PASTE . . . . Mar/Apr 95   19

Tapioca
What Is Tapioca? . . . . Jul/Aug 95   7

Tarragon
BRAISED BRUSSELS SPROUTS
WITH TARRAGON-MUSTARD
BUTTER . . . . Nov/Dec 95   21
FENNEL AND OLIVE SALAD WITH CREAMY
TARRAGON VINAIGRETTE . . . May/Jun 95   23
FRENCH-STYLE POTATO SALAD WITH
TARRAGON VINAIGRETTE . . . . Jul/Aug 94   7
GREEN BEANS WITH TOASTED WALNUTS
AND TARRAGON . . . . Nov/Dec 96   7
ROASTED BUTTERFLIED CHICKEN
WITH TARRAGON-MUSTARD PAN
SAUCE . . . . Sep/Oct 94   25
SHIITAKE-STUFFED SALMON ROLLS WITH
TARRAGON-TOMATO SAUCE . . Jul/Aug 95   11
TARRAGON MAYONNAISE . . . . . Jul/Aug 97   10

Tarts (See Pies and Tarts)

Tea
Chinese Tea and Spices for
Smoking (S&R) . . . . May/Jun 95   32
Exotic Teas by Mail (S&R) . . . . . . Mar/Apr 94   32
Fresh Water for Tea (Notes) . . . . . . Nov/Dec 95   3
Mesh Tea Balls (S&R) . . . . May/Jun 95   32
Specialty Teas (S&R) . . . . Mar/Apr 96   32
STOVE-TOP TEA-SMOKED
CHICKEN . . . . May/Jun 95   15
Tea Bag Squeezer (Notes,

Cook's Illustrated 1993–1997 Index

What Is It?) . . . . Nov/Dec 96   3
Tea-Smoked Chicken . . . . May/Jun 95   14

Techniques

all-purpose tips

Adapting Your Carving Board
   (to Collect Juices) (QT) . . . . Jul/Aug 97   5
Blanching Salted Nuts (QT) . . . . . . Sep/Oct 97   5
Cheese Grating (QT) . . . . Sep/Oct 95   4
Clarifying Broth (Notes) . . . . Nov/Dec 96   3
Clarifying Butter (Notes) . . . . Jan/Feb 97   3
Controlling Your Tongs . . . . Sep/Oct 97   4
Creating a Vacuum Seal (QT) . . . . Nov/Dec 94   5
Cookbook Holder, Making (QT) . . . Mar/Apr 95   4
Cooking in Copper (Notes) . . . . Nov/Dec 97   2
Easy Rice Handling and
   Storage (QT) . . . . Sep/Oct 97   4
Filling Salt and Pepper
   Shakers (QT) . . . . Nov/Dec 97   4
Grating Hard Cheeses (QT) . . . . . . Sep/Oct 95   4
Holding Bowl Steady (QT) . . . . Nov/Dec 96   5
Holding Recipe Cards (QT) . . . . . . Mar/Apr 97   5
Instant Cooling Rack (QT) . . . . Sep/Oct 97   5
Keeping a Cookbook Flat (QT) . . . . Mar/Apr 97   4
Keeping Can Tops Afloat (QT) . . . . . Jul/Aug 97   5
Keeping Whipped Cream (Notes) . . Sep/Oct 97   2
Kitchen Timer Memory (Notes) . . . . Jan/Feb 97   2
Lifting Hot Lids (QT) . . . . Nov/Dec 96   4
Lifting Hot Pot Lids (QT) . . . . Mar/Apr 97   5
Listing New Proportions (QT) . . . . . Sep/Oct 97   5
Loosening Small Jar Tops (QT) . . . Nov/Dec 97   5
Making Canned Broth Fat-
   Free (QT) . . . . May/Jun 97   5
Making Extra Counter
   Space (QT) . . . . Nov/Dec 97   5
Milk, Preventing Boil-over (QT) . . . Nov/Dec 96   4
Olives, Pitting (QT) . . . . Sep/Oct 93   5
Oven Reminder (QT) . . . . May/Jun 97   4
Packed Brown Sugar (QT) . . . . Mar/Apr 97   5
Quick Shaker Jar (QT) . . . . Sep/Oct 97   4
Recipe Card Holder (QT) . . . . Mar/Apr 96   5
Recipe Holder (QT) . . . . Nov/Dec 96   5
Rehydrating Dried
   Ingredients (QT) . . . . Nov/Dec 95   5
Stain-Free Plastic
   Containers (QT) . . . . Nov/Dec 97   4
Stir-frying . . . . Mar/Apr 96   19
Stock Freezing (QT) . . . . Jul/Aug 96   3
Stock, Removing Fat From (QT) . . . Sep/Oct 94   4

Testing Ingredient Additions (QT) . . Sep/Oct 97   4
Vanilla Beans, Preparing . . . . Jul/Aug 93   27

baking

Always Ready to Dip and Sweep
   (Flour) . . . . Sep/Oct 97   5
Avoiding Splatters When
   Mixing (QT) . . . . May/Jun 94   4
(Baking) Soda or Powder? The Lift
   Questions . . . . Jan/Feb 97   23
Biscuits, Rolling . . . . May/Jun 93   11
Biscuits, Shaping . . . . May/Jun 93   10
Butter, Cutting for Pastry (QT) . . . May/Jun 94   5
Butter, Cutting Into Flour (QT) . . . . Jan/Feb 95   5
Butter, Melting . . . . Nov/Dec 95   7
Butter, Softening for Mixing (QT) . . Jul/Aug 94   4
Choosing Your Mixing Method . . . . Jan/Feb 97   19
Easy Dusting Technique (QT) . . . . . Jul/Aug 97   4
Egg (Pastry) Doughs Lift Off . . . . . Sep/Oct 97   11
Filling a Pastry Bag (QT) . . . . May/Jun 97   5
Fitting Pastry into Pie Dishes . . . . Sep/Oct 97   10
foil-lining springform pans . . . . Sep/Oct 95   7
Forming and Cooking (Bagel
   Dough) . . . . Sep/Oct 97   15
Freezing Pie Pastry (QT) . . . . Nov/Dec 97   4
greasing pans (QT) . . . . Mar/Apr 95   5
Instant Cooling Rack (QT) . . . . Sep/Oct 97   5
Keeping Dough from Sticking (QT) . Jan/Feb 97   5
Leaving Visual Cues When
   Baking (QT) . . . . Nov/Dec 97   4
Lightening Batters Without
   Waste (QT) . . . . Jul/Aug 97   5
Lining a Loaf Pan . . . . May/Jun 94   19
Loosening a Sticky Mixing
   Bowl (QT) . . . . Nov/Dec 97   5
Measuring Dough Height, (QT) . . . . Sep/Oct 94   5
Measuring Extracts (QT) . . . . Jul/Aug 95   5
Measuring Flour . . . . Sep/Oct 93   6
Measuring Shortening (Notes) . . . . May/Jun 95   2
Measuring Shortening (Notes) . . . . Sep/Oct 94   2
Meringues, Shaping . . . . May/Jun 95   12
New Uses for Your Cake
   Tester (QT) . . . . Jan/Feb 97   5
Packed Brown Sugar (QT) . . . . Mar/Apr 97   5
Parchment Paper Liner,
   Sizing (QT) . . . . May/Jun 93   4
Pastry Bag, Filling (QT) . . . . Jan/Feb 95   4
Puff Pastry, Making Quickest . . . . . Mar/Apr 94   15
Rolling Out Sticky Dough (QT) . . . Mar/Apr 97   5
Testing Ingredient Additions (QT) . . Sep/Oct 97   4

Cook's Illustrated 1993–1997 Index

Water Baths (QT) . . . . Sep/Oct 95   5

Water Baths . . . . Sep/Oct 95   8

(The Water in) Pastry Dough

   (Notes) . . . . Sep/Oct 97   3

barbecuing

Barbecued Ribs, Making

   Homemade . . . . Jul/Aug 94   11

Essential Steps to Homemade Pork

   Barbecue . . . . Jul/Aug 97   20

How to Make Authentic Barbecued

   Ribs at Home . . . . Jul/Aug 94   10

beef

Burger Shaping . . . . Jul/Aug 95   15

Carving Prime Ribs . . . . Nov/Dec 95   13

Freezing Ground Beef (QT) . . . . . . May/Jun 97   4

Raw Beef Safety (Notes) . . . . Jan/Feb 97   3

Steak, Carving Two-Part . . . . May/Jun 96   24

Steak, Checking For Doneness . . . May/Jun 96   24

Steak, Cuts for . . . . May/Jun 96   24

Stew, Cuts for . . . . Jan/Feb 96   19

Tying Prime Ribs . . . . Nov/Dec 95   13

bread

Bread Blowout (on Tearing During Baking)

   (Notes) . . . . Mar/Apr 97   2

Bread Crumbs . . . . May/Jun 95   25

Bread Dough, Braiding . . . . Mar/Apr 94   4

Bread Shapes, Forming . . . . Jan/Feb 95   16

Cleaning Up After

   Breadmaking (QT) . . . . Nov/Dec 96   4

Dinner Rolls, Preparing the Dough . . Nov/Dec 93   15

Dinner Rolls, Shaping . . . . Nov/Dec 93   16

Draft-Free Rising Location (QT) . . . Jan/Feb 96   4

How to Shape and Bake a Loaf . . . May/Jun 96   10

Making Smaller Bread

   Loaves (QT) . . . . Jan/Feb 96   5

Pita Slicing (QT) . . . . May/Jun 96   5

Proofing Bread (QT), ... Nov/Dec 96   4

The Right Speed to Knead (Notes) . Jan/Feb 97   2

Shaping Dough . . . . Charter Issue   25

Shaping Dough for Rising . . . . Jan/Feb 95   8

Slashing Tops of Loaves . . . . Charter Issue   23

Slashing Tops of Loaves (QT) . . . . Nov/Dec 94   5

cakes

Angel Food Cake, Unmolding . . . Charter Issue   12

Cake Filling Prevented From Bleeding

   Into Frosting (QT) . . . . Mar/Apr 95   4

Chiffon Cake Making . . . . May/Jun 96   7

Genoise . . . . Nov/Dec 95   10

Jelly Roll, Making . . . . Jan/Feb 94   15

Layers, Making Even (QT) . . . . . . May/Jun 95   4

Layers, Moving (QT) . . . . Sep/Oct 94   5

Leveling a Cake Layer (QT) . . . . . Mar/Apr 96   4

Magi-Cake Strips,

   replicating (QT) . . . . Mar/Apr 95   5

Measuring Cake Batter (QT) . . . . . Jul/Aug 94   5

Pudding Cakes . . . . Jan/Feb 95   25

Removing From Bundt Pan (QT) . . . Nov/Dec 96   5

cast-ironware

How to Season a Cast-Iron Pan . . May/Jun 97   9

Can You Deglaze a Cast-Iron Pan? May/Jun 97   8

chocolate

Chopping a Block of

   Chocolate (QT) . . . . Mar/Apr 94   4

Elegant Dipped

   Strawberries (QT) . . . . Jul/Aug 97   5

Making Perfect Dipped

   Berries (QT) . . . . Mar/Apr 96   5

Melting and Holding

   Chocolate (QT) . . . . Jan/Feb 94   4

The Perfect Chocolate Truffle . . . . Nov/Dec 97   25

coffee

Cleaning a Burr Coffee Grinder,

   Carefully (Notes) . . . . Jan/Feb 97   2

Coffee Grinders, Cleaning (QT) . . . Jul/Aug 95   4

For Dirty Blade-Type Coffee

   Grinders (Notes) . . . . Jan/Feb 97   2

Undiluted Ice Drinks (Notes) . . . . . Jul/Aug 97   2

cookies

Bar Cookies, Chocolate-

   Coating (QT) . . . . May/Jun 96   4

Bar Cookies, Cutting (QT) . . . . Mar/Apr 96   5

Bookie Crumbs, Making (QT) . . . . . Sep/Oct 94   5

Cookies (QT) . . . . Nov/Dec 94   5

Icebox, Forming (QT) . . . . Mar/Apr 95   5

Indenting Cookies for Filling (QT) . Nov/Dec 97   4

Macaroon Shaping . . . . Sep/Oct 96   7

Marble Cookie Making . . . . Nov/Dec 96   19

Shaping . . . . Nov/Dec 93   8

Shaping Rounds Without a

   Rolling Pin . . . . Nov/Dec 96   20

Solving the Mystery of the Chewy Chocolate

   Chip Cookie . . . . Jan/Feb 96   22

decorating cakes

Basket Weave . . . . May/Jun 95   17

Borders . . . . May/Jun 95   17

Cakes . . . . Jul/Aug 94   23

Chocolate Curls . . . . Mar/Apr 96   17

Chocolate Shards . . . . Mar/Apr 96   17

Cook's Illustrated 1993–1997 Index

Chocolate Splinters . . . . Mar/Apr 96   17
Citrus Spirals (QT) . . . . Jul/Aug 95   5
Decorating Tube, Making a
  Quick (QT) . . . . Mar/Apr 94   5
Filling and Holding Pastry Bags . . May/Jun 95   16
Fine Chocolate Shavings . . . . Mar/Apr 96   16
Fitting Pastry Bags with Plastic
  Coupler . . . . May/Jun 95   16
Giving Cakes a Silky Look (QT) . . . Jul/Aug 95   4
Pastry Bag Filling (QT) . . . . Sep/Oct 96   5
Piping Cone, Making a
  Disposable (QT) . . . . Nov/Dec 93   5
Piping From Pastry Bag (QT) . . . . Sep/Oct 95   5
Quick Cake Decorations (QT) . . . . . Jul/Aug 97   4
Rosettes and Stars . . . . May/Jun 95   17
Side Swags . . . . May/Jun 95   16
Thick Chocolate Shavings . . . . Mar/Apr 96   16
Torting (QT) . . . . Jan/Feb 94   5
Writing . . . . May/Jun 95   17

decorating cookies
Crimped Edge Decoration . . . . Nov/Dec 96   17
Decorating (QT) . . . . Nov/Dec 94   5
Diamond Cut Decoration . . . . Nov/Dec 96   16
Floral Design Decoration . . . . Nov/Dec 96   16
Geometric Design Decoration . . . . . Nov/Dec 96   17
Gingerbread Coiffure (QT) . . . . Nov/Dec 97   4
Grooved Look Decoration . . . . Nov/Dec 96   16
Polka-Dot Effect . . . . Nov/Dec 96   16
Quilted Look . . . . Nov/Dec 96   17
Ricrac Design Decoration . . . . Nov/Dec 96   17
Spiraled Effect . . . . Nov/Dec 96   17
Star Pattern Decoration . . . . Nov/Dec 96   17
Subtle Groove Decoration . . . . Nov/Dec 96   16
Tailored Crosshatch Decoration . . . Nov/Dec 96   17
Waffle Texture Decoration . . . . Nov/Dec 96   16
Wavy Pleats Decoration . . . . Nov/Dec 96   17
Zigzag Look Decoration . . . . Nov/Dec 96   17

eggs
Chopping Hard-Boiled (QT) . . . . . . Jul/Aug 96   4
Custard, Judging Doneness . . . . . . Jul/Aug 93   27
Folding Egg Whites Gently (QT) . . Nov/Dec 95   4
Folding in Beaten Whites . . . . Sep/Oct 96   19
Hollandaise Sauce, Saving
  "Broken" (QT) . . . . May/Jun 95   4
Omelets . . . . Sep/Oct 93   21
Separating . . . . Jul/Aug 93   5
Setting, for a Frittata . . . . Mar/Apr 96   11
Storing Poached Eggs (QT) . . . . . . May/Jun 97   4
Whites, Beating . . . . Charter Issue   11

equipment
Food Processor, Pouring From (QT) . . Jul/Aug 96   4
Food Processor Lid Kept
  Clean (QT) . . . . Sep/Oct 96   4
Steamer Set Up (QT) . . . . Jan/Feb 96   5
Tong Storage (QT) . . . . Sep/Oct 96   4
Using and Rating Immersion
  Blenders (ER) . . . . May/June 93   28

fish
Breading Fillets . . . . Sep/Oct 95   23
Cleaning . . . . Mar/Apr 95   16
Freezing (QT) . . . . Nov/Dec 94   4
Keeping Fresh (QT) . . . . Jan/Feb 94   4
Monkfish, Preparing (QT) . . . . Sep/Oct 93   4
Removing Pin Bones from
  Salmon . . . . Jul/Aug 97   6
Roundfish, Filleting . . . . Charter Issue   2
Salmon, Boning . . . . Jul/Aug 93   24
Salmon Rolls . . . . Jul/Aug 95   10
Scaling (QT) . . . . May/Jun 94   20
Skinning Fillets . . . . Sep/Oct 95   24
Trimmings Prepared for Stock . . . . Nov/Dec 94   20

fruit
Apple Coring . . . . Sep/Oct 95   12
Apples, Coring Quarters (QT) . . . . . Jan/Feb 96   4
Apples, Peeling, Coring, and
  Slicing . . . . Nov/Dec 97   22
Berries, Dipping (QT) . . . . Mar/Apr 96   5
Citrus Fruit . . . . Jan/Feb 97   16
Citrus Rinds, Grating . . . . May/Jun 94   4
Citrus Rinds, Mincing . . . . Charter Issue   9
Coconut, Opening and Cleaning . . . Mar/Apr 94   21
Cranberries, Halving (QT) . . . . Jan/Feb 95   4
Dried, Cutting up (QT) . . . . Jan/Feb 96   5
Lemon Peel, Grating . . . . May/Jun 93   51
Lemons, Juicing (QT) . . . . May/Jun 95   5
Mangoes, Cutting (QT) . . . . Jul/Aug 93   4
Melon Carving . . . . Jul/Aug 95   16
Melons, Peeling and Seeding (QT) . . Jul/Aug 94   4
Oranges, Segmenting . . . . Charter Issue   3
Pears, Coring . . . . May/Jun 93   25
Persimmon, Preparing (QT) . . . . . . Nov/Dec 94   5
Pineapple, Slicing . . . . May/Jun 93   25
Poaching . . . . May/Jun 93   24
Pomegranate Juicing (QT) . . . . Jan/Feb 95   5
Pomegranate Seeds, Extracting . . . Nov/Dec 93   4
Rhubarb, Stringing (QT) . . . . May/Jun 93   4
Strawberries, Keeping Fresh (QT) . . . Jul/Aug 96   3
Tropical, Preparing . . . . Jan/Feb 94   16

Cook's Illustrated 1993–1997 Index

Watermelon, Seeding (QT) . . . . Jul/Aug 94   4

garlic

Blanching (QT) . . . . Jul/Aug 96   3

Chopping with Herbs (QT) . . . . May/Jun 94   5

Crushing (QT) . . . . Sep/Oct 94   5

Hand-Pureeing Garlic (QT) . . . . . . Jan/Feb 97   4

New Uses for Cheese Slicer (QT) . . Jan/Feb 97   4

Peeling (QT), ... Sep/Oct 96   5

Pureeing (QT) . . . . Nov/Dec 95   5

Roasting. Sep/Oct 93   20

Separating and Peeling Large
  Amounts (QT) . . . . Jan/Feb 95   5

ginger

Juice, Extracting (QT) . . . . Jul/Aug 93   5

Mincing . . . . May/Jun 93   21

Peeling (QT). . . . . Sep/Oct 96   5

grilling

Arranging the Fire . . . . Jul/Aug 97   16

Building a Two-Level Fire . . . . May/Jun 96   23

Checking Fuel Level . . . . Jul/Aug 97   17

Chimney Starter (S&R) . . . . Jul/Aug 97   32

Chimney Starter (S&R) . . . . Jul/Aug 93   32

Coating Grilled Food (QT) . . . . Jan/Feb 97   5

Dousing flames . . . . May/Jun 96   24

Fish . . . . Jul/Aug 97   17

Fuels . . . . Jul/Aug 97   16

Grill-Roasting Over Charcoal . . . . . Jul/Aug 93   19

Grill-Roasting Over Gas . . . . Jul/Aug 93   20

Lobster . . . . Jul/Aug 97   17

Maintaining (grill) Temperature . . Jul/Aug 97   15

Onions . . . . Jul/Aug 97   17

Preventing Sticking . . . . Jul/Aug 97   17

With Skewers . . . . Jul/Aug 97   17

Smoke and Fire (hardwood
  charcoals) (S&R) . . . . Jul/Aug 97   32

Starting the Fire . . . . Jul/Aug 97   16

Steaks (on Cast-iron Grate) (Notes). . Jul/Aug 97   3

Vegetables . . . . Jul/Aug 97   17

ham

Country Ham, Trimming and
  Stuffing . . . . Nov/Dec 93   13

Half-ham, Carving (QT) . . . . Charter Issue   5

Preparing for Cooking . . . . Nov/Dec 96   13

Simmered, Boning . . . . Nov/Dec 96   13

Whole Ham Carving (QT) . . . . . . Charter Issue   5

herbs

Basil, Bruising for Pesto . . . . Jul/Aug 96   29

Bouquet, Garni (QT) . . . . Nov/Dec 94   4

Chopping Small Quantities (QT) . . Nov/Dec 94   4

Dried, Making the Best Use
  of (QT) . . . . May/Jun 95   5

Drying (QT) . . . . Sep/Oct 94   5

Ginger, Mincing (QT) . . . . May/Jun 96   4

Keeping Fresh (QT) . . . . Jul/Aug 96   3

Keeping Fresh (QT) . . . . Mar/Apr 96   5

knives

Cleaver Quick Tips . . . . Sep/Oct 97   17

Cutting Techniques . . . . Jan/Feb 96   17

Gripping . . . . Mar/Apr 94   27

Guiding Hand . . . . Jan/Feb 96   16

Knife Grips . . . . Jan/Feb 96   16

Mincing with a Vegetable
  Cleaver . . . . Sep/Oct 97   17

Sharpening by Hand . . . . Mar/Apr 97   28

Slicing with a Meat Cleaver . . . . . . Sep/Oct 97   16

Slicing with a Vegetable Cleaver . . Sep/Oct 97   16

Steeling . . . . Mar/Apr 94   28

Will Electric Sharpeners Reduce the
  Life of Your Knives? . . . . Mar/Apr 97   28

lamb

Lamb Shanks, Trimming. . . . . Jan/Feb 95   18

Leg of Lamb, Cleaning, Boning and
  Carving . . . . Mar/Apr 94   9

Leg of Lamb, Tying . . . . Mar/Apr 94   8

Leg of Lamb, Tying . . . . May/Jun 93   23

measuring

Glass measuring cups (QT) . . . . . . Sep/Oct 96   5

How to Measure (Notes). . . . . Mar/Apr 95   2

Keeping Count (of Many Measurements)
  (Notes) . . . . Jul/Aug 97   3

Measuring Cake Batter (QT) . . . . . Jul/Aug 94   5

Measuring Dough Height (QT) . . . . Sep/Oct 94   5

Measuring Extracts (QT) . . . . Jul/Aug 95   5

Measuring Flour (Notes) . . . . Jul/Aug 95   3

Measuring Liquid
  Ingredients (QT) . . . . Sep/Oct 96   5

Measuring Shortening (Notes) . . . . May/Jun 95   2

Measuring Shortening (Notes) . . . . Sep/Oct 94   2

Packed Brown Sugar (QT) . . . . Mar/Apr 97   5

Portioning Tomato Paste (QT) . . . . Jan/Feb 96   4

muffins

Avoiding Soggy Muffin
  Bottoms (QT) . . . . Jan/Feb 97   5

Do Muffin Papers Help? . . . . Jan/Feb 97   19

Muffins . . . . Sep/Oct 93   8

pasta

Cavatelli, Shaping . . . . Jan/Feb 94   20

Fusilli, Shaping . . . . Jan/Feb 94   20

Cook's Illustrated 1993–1997 Index

Heating Bowl for (QT) . . . . Nov/Dec 94   4
Kneading Dough in Food Processor . . Sep/Oct 93   15
Lasagne Construction Tips . . . . Nov/Dec 94   10
Orechiette, Shaping . . . . Jan/Feb 94   20
Ravioli Making . . . . Sep/Oct 93   17
Rolling With a Machine . . . . Sep/Oct 93   16
Testing Pasta Doneness (QT) . . . . . May/Jun 97   4
Tortellini Making . . . . Sep/Oct 93   17
Twisted Tortellini Making . . . . Sep/Oct 93   17

pies

Bold Crosshatch Edging . . . . Sep/Oct 96   16
Checkerboard Edging . . . . Sep/Oct 96   16
Crimped Edging . . . . Sep/Oct 96   17
Crumb Crusts (QT) . . . . Jan/Feb 95   4
Crust Rims, Protecting (QT) . . . . . . Jul/Aug 95   4
Crusts . . . . Charter Issue   17
Crusts (QT) . . . . May/Jun 95   5
Crusts (QT) . . . . Jan/Feb 95   4
Crusts for Cream Pies . . . . Mar/Apr 96   23
Crusts for Pecan Pies . . . . Nov/Dec 95   7
Crust Transfers (QT) . . . . Nov/Dec 95   5
Dough Moistening (QT) . . . . Jul/Aug 95   5
Easy Decorative Pie Edgings . . . . . Sep/Oct 96   16
Fine Crosshatch Edging . . . . Sep/Oct 96   17
Fluted Edging . . . . Sep/Oct 96   17
Free-Form Pastry Shells, Making . . May/Jun 94   15
Herringbone Edging . . . . Sep/Oct 96   17
Horizontal Crosshatch Edging . . . . Sep/Oct 96   17
Lemon Meringue Tips . . . . Nov/Dec 94   24
Moving Pastry (QT) . . . . May/Jun 94   4
Rope Edging . . . . Sep/Oct 96   17
Rolling and Transferring Pie
   Dough (QT) . . . . Jul/Aug 96   4
Rolling Out Perfect Cookie (or pie)
   Dough (QT) . . . . Jan/Feb 96   5
Rounded Points Edging . . . . Sep/Oct 96   16
Scalloped Edging . . . . Sep/Oct 96   16
Sharp Points Edging . . . . Sep/Oct 96   17
Sheaves of Wheat Edging . . . . Sep/Oct 96   16
Triple Scallop Edging . . . . Sep/Oct 96   16
Tarte Tatin, Assembling . . . . Jan/Feb 96   15
Tartlets (QT) . . . . Mar/Apr 96   5

pork

Preparing (Pork) Tenderloin . . . . . . Jul/Aug 97   19
Preparing the Roast (Rack of Pork) Nov/Dec 97   13

poultry

Carving, Chinese-style . . . . Sep/Oct 95   11
Chicken, Butchering . . . . May/Jun 94   7
Chicken, Butterflying . . . . Sep/Oct 94   24

Chicken, Carving . . . . Charter Issue   26
Chicken, Frying (QT) . . . . Nov/Dec 95   5
Chicken, Trussing . . . . May/Jun 93   3
Chicken, Weighting Butterflied . . . Sep/Oct 94   25
Chicken Breast, Butterflying (QT) . . May/Jun 94   5
Chicken Breast, Cutting . . . . May/Jun 93   20
Chicken Breast, Fanning . . . . Sep/Oct 93   11
Chicken Breast, Preparing for
   Sauté . . . . Sep/Oct 93   10
Chicken Thigh, Boning (QT) . . . . . . Nov/Dec 94   4
Cutting and Boning . . . . May/Jun 93   16
Drumstick Tendons Removal (QT) . . Nov/Dec 96   5
Duck, Preparing for Air Drying . . . . Sep/Oct 93   13
Goose, Preparing and Stuffing . . . . Nov/Dec 94   8
How to Cut Up a Chicken . . . . Mar/Apr 97   7
Important Steps in Roasting Hens . Jul/Aug 97   21
Preflavoring Frozen Chicken
   Breasts (QT) . . . . Sep/Oct 97   5
Preparing Steamed/Roasted . . . . . . Sep/Oct 95   10
Preparing the Chicken (for Chicken
   Salad) . . . . Jul/Aug 97   8
The Real Lowdown on Turkey
   Safety . . . . Nov/Dec 97   9
Stabilizing Stuffed Chicken
   Breasts (QT) . . . . Nov/Dec 96   4
Steps for Making Chicken Sausage Mar/Apr 96   13
Stuffing Removal (QT) . . . . Jul/Aug 95   4
Stuffing the Skin . . . . May/Jun 93   17
Temperature Taking (QT) . . . . May/Jun 94   5
Turkey and Goose, How to Carve . . Nov/Dec 94   16
Turkey Trussing . . . . Nov/Dec 93   18
Wishbone Removal Before
   Roasting . . . . Jan/Feb 96   9

roasting

Adapting Your Carving Board (to Collect
   Juices) (QT) . . . . Jul/Aug 97   5
Basket Roasting Rack (S&R) . . . . . . Jan/Feb 97   32
Customizing a Roasting Pan . . . Charter Issue   27
A Different Take on Vertical
   Roasters . . . . May/Jun 97   2
Important Steps in Roasting
   Hens . . . . Jul/Aug 97   21
Preparing a Lobster for Roasting . May/Jun 97   16
Preparing a Turkey Breast for
   Roasting . . . . Jan/Feb 97   25
Preparing the Roast (Rack of Pork) Nov/Dec 97   13
Rating Roasting Racks for
   Poultry (ER) . . . . Jan/Feb 97   28
Roasts, Tying . . . . Jan/Feb 94   7

Cook's Illustrated 1993–1997 Index

Roasts (Cheap), Cuts for . . . . Sep/Oct 96   11
Roast/Turkey Lifters . . . . Nov/Dec 97   9
Stuffing and Roasting The
    Big Bird (The Turkey) . . . . Nov/Dec 97   9
Tying a Roast . . . . May/Jun 95   21
Tying Prime Ribs . . . . Nov/Dec 95   13
We're Not High on Vertical
    Roasters . . . . Jan/Feb 97   28

safety
Raw Beef Safety (Notes) . . . . Jan/Feb 97   3
Raw Fish Safety (Notes) . . . . Jan/Feb 97   3
The Real Lowdown on Turkey
    Safety . . . . Nov/Dec 97   9
Safe Bagel Slicing (QT) . . . . Sep/Oct 97   4

seasonings and spices
Cooking Spices: a Matter of
    Temperature . . . . Jan/Feb 97   7
Cracking Peppercorns
    Neatly (QT) . . . . Jul/Aug 97   4
Fennel Seeds, Chopping (QT) . . . . . Mar/Apr 95   4
Filling Salt and Pepper
    Shakers (QT) . . . . Nov/Dec 97   4
Getting The Most Mustard (QT) . . . Jul/Aug 97   5
Grinding Spices . . . . Jan/Feb 97   7
Saffron, Pulverizing (QT) . . . . May/Jun 95   5
Spices, Removing Easily (QT) . . . . May/Jun 95   4
Spice Funnel (QT) . . . . Mar/Apr 97   5
Taming Toasted Seeds (QT) . . . . . . Nov/Dec 97   5
Zest . . . . Jan/Feb 97   16

shellfish
Cleaning Shrimp, Squid, and Soft-
    Shell Crab . . . . May/Jun 94   16
Crabs, Cleaning Soft-Shell . . . . May/Jun 95   7
Lobster, Keeping Tails
    Straight (QT) . . . . May/Apr 94   5l
Lobster, Preparing and Eating . . . . Jul/Aug 93   16
Lobster, Preparing for Stew . . . . . . Nov/Dec 94   21
Oyster, Shucking (QT) . . . . Charter Issue   4
Scallop Cooking . . . . Mar/Apr 96   7
Scallop Muscle Removal . . . . Mar/Apr 96   6
Shrimp, Peeling and Deveining . . . May/Jun 94   17
Shrimp, Preparing for The Grill . . . Jul/Aug 94   19
Soft-Shell Crabs, Cleaning . . . . May/Jun 94   17
Spices, Crushing (QT) . . . . Sep/Oct 94   5
Squid Cleaning . . . . May/Jun 94   16
Shrimp, Extending Quantities (QT) Jul/Aug 95   4

smoking
Smoke-Cooking . . . . Jul/Aug 95   19
Stove-Top Smoking . . . . May/Jun 95   15

stovetop
Achieving Low Flame (QT) . . . . Mar/Apr 97   5
Crepe Pan Technique . . . . Mar/Apr 97   15
Different Pans for Different
    Stoves? . . . . May/Jun 97   25
Hollandaise Sauce, Saving
    "Broken" (QT) . . . . May/Jun 95   4
Stove-Top Smoking . . . . May/Jun 95   15
Thickening Macaroni and
    Cheese (Notes) . . . . May/Jun 97   2

temperature reading/testing
Meat Thermometer, Testing (QT) . . May/Jun 95   5
Temperature Taking (QT) . . . . May/Jun 94   5
Thermometer, Reading (QT) . . . . . . Jul/Aug 94   5

vegetables
Artichokes, Preparing for
    Steaming . . . . May/Jun 94   11
Artichokes, Removing Heart . . . . . May/Jun 94   11
Artichokes, Trimming and
    Coring (QT) . . . . May/Jun 93   5
Asparagus, Roll Cutting . . . . May/Jun 93   6
Avocados, Extracting Meat
    From (QT) . . . . Sep/Oct 94   4
Avocados, Pitting (QT) . . . . Sep/Oct 93   5
Basil, Keeping It Green (Notes) . . . May/Jun 97   3
Bean "Frenching" . . . . Nov/Dec 96   7
Beets, Peeling (QT) . . . . Mar/Apr 94   5
Bell Peppers, Roasting (QT) . . . . . . May/Jun 95   4
Bell Peppers, Trimming (QT) . . . . . May/Jun 93   4
Broccoli, Keeping It Fresh (QT) . . . . Jan/Feb 97   4
Broccoli, Quick Prep . . . . Sep/Oct 97   8
Brussels Sprouts, Preparing . . . . . . Nov/Dec 95   20
Brussels Sprouts, Preparing (QT) . . Jan/Feb 94   5
Cabbages, Removing Leaves (QT) . . Sep/Oct 95   4
Cabbages, Shredding . . . . Jul/Aug 95   13
Cauliflower, Breaking Into
    Florets (QT) . . . . Sep/Oct 93   5
Celery, Chopping (QT) . . . . Nov/Dec 94   5
chiffonading . . . . Jul/Aug 94   16
Chile Pepper Handling (QT) . . . . . . Nov/Dec 95   4
Chiles, Dried, Cutting and
    Seeding (QT) . . . . Sep/Oct 93   4
Chiles, Fresh, Seeding (QT) . . . . . . Mar/Apr 94   4
Corn, Double-Cutting . . . . Jul/Aug 93   9
Corn, Grating and Scraping . . . . . . Jul/Aug 93   9
Corn, Silking Without Husking . . . . Jul/Aug 95   22
Cucumber, Dicing . . . . Charter Issue   8
Cucumbers, Salting and Draining . . Jul/Aug 97   11
Cucumbers, Seeding (QT) . . . . Jul/Aug 93   4

Cook's Illustrated 1993–1997 Index

Dégorger (Notes) . . . . Sep/Oct 97   3
Dicing . . . . Jul/Aug 94   17
Eggplant, Male Vs. Female (QT) . . May/Jun 93   5
Eggplant, Squeezing Moisture
    From (QT). . . . . Sep/Oct 94   4
Fava Bean Preparation (QT) . . . . . . Jul/Aug 95   5
Fennel Preparation . . . . May/Jun 96   19
Fennel, Trimming and Slicing (QT) . Sep/Oct 94   21
French Fries, Better (Notes) . . . . . . Jan/Feb 95   2
Grating With Citrus Zester (QT) . . May/Jun 96   5
Greens, Drying (QT) . . . . Sep/Oct 95   4
Greens, Drying Cooked (QT) . . . . . Mar/Apr 97   5
Greens, Squeezing Water From . . . May/Jun 95   4
Greens, Stemming . . . . Jan/Feb 95   14
Greens, Stemming . . . . Sep/Oct 94   21
Greens, Stemming and
    Cutting (QT) . . . . Nov/Dec 93   4
Grilling Vegetables . . . . Jul/Aug 97   16
Guacamole Prepared Quickly (QT) May/Jun 96   5
How To Cut Vegetables . . . . Jul/Aug 94   16
Jicama, Preparing (QT) . . . . Jul/Aug 94   5
Julienning . . . . Jul/Aug 94   16
Leeks, Cleaning (QT) . . . . Jul/Aug 93   4
Leeks, Cutting . . . . Charter Issue   8
Leeks, Trimming and Cleaning . . . Mar/Apr 95   15
Lettuce, Corning and
    Washing (QT) . . . . Jan/Feb 94   4
Mushrooms, Cleaning (QT) . . . . . . Jan/Feb 95   4
Mushrooms, Making Room In (QT) . Jul/Aug 97   4
Mushrooms, Rehydrating
    Dried (QT) . . . . Jan/Feb 97   4
Mushrooms, Submerging
    Rehydrated (QT) . . . . Nov/Dec 97   5
Mushrooms, Slicing (QT) . . . . Nov/Dec 94   5
Onion Peeling (QT) . . . . Sep/Oct 96   4
Onions, Dicing (QT) . . . . Charter Issue   5
Parsnips, Preparing . . . . Sep/Oct 94   9
Pearl Onions, Preparing (QT) . . . . Mar/Apr 94   5
Peppers, Preparing for
    Stuffing (QT) . . . . Jan/Feb 97   5
Pepper Roasting . . . . May/Jun 96   21
Peppers, Roasted, Peeling and
    Seeding (QT). . . . . Jul/Aug 93   5
Potato Chips, Herbed, Making (QT) Mar/Apr 94   5
Potato Preparation for French
    Fries . . . . Jul/Aug 96   13
Potatoes, Retrieving Baked (QT) . . May/Jun 96   5
Pumpkin and Winter Squash,
    Cleaning (QT). . . . . Sep/Oct 96   4

Roll-Cut . . . . May/Jun 93   20
Root, Cutting for Roasting. . . . . . . Jan/Feb 94   11
Root, Slicing (QT) . . . . May/Jun 94   5
Scallion Brushes, Making . . . . Sep/Oct 93   4
Shallot, Dicing (QT) . . . . Jan/Feb 94   5
Shredding. . . . . May/Jun 93   20
Slicing . . . . Jul/Aug 94   16
Slicing . . . . May/Jun 93   20
Tomatoes, Cutting Whole
    Canned (Notes) . . . . May/Jun 97   2
Tomatoes, Dicing . . . . Jul/Aug 93   15
Tomato Peeling (QT) . . . . May/Jun 96   4
Tomatoes, Peeling (QT) . . . . Jul/Aug 94   5
Tomatoes, Peeling . . . . Jul/Aug 93   15
Tomatoes, Peeling and
    Seeding (QT) . . . . Charter Issue   4
Tomatoes Prepared for Drying . . . . Sep/Oct 96   20
Tomatoes, Skinning (QT) . . . . Mar/Apr 95   5
Tomato Slicing (QT). . . . . Jul/Aug 96   4
Vary Slices of Long Vegetables. . . . May/Jun 93   20
Vidalia Onion Storage (QT) . . . . . . May/Jun 95   5
Weighting Evenly (QT) . . . . Jan/Feb 95   5
Wilting Cabbage Leaves for
    Stuffing (Notes). . . . . May/Jun 97   3
Winter Squash Slicing (QT) . . . . . May/Jun 96   4
Zucchini, Shredding. . . . . Jul/Aug 95   8
Zucchini, Slicing . . . . Jul/Aug 95   8

Thickeners

Cornstarch Connection . . . . Nov/Dec 93   9
Cornstarch Problems (Notes). . . . . Sep/Oct 94   3
Potato Starch (Notes) . . . . Jan/Feb 95   2

Thyme

BRAISED CABBAGE WITH PARSLEY AND
    THYME . . . . Sep/Oct 96   9
BRAISED ONIONS WITH RED WINE, THYME,
    AND PANCETTA . . . . Jan/Feb 96   26
CHICKEN IN THE POT WITH CARROTS, MUSH-
    ROOMS, AND THYME. . . . . Sep/Oct 95   19
COUNTRY MUSTARD–SHALLOT SAUCE WITH
    THYME. . . . . May/Jun 95   22
GRILLED ITALIAN VEGETABLES WITH THYME
    AND GARLIC. . . . . Jul/Aug 96   8
QUICK-COOKED CARROTS WITH VINEGAR
    AND THYME . . . . Mar/Apr 96   25
RAISIN COMPOTE WITH ROSEMARY AND
    THYME . . . . Jan/Feb 95   23
ROAST CHICKEN WITH DIJON

Cook's Illustrated 1993–1997 Index

MUSTARD–THYME SAUCE . . . May/Jun 93   28
ROASTED BUTTERNUT SQUASH WITH SHAL-
    LOTS AND THYME . . . . Nov/Dec 94   15
ROASTED POTATOES WITH ONION, BACON,
    AND THYME . . . . Jan/Feb 94   11
TOASTED BREAD CRUMBS WITH MARJORAM,
    THYME, AND LEMON ZEST . . May/Jun 95   25
ZUCCHINI, RED PEPPER, AND TOMATO SAUCE
    WITH THYME AND MINT . . . . . Sep/Oct 94   22

Timing
Kitchen Timer Memory (Notes). . . . Jan/Feb 97   2

Toasters
Building a Better Toaster (ER) . . . . Sep/Oct 94   28
Dualit Toaster (Notes) . . . . Mar/Apr 95   3
More on Dualit Toasters (Notes). . . Nov/Dec 95   2
Top Toasters (S&R) . . . . Sep/Oct 94   32

Tofu
STIR-FRY, MASTER RECIPE
    FOR. . . . . Mar/Apr 96   20

Tomatillos
FRESH CORN TAMALES WITH TOMATILLO
    CHILE SAUCE. . . . . Jul/Aug 94   14

Tomatoes
AND CILANTRO. . . . . Sep/Oct 94   21
AND GARLIC . . . . May/Jun 94   12
Another Kind of Pomi Tomatoes
    (Notes) . . . . Sep/Oct 97   2
BEEF STEW WITH TOMATOES, CINNAMON,
    AND CLOVES . . . . Jan/Feb 96   20
BEEF STEW WITH TOMATOES, ORANGE ZEST,
    AND OLIVES. . . . . Jan/Feb 96   20
BRAISED ARTICHOKES WITH TOMATOES
BREAD SALAD WITH TOMATOES, HERBS, AND
    RED ONIONS . . . . Sep/Oct 95   14
BRUSCHETTA WITH TOMATOES AND
    BASIL. Sep/Oct 96   8
CHICKEN IN THE POT WITH TOMATOES,
    BLACK OLIVES, AND CAPERS . Sep/Oct 95   19
CLASSIC RED TABLE SALSA. . . . Jul/Aug 96   21
Crushed Can Tomatoes
    Evaluated (BT) . . . . Mar/Apr 97   26
Cutting Whole Canned Tomatoes
    (Notes). . . . . May/Jun 97   2
Dicing Tomatoes . . . . Jul/Aug 93   15

Easily Skin Tomatoes (QT). . . . . . Mar/Apr 95   5
Freezing and Peeling Tomatoes
    (Notes) . . . . Jul/Aug 94   2
FRESH TOMATO PIZZA WITH ARUGULA AND
    PROSCIUTTO . . . . May/Jun 95   11
FUSILLI WITH ARUGULA AND TOMATO
    SAUCE. Jan/Feb 94   21
GREEN BEANS BRAISED IN
    TOMATOES . . . . Nov/Dec 96   7
GRILLED BREAD WITH ROASTED GARLIC AND
    FRESH TOMATO SAUCE . . . . . . Sep/Oct 93   19
GRILLED JALAPEÑO SALSA . . . . Jul/Aug 96   21
GRILLED SHRIMP TOPPING WITH ROASTED
    TOMATOES AND FARMER'S
    CHEESE. . . . . May/Jun 93   9
GRILLED ZUCCHINI SALAD WITH TOMATOES
    AND BASIL . . . . Jul/Aug 95   9
HEARTY CHICKEN SOUP WITH SHELLS, TOMA-
    TOES, AND ZUCCHINI . . . . Mar/Apr 96   15
MEXICAN-STYLE SALSA CRUDA Jul/Aug 93   14
Muir Glen Diced Tomatoes (S&R) . May/Jun 97   32
MUSSELS STEAMED IN WHITE WINE WITH
    TOMATO AND BASIL . . . . Nov/Dec 96   15
Paste, Portioning (QT). . . . . Jan/Feb 96   4
Peeling a Few Tomatoes (QT). . . . . May/Jun 96   4
Peeling and Seeding
    Tomatoes (QT) . . . . Charter Issue   4
Peeling Ripe Tomatoes (QT) . . . . . . Jul/Aug 94   5
PITA BREAD SALAD WITH CUCUMBERS,
    CHERRY TOMATOES, AND FRESH
    HERBS. Sep/Oct 95   14
PLUM TOMATO SALSA WITH SHERRY
    VINEGAR. . . . . May/Jun 94   13
QUICK-COOKED TOMATOES WITH
    OLIVE OIL . . . . Mar/Apr 94   26
Ranking Tomatoes . . . . Mar/Apr 97   25
RISOTTO WITH TOMATOES AND
    BASIL . . . . Mar/Apr 94   19
ROASTED TOMATO TOPPING WITH FENNEL
    AND ASIAGO . . . . May/Jun 93   9
Slicing a Tomato (QT) . . . . Jul/Aug 96   4
TENDER GREENS WITH CUMIN, TOMATOES,
    TOMATO BASE WITH POBLANOS AND
    CILANTRO. . . . . Jan/Feb 95   11
Two Ways to Peel Tomatoes. . . . . . . Jul/Aug 93   15
Which Canned Tomatoes Should You
    Buy? (BT) . . . . Mar/Apr 94   24
WHITE BEAN AND TOMATO
    CASSEROLE. . . . . Charter Issue   9

sauces

ALL-PURPOSE TOMATO SAUCE Mar/Apr 94   26
AROMATIC TOMATO SAUCE . . . Mar/Apr 94   26
CLAM SAUCE WITH TOMATOES AND
GARLIC . . . . Mar/Apr 96   9
FRESH TOMATO-HERB SAUCE, MASTER
RECIPE FOR . . . . Jul/Aug 93   14
GARDEN TOMATO SAUCE . . . . . . Sep/Oct 93   18
The Happy Marriage of Sweet and Tart
(in Tomato Sauce) . . . . May/Jun 97   11
LASAGNE WITH HERBED MEATBALLS,
TOMATO SAUCE, AND
MOZZARELLA . . . . Nov/Dec 94   11
POLENTA WITH ITALIAN SAUSAGES AND
TOMATO SAUCE . . . . Jan/Feb 95   21
POTATO GNOCCHI WITH TOMATO-MINT
SAUCE . . . . Mar/Apr 95   10
POTATO GRATIN WITH SWEET PEPPERS AND
TOMATOES . . . . Nov/Dec 95   19
PROVENÇAL TOMATO SAUCE WITH BASIL
AND ORANGE . . . . Sep/Oct 95   24
QUICK-COOKED TOMATOES WITH
OLIVE OIL . . . . Mar/Apr 94   26
QUICK TOMATO SAUCE FOR
PIZZA . . . . May/Jun 95   10
Raw Tomato Sauces . . . . Jul/Aug 93   14
SAUTÉED EGGPLANT IN TOMATO SAUCE
WITH BASIL . . . . Jul/Aug 93   7
SHIITAKE-STUFFED SALMON ROLLS WITH
SIMPLE TOMATO SAUCE . . . . . Nov/Dec 94   11
STEWED TOMATO SAUCE WITH BASIL AND
OLIVE OIL . . . . Mar/Apr 94   26
TARRAGON-TOMATO SAUCE . . . Jul/Aug 95   11
TOMATO-BASIL SAUCE WITH
CAPERS . . . . Sep/Oct 93   11
TOMATO FIREWORKS SAUCE . . May/Jun 93   19
TOMATO-ROSEMARY CREAM
SAUCE . . . . May/Jun 95   22
Tomato Sauces for Pasta . . . . Mar/Apr 94   26
TOMATO SAUCE WITH ANCHOVIES AND
OLIVES . . . . May/Jun 97   11
TOMATO SAUCE WITH ARUGULA AND BLACK
OLIVES . . . . Mar/Apr 95   11
TOMATO SAUCE WITH BACON AND
PARSLEY . . . . May/Jun 97   11
TOMATO SAUCE WITH BELL PEPPERS AND
BALSAMIC VINEGAR . . . . Mar/Apr 95   20
TOMATO SAUCE WITH PORCINI
MUSHROOMS . . . . Jan/Feb 97   15
TOMATO SAUCE WITH TUNA AND GREEN
OLIVES . . . . Mar/Apr 96   9
TOMATO SAUCE WITH VODKA AND
CREAM . . . . May/Jun 97   11
TOMATO YOGURT SAUCE . . . . . . Jul/Aug 93   14
ZUCCHINI, RED PEPPER AND TOMATO SAUCE
WITH THYME AND MINT . . . . . Sep/Oct 94   22

Trifle

ALMOND COOKIES . . . . Nov/Dec 96   9
Classic Trifle . . . . Nov/Dec 96   8
Cleaning the Trifle Bowl (QT) . . . . Nov/Dec 96   4
FRESH RASPBERRY PUREE . . . . Nov/Dec 96   9
LEMON WHIPPED CREAM . . . . . Nov/Dec 96   10
RICH BAKED CUSTARD . . . . Nov/Dec 96   9
SPONGE SHEET CAKE . . . . Nov/Dec 96   9
Trifle Bowl (S&R) . . . . Nov/Dec 96   32

Truffles

CHOCOLATE COCONUT
TRUFFLES . . . . Nov/Dec 97   25
CHOCOLATE NUT TRUFFLES . . Nov/Dec 97   25
The Perfect Chocolate Truffle . . . . Nov/Dec 97   25
PERFECT CHOCOLATE TRUFFLES, MASTER
RECIPE FOR . . . . Nov/Dec 97   25

Tuna

GRILLED TUNA WITH GINGER AND
GARLIC . . . . Jul/Aug 93   12
SICILIAN GRILLED TUNA
STEW . . . . Nov/Dec 94   21
TOMATO SAUCE WITH TUNA AND GREEN
OLIVES . . . . Mar/Apr 96   9

Turkey (*See also Poultry*)

THE BEST GRILL-ROASTED
TURKEY . . . . Nov/Dec 93   21
THE BEST OVEN-ROASTED TURKEY WITH
GIBLET PAN SAUCE . . . . Nov/Dec 93   20
BEST TURKEY GIBLET GRAVY . Nov/Dec 96   24
Grilling the Holiday Bird . . . . Nov/Dec 93   20
The Holiday Turkey Perfected . . . . Nov/Dec 93   18
How to Carve Turkey and Goose . . Nov/Dec 94   16
Internal Temperature-How Much Is
Enough? . . . . Nov/Dec 93   21
Preparing a Turkey Breast for
Roasting . . . . Jan/Feb 97   25
The Real Lowdown on Turkey
Safety . . . . Nov/Dec 97   9

Cook's Illustrated 1993–1997 Index

ROAST BRINED TURKEY BREAST WITH CRISP
SKIN . . . . Jan/Feb 97   25
Roasted Turkey Revisited. . . . . Nov/Dec 95   9
Roast/Turkey Lifters . . . . Nov/Dec 97   9
ROAST TURKEY WITH GIBLET PAN
SAUCE . . . . Nov/Dec 95   9
The Science of Brining . . . . Nov/Dec 93   19
Selecting a Turkey Breast . . . . Jan/Feb 97   24
SMOKED TURKEY BREAST WITH GINGER-
CARDAMOM RUB. . . . . Jul/Aug 95   20
STUFFED ROAST TURKEY . . . . . Nov/Dec 97   9
Stuffing and Roasting the Big
Bird . . . . Nov/Dec 97   9

Turnips
CHICKEN IN THE POT WITH TURNIPS AND
NORTH AFRICAN SPICES . . . . . Sep/Oct 95   19
PICKLED TURNIPS . . . . Sep/Oct 94   19
QUICK-BRAISED BOK CHOY, TURNIPS,
AND WATERCRESS WITH GINGER
AND SOY . . . . Jan/Feb 96   26
ROASTED TURNIPS, SHALLOTS, AND GARLIC
WITH ROSEMARY . . . . Jan/Feb 94   11

Upside-Down Cake
Doing Upside-Down Cake Right . . . Jul/Aug 97   25
Fruit for Upside-Down Cake . . . . . . Jul/Aug 97   25
MASTER RECIPE FOR FRUIT UPSIDE-DOWN
CAKE . . . . Jul/Aug 97   25
Upside-Down Cake Pan (S&R) . . . . Jul/Aug 97   32

Vacuum Seal
Creating a Vacuum Seal (QT). . . . . Nov/Dec 94   5

Vanilla
The Best Homemade Vanilla Ice
Cream. . . . . Jul/Aug 93   26
Homemade Vanilla Extract
(Notes). Nov/Dec 93   2
Rating Vanilla Extracts (BT) . . . . . May/Jun 95   26
Rating Vanilla Ice Creams (BT). . . . Jul/Aug 94   27
SIMPLE VANILLA CAKE . . . . Mar/Apr 94   21
Vanilla Beans, Preparing. . . . . Jul/Aug 93   27
VANILLA-BOURBON PUDDING
CAKE. . . . . Jan/Feb 95   25
VANILLA FROZEN YOGURT . . . . May/Jun 96   15
VANILLA ICE CREAM, MASTER
RECIPE FOR . . . . Jul/Aug 93   27

Veal
BACON-WRAPPED MEAT LOAF WITH BROWN-
SUGAR KETCHUP GLAZE . . . . . Sep/Oct 96   22
BRAISED VEAL BREAST WITH SAUSAGE,
LOAF PAN VARIATION FOR MEAT
LOAF . . . . Sep/Oct 96   22
OLIVE, AND SWISS CHARD
STUFFING (Notes) . . . . Sep/Oct 93   3
Simple Veal Stock (Notes) . . . . Sep/Oct 93   3
Stuffed Veal Breast (Notes). . . . . . . Sep/Oct 93   3

Vegetables (See also specific kinds)
Braised Winter Vegetables . . . . Jan/Feb 96   26
Country Italian Vegetable Pasta
Sauces. . . . . Mar/Apr 95   11
Exotic Produce by Mail (S&R) . . . . Nov/Dec 93   32
Grating with citrus zester (QT) . . . May/Jun 96   5
Great Grilled Vegetables . . . . Jul/Aug 96   8
GRILLED ITALIAN VEGETABLES WITH THYME
AND GARLIC. . . . . Jul/Aug 96   8
Grilling Vegetables . . . . Jul/Aug 97   16
Guide to Marinating for Flavor . . . . Jul/Aug 93   11
HEARTY CHICKEN SOUP WITH ORZO AND
SPRING VEGETABLES . . . . Mar/Apr 96   15
How to Cut Vegetables . . . . Jul/Aug 94   16
Impromptu Steamer (QT) . . . . Sep/Oct 97   5
Improvising Vegetable Soups . . . Charter Issue   28
Japanese Vegetable Shredder
(S&R). . . . . Nov/Dec 94   32
MOROCCAN LAMB BROTH WITH CHICKPEAS
AND VEGETABLES . . . . Mar/Apr 95   13
PAN-BRAISED ROOT VEGETABLES WITH RED
CABBAGE AND ROSEMARY . . . Jan/Feb 96   26
Preparing Vegetables for Lasagne . Sep/Oct 97   7
Pre-Soaking Vegetables (Notes) . . . May/Jun 93   20
PUREED VEGETABLE SOUP, MASTER RECIPE
FOR . . . . Nov/Dec 96   23
Quick-Shred Long, Round
Vegetables. . . . . May/Jun 93   20
Roll-Cut Vegetables . . . . May/Jun 93   20
Sharp Vegetable Peeler (S&R) . . . . Nov/Dec 93   32
Smoke-Cooking Times . . . . Jul/Aug 95   20
SOUP BASE . . . . Charter Issue   29
Spring Vegetable Salads . . . . May/Jun 95   23
SPRING VEGETABLE SOUP WITH EGG NOO-
DLES AND MINT . . . . Charter Issue   29
STIR-FRY, MASTER
RECIPE FOR . . . . Mar/Apr 96   20
SUMMER HARVEST SOUP

WITH BASIL . . . . Charter Issue   29
SUMMER VEGETABLE AND RICE
    STUFFING . . . . Jul/Aug 93   25
Vary Slices of Long Vegetables . . . . May/Jun 93   20
Vegetable Pasta Sauces . . . . Sep/Oct 94   22
The Very Best Beef Stew: The Vegetables
    Last . . . . Jan/Feb 96   20
Weighting Food Evenly (QT) . . . . . . Jan/Feb 95   5

cleavers
Mincing With a Vegetable Cleaver . Sep/Oct 97   17
Slicing With a Vegetable Cleaver . . Sep/Oct 97   16
Vegetable Cleavers (S&R) . . . . Sep/Oct 97   32

Vinaigrette
ALFRED PORTALE'S JUMBO ASPARAGUS
    SALAD WITH PARMA HAM, PARMESAN, AND
    LEMON VINAIGRETTE . . . . . . May/Jun 93   7
ARTICHOKE CUPS WITH SEAFOOD SALAD
    AND HERB VINAIGRETTE . . . . May/Jun 93   BC
BALSAMIC VINAIGRETTE . . . . . May/Jun 94   12
CREAMY VINAIGRETTE . . . . May/Jun 97   24
HONEY-PEPPER VINAIGRETTE . May/Jun 94   13
HOT-AND-SWEET MUSTARD
    VINAIGRETTE . . . . Jan/Feb 94   18
LEMON-CHIVE VINAIGRETTE . . May/Jun 94   12
LIME-GINGER VINAIGRETTE . . May/Jun 94   28
TARRAGON VINAIGRETTE . . . . . Jul/Aug 94   7
MIXED GREEN SALAD WITH CLASSIC
    FRENCH DRESSING . . . . Jul/Aug 96   14
MUSTARD VINAIGRETTE . . . . . . Mar/Apr 95   15
Salad Dressing 101 . . . . Jul/Aug 96   14
SMOKED SALMON AND MUSTARD-HORSERAD-
    ISH VINAIGRETTE . . . . May/Jun 97   BC
VINAIGRETTE WITH MEDITERRANEAN
    FLAVORS . . . . Jul/Aug 96   14
WARM BALSAMIC VINAIGRETTE WITH
    HERBS . . . . Sep/Oct 95   24

Vinegar (See also Balsamic Vinegar)
Flavored Vinegars (S&R) . . . . Sep/Oct 96   32
GERMAN-STYLE POTATO SALAD WITH BACON
    AND BALSAMIC VINEGAR . . . . Jul/Aug 94   8
Glass Vinegar Flasks (S&R) . . . . . . Sep/Oct 93   32
Making Your Own Vinegar . . . . Sep/Oct 93   23
PLUM TOMATO SALSA WITH SHERRY
    VINEGAR . . . . May/Jun 94   13
QUICK-COOKED CARROTS WITH VINEGAR
    AND THYME . . . . Mar/Apr 96   25
Rating Red Wine Vinegars (BT) . . . Sep/Oct 93   25

ROASTED CARROTS AND RED ONION WITH
    BALSAMIC VINEGAR . . . . Jan/Feb 94   11
Vinegar Equipment (S&R) . . . . Sep/Oct 93   32

Waffles
ALMOST-AS-GOOD-AS-BUTTERMILK
    WAFFLES . . . . Nov/Dec 93   28
THE BEST BUTTERMILK
    WAFFLES . . . . Nov/Dec 93   28
The Mystery of the Ideal Waffle . . . Nov/Dec 93   27
RAISED WAFFLES (Notes) . . . . Charter Issue   2
Rating Waffle Irons (ER) . . . . Nov/Dec 93   29
Waffle Irons (S&R) . . . . Nov/Dec 93   32

Walnuts
APPLE-CRANBERRY SALAD WITH CREAMY
    LEMON VINAIGRETTE . . . . Nov/Dec 96   21
APPLE-WALNUT WHEAT
    BREAD . . . . May/Jun 94   29
CINNAMON-WALNUT FILLING . . Sep/Oct 95   15
CLASSIC BAKLAVA FILLING . . . Nov/Dec 95   15
Cooking with Walnuts . . . . Jan/Feb 96   21
GINGER WALNUT MISO
    DRESSING . . . . Charter Issue   30
GREEN BEANS WITH TOASTED WALNUTS
    AND TARRAGON . . . . Nov/Dec 96   7
LINGUINE WITH WALNUT, GARLIC, AND
    HERB SAUCE . . . . Jan/Feb 96   21
MOCHA-NUT CHIFFON CAKE . . May/Jun 96   8
PEAR SALAD WITH ARUGULA, WALNUTS,
    AND GORGONZOLA . . . . Nov/Dec 96   21
POACHED PEARS ON SALAD GREENS WITH
    WALNUTS AND STILTON . . . . . Jan/Feb 94   BC
SAUTÉED ZUCCHINI WITH WALNUTS AND
    HERBS . . . . Jul/Aug 95   9
TOASTED WALNUTS WITH CURRY SPICES
    Jan/Feb 96 21
WALNUT-RAISIN BAKED APPLES WITH
    MAPLE SYRUP . . . . Sep/Oct 95   13
WALNUT WAFERS . . . . Charter Issue   15

Water
Floral Waters (S&R) . . . . May/Jun 94   32
Taste-Testing Sparkling
    Waters (BT) . . . . Jul/Aug 93   22
The Water in Bread . . . . Sep/Oct 97   2
(The Water in) Pastry Dough
    (Notes) . . . . Sep/Oct 97   3
Squeeze Water from Cooked

Greens (QT) . . . . May/Jun 95   4

Water Bath
Pouring Boiling Water into a Pan in
   the Oven (QT). . . . . Sep/Oct 95   5
Preparing for a Bath . . . . Sep/Oct 95   8
Water Baths (QT) . . . . Sep/Oct 95   5
Water Baths. . . . . Sep/Oct 95   8

Watercress
QUICK-BRAISED BOK CHOY, TURNIPS,
   AND WATERCRESS WITH GINGER
   AND SOY . . . . Jan/Feb 96   26
WATERCRESS SALAD WITH SEARED SCALLOPS
   AND ORANGE VINAIGRETTE . Mar/Apr 96   8

Watermelon (*See* also Melon)
Carving a Watermelon to Resemble a
   Wooden Apple Basket . . . . Jul/Aug 95   17
Fruit Sorbets at a Glance . . . . Jul/Aug 95   25
Seeding a Watermelon (QT) . . . . . . Jul/Aug 94   4

Whipped Cream
Keeping Whipped Cream (Notes) . . Sep/Oct 97   2
LEMON WHIPPED CREAM . . . . . Nov/Dec 96   10
PERFECT WHIPPED CREAM . . . May/Jun 97   19
WHIPPED CREAM . . . . May/Jun 97   19

Whiskey
DRIED PEACH COMPOTE WITH MINT AND
   WHISKEY . . . . Jan/Feb 95   23

White Beans
BRAISED LAMB SHANKS WITH WHITE
   BEANS, SWISS CHARD, AND
   MARJORAM . . . . Jan/Feb 95   19
CANNELLINI BEANS . . . . Jan/Feb 95   19
COOKED DRIED BEANS. . . . . . . Jan/Feb 95   14
QUICK-COOKED GREENS WITH WHITE BEANS
   AND ROSEMARY . . . . Jan/Feb 95   14

White Chocolate
Rating White Chocolate (BT) . . . . . Nov/Dec 97   27

White Wine (*See* also Wines)
BRAISED ARTICHOKE SAUCE WITH WHITE
   WINE, GARLIC, AND LEMON. . Mar/Apr 95   11
BRAISED FENNEL WITH WHITE WINE AND
   PARMESAN . . . . May/Jun 96   18

German Wine Information (S&R) . . Jul/Aug 96   32
Italian white wines (BT) . . . . May/Jun 97   30
Lively (and Inexpensive) Sauvignon Blancs Sweep
   Tasting (BT) . . . . May/Jun 94   30
MUSSELS STEAMED IN WHITE WINE WITH
   CURRY AND BASIL . . . . Nov/Dec 96   15
MUSSELS STEAMED IN WHITE WINE WITH
   TOMATO AND BASIL . . . . Nov/Dec 96   15
MUSSELS STEAMED IN WHITE WINE, MASTER
   RECIPE FOR . . . . Nov/Dec 96   15
Non-Chablis Dominate "Chablis"
   Tasting (BT) . . . . Jul/Aug 93   30
Nonchardonnay white wines (BT) . Mar/Apr 97   30
A Sampling of German
   Rieslings (BT) . . . . Jul/Aug 96   30
SAUTÉED PORK CHOPS WITH WHITE
   WINE PAN SAUCE, MASTER
   RECIPE FOR . . . . Sep/Oct 94   13
STEAMED MUSSEL SAUCE WITH LEMON AND
   WHITE WINE . . . . Mar/Apr 96   9
TOASTED BREAD CRUMBS WITH WHITE WINE
   AND BUTTER . . . . May/Jun 95   25
"Vacation" Whites You Can Live
   With (BT). . . . . May/Jun 95   30
WHITE WINE-BUTTER SAUCE
   WITH CAPERS . . . . Mar/Apr 95   19

Whole Wheat Bread
Basic Sandwich Style Loaf . . . . Jan/Feb 97   13
Dinner Rolls . . . . Jan/Feb 97   13
HAND-KNEADED WHOLE
   WHEAT BREAD . . . . Jan/Feb 97   14
Sandwich Style . . . . Jan/Feb 97   13
Twisted Loaf Baked in a Loaf Pan . Jan/Feb 97   13
The Water in Bread (Notes). . . . . . Sep/Oct 97   2
When Things Go Wrong . . . . Jan/Feb 97   14
WHOLE WHEAT BREAD WITH WHEAT GERM
   AND RYE. . . . . Jan/Feb 97   14

Wild Rice
HEARTY CHICKEN SOUP WITH LEEKS, WILD
   RICE, AND MUSHROOMS . . . . Mar/Apr 96   15
WILD RICE STUFFING WITH CARROTS,
   MUSHROOMS, AND THYME . . . . Jul/Aug 97   21
WILD RICE STUFFING WITH CRANBERRIES
   AND TOASTED PECANS . . . . . . Jul/Aug 97   21

Wines (*See* also Red Wine; Rosé Wine; White Wine)
Alcohol-Free Wine for Cooking (Notes) Sep/Oct 94   2

More Orderly Bubbles (Notes) . . . . Nov/Dec 94   3
Orderly Bubbles (Notes) . . . . Jul/Aug 94   2
POACHED PLUM AND RASPBERRY COMPOTE
    IN SWEET WINE SYRUP . . . . . Jul/Aug 96   BC
WINE SYRUP . . . . Jul/Aug 96   BC

accessories

Corkscrews (S&R) . . . . Nov/Dec 97   32
Home-Style Wine Cooler (QT) . . . . Jan/Feb 97   4
Rating Corkscrews . . . . Nov/Dec 97   28
Wine Tasting Wheels (S&R) . . . . . . Nov/Dec 97   32

taste tests

Acceptable Cheap Reds (BT) . . . . . Sep/Oct 96   30
American Pinot Noirs Eclipse French
    Burgundies (BT) . . . . Sep/Oct 93   30
American "Rhone" Wine Wins
    Tasting (BT) . . . . Mar/Apr 95   30
The Best Red Wines for Grilled
    Foods (BT) . . . . Jul/Aug 95   30
Bordeaux (BT) . . . . Sep/Oct 97   30
Burgundies (BT) . . . . Jan/Feb 97   30
Cheap, Drinkable Red Wines (BT) . May/Jun 96   30
Dessert wines (BT) . . . . Nov/Dec 97   30
Finding the Best California
    Sparklers (BT) . . . . Nov/Dec 94   30
French Rosés Still the Best–
    Barely (BT) . . . . May/Jun 93   31
Inexpensive Chianti Wins Blind
    Tasting (BT) . . . . Charter Issue   32
Inexpensive Pinot Noirs
    Disappoint (BT) . . . . Sep/Oct 94   30
Inexpensive Ports Fail Test (BT) . . . Jan/Feb 94   30
Italian white wines (BT) . . . . May/Jun 97   30
Judging Merlots (Notes) . . . . Mar/Apr 96   2
Lively (and Inexpensive) Sauvignon
    Blancs Sweep Tasting (BT) . . . . May/Jun 94   30
Non-Chablis Dominate "Chablis"
    Tasting (BT) . . . . Jul/Aug 93   30
Nonchardonnay white wines (BT) . Mar/Apr 97   30
Pricey Champagnes Fizzle in
    Tasting (BT) . . . . Nov/Dec 93   30
Ranking Inexpensive
    Bordeaux (BT) . . . . Jan/Feb 96   30
Ranking Inexpensive
    Merlots (BT) . . . . Sep/Oct 95   30
Rating California's Best
    Reds (BT) . . . . Jan/Feb 95   30
Rating the Bargains of
    Spain (BT) . . . . Mar/Apr 94   30
Rating Tuscan Wines (BT) . . . . . . Mar/Apr 96   30

A Sampling of German
    Rieslings (BT) . . . . Jul/Aug 96   30
Tasting Finds Both Sweet and Dry Chemin Blancs
    Enjoyable (BT) . . . . Jul/Aug 94   30
"Vacation" Whites You Can Live
    With (BT) . . . . May/Jun 95   30

Yeast

Best Yeast for American Sandwich
    Bread? . . . . May/Jun 96   11
Bread Machine Yeast (Notes) . . . . . Mar/Apr 97   2
Cake Yeast (Notes) . . . . Jul/Aug 97   3
Instant Yeast (Notes) . . . . Mar/Apr 95   3
Instant Yeast (S&R) . . . . May/Jun 96   32

Yogurt

BREAKFAST BAKED APPLES WITH YOGURT
    AND GRANOLA . . . . Sep/Oct 95   13
CHOCOLATE FROZEN YOGURT   May/Jun 96   15
COFFEE FROZEN YOGURT . . . . May/Jun 96   15
Dannon Lowfat Wins Yogurt
    Tasting (BT) . . . . Jul/Aug 96   24
GRILLED SKEWERED LAMB WITH YOGURT,
    CURRY, AND MINT . . . . Jul/Aug 93   12
Homemade Frozen Yogurt . . . . May/Jun 96   14
Homemade Yogurt Cheese (Notes) . May/Jun 95   2
Making Yogurt Cheese (QT) . . . . . . Mar/Apr 96   4
Making Yogurt Cheese (QT) . . . . . . Sep/Oct 94   4
RASPBERRY FROZEN YOGURT . May/Jun 96   15
STRAWBERRY FROZEN
    YOGURT . . . . May/Jun 96   15
TOMATO YOGURT SAUCE . . . . . Jul/Aug 93   14
VANILLA FROZEN YOGURT . . . . May/Jun 96   15
YOGURT-CREAMED OATS WITH BERRIES AND
    APPLES . . . . May/Jun 94   BC

Zest

CELERY ROOT AND POTATO ROESTI WITH
    LEMON AND PARSLEY . . . . . . Jan/Feb 95   22
Freezing Lemon Zest (Notes) . . . . . Mar/Apr 95   3
Handheld Grater . . . . Jan/Feb 97   16
Making Decorative Citrus
    Spirals (QT) . . . . Jul/Aug 95   5
QUICK-COOKED GREENS WITH BLACK OLIVES
    AND LEMON ZEST . . . . Jan/Feb 95   13
TOASTED BREAD CRUMBS WITH MARJORAM,
    THYME, AND LEMON ZEST . . May/Jun 95   25
Types of zest . . . . Jan/Feb 97   16
Zester . . . . Jan/Feb 97   16

Zucchini

CORN AND ZUCCHINI SAUTÉ WITH
CHILES . . . . Jul/Aug 93   9

CREAMED ZUCCHINI WITH
HERBS. . . . . Jul/Aug 95   9

GRILLED ITALIAN VEGETABLES WITH
THYME AND GARLIC. . . . . Jul/Aug 96   8

GRILLED ZUCCHINI SALAD WITH TOMATOES
AND BASIL . . . . Jul/Aug 95   9

HEARTY CHICKEN SOUP WITH SHELLS, TOMA-
TOES, AND ZUCCHINI . . . . Mar/Apr 96   15

How to Quick-Cook Zucchini . . . . . . Jul/Aug 95   8

MARINATED ZUCCHINI WITH
PARMESAN . . . . May/Jun 96   16

SAUTÉED ZUCCHINI WITH LEMON AND
HERBS. . . . . Jul/Aug 95   9

SAUTÉED ZUCCHINI WITH OLIVES AND
LEMON . . . . Jul/Aug 95   9

SAUTÉED ZUCCHINI WITH PANCETTA AND
PARSLEY. . . . . Jul/Aug 95   9

SAUTÉED ZUCCHINI WITH WALNUTS AND
HERBS. . . . . Jul/Aug 95   9

SHREDDED ZUCCHINI AND CARROT SAUTÉ
WITH GARLIC AND HERBS . . . Jul/Aug 95   9

SHREDDED ZUCCHINI SAUTÉ WITH
GARLIC AND HERBS, MASTER
RECIPE FOR . . . . Jul/Aug 95   9

VEGETABLE RISOTTO IN CARROT AND CELERY
BROTH. . . . . Jan/Feb 94   27

ZUCCHINI FRITTATA WITH PARMESAN AND
HERBS. . . . . Jul/Aug 95   9

ZUCCHINI, RED PEPPER, AND TOMATO SAUCE
WITH THYME AND MINT . . . . . Sep/Oct 94   22